To Cheri
I hope you enjoy my book
all the best
James F "Jim" Grey

VANISHING CONTRAILS

The Complete Memoirs of

Lt. Col. James Franklin Grey, Ret.

Edited by

James Hunter Grey

Wordclay
1663 Liberty Drive, Suite 200
Bloomington, IN 47403
www.wordclay.com

First published by Wordclay on 11/21/2011.

ISBN: 978-1-6048-1950-2

Library of Congress Control Number: 2011943955

Printed in the United States of America.

This book is printed on acid-free paper.

Table of Contents

Selected Illustrations

Note: All images are digital reproductions of originals from the author's private collection of photos, records and paraphernalia.

Foreword

As it travels across the sky, an airplane often leaves a vapor trail that is visible from the ground. This contrail, the memory of the plane's passage, may hang in the air for a long time before eventually dissipating, like a message written by a skywriter. Because of Dad's lifelong involvement in flying, he and I agreed that *Vanishing Contrails* would be a fitting title for his memoirs.

Dad enjoyed a full career in the Air Force that ended in 1964, but he never stopped flying. A huge part of his self-identity is that of aviator. Flying is what he loved more than anything else, and all he ever really wanted to do professionally. After the Air Force, he continued to fly and teach other pilot friends until 2008. Almost all his friendships, and certainly his closest ones, were with Air Force guys, pilots and private aircraft owners. Dad has led a rich and active life, and did have other professional, social, and recreational interests like golf, fishing, boating and hunting. But flying superseded them all, and was really at the center of his life.

He began working on this project one small section at a time in the summer of 2005, and kept at it through the spring of 2006. During this time, most of the content covering the period from 1924 to about 1962 was developed. After that surge of productivity, his interest in the project waned, he set it aside, and almost nothing happened again until 2010. That is when we discovered the online self-publishing industry. Before that, we wondered what we were ever going to do with his manuscript once it was finished (maybe run a few copies at Kinko's and give them to the family and friends on his list?). It is amazing how simple, convenient and inexpensive it has become to publish a book now, regardless of the quantities produced.

Dad's enthusiasm for the project was reinvigorated and he finished the rest of the content during the fall of 2010 through the summer of 2011. Some of his stories he delivered in a combination of live and recorded interviews, but mostly Dad typed short sections into simple word processing files. He has always had an incredible memory for exact dates, not merely for the sorts of things everyone remembers like birthdays and anniversaries, but even the most trivial of events. And he delivered all this information from memory while in his eighties.

My job was to proofread, merge and organize the passages he provided, and do some of the research necessary for verifying and clarifying facts. For the photos, Dad and I went through all his dusty old albums and storage boxes and catalogued everything. This was a tedious exercise, but necessary for selecting photos that best complemented the narrative.

Dad lived in interesting times and has stories worth knowing. Like most people born and raised during the Great Depression, his is a classic story of "rags to riches." He lived through that most economically deprived period in our nation's history, as well as the most prosperous and abundant one (the post-WWII era). In many ways, Dad's life is not so different from other people his age. But he belongs to a truly extraordinary generation, today justifiably referred to as America's "greatest." The heroic acts of men like Dad during WWII and the tremendous victory they won in a nearly pure contest of good against evil are impossible to imagine in today's world. Men like Dad lived to see the American empire rise to its zenith, because they took it there.

Most of the stories in this book are ones with which I was already familiar, but as the project unfolded, a lot of details about Dad's life came to light that I had never known or thought about. The most revealing aspect of this for me was not what he chose to include in the book, but instead what he chose not to include. We spent many hours in conversation about his life, talking through all the details and unraveling several mysteries. The experience was bittersweet for Dad because along with the good memories he also had to confront some painful ones that had been long buried, many of which he had not given thought to for a very long time. Dad wanted these memoirs to be honest and to include every essential aspect of who he is, and he candidly shares some very personal information, thoughts and feelings. On the other hand, Dad also wanted them to be a positive presentation of his life, and in this book he has for the most part chosen to accentuate the good things from his past experiences and relationships. Besides talking about what happened, in this book Dad reveals quite a lot about his values, attitudes, beliefs and opinions, leaving little to the imagination. I appreciate having been able to work with Dad on this project. It was a great experience that brought us closer together, and one that I will always cherish.

Preface: The Dream

My arms are stretched out in front of me. I am soaring at a low altitude over a landscape covered by a dense black forest. I am moving slowly, smoothly through the air. I can bank right, or left. I can stop and hover if I wish. Everything is dark and dusky, colorless. I feel happy, content. I see a rugged, jagged coastline ahead, and then calm, black water that merges in the distance with the dark gray sky, obscuring the horizon. I am looking for something along that coastline that I am supposed to find. Just when I am about to reach the place where it must be, I awaken.

This is a recurring dream I have had since I was a very young boy. It's the first dream I have a memory of, and I have had it again and again, exactly the same, throughout my entire lifetime. I never discover what it is that I am supposed to find there. But it reminds me that air is my element. It is where I always want to be, and where I feel I belong.

My son Jimmy urged me to recount some of my lifetime experiences so they could be preserved for my family and posterity. I really only expected to hand out a few copies to relatives and friends. As the subject of this project came up in conversations, many friends and acquaintances began expressing an interest in reading my book when it was published, and I had to start taking orders.

We seniors are always looking for ways to exercise our minds, and it has been a fun and interesting experience to recall and recount all the interesting things that have happened to me over this long life, many to which I had not given thought for a long, long time.

I am glad that you are reading this, and hope you enjoy it.

Carmichael, California, October 28, 2011.

Part One: Family & Childhood

Family Background

I was nicknamed "Jack" by my maternal grandfather when I was still an infant, and that is what everyone called me until I left for the service at age eighteen. My given name, James, was after my father. It is a popular name in my family that recurs through many generations. My middle name, Franklin, was the maiden name of my paternal grandmother, Annie.

My people—originally from England, Scotland and Holland—began arriving in New England and Canada in the 1620s, migrating gradually through upstate New York and Pennsylvania to Wisconsin, where my family has lived for about the last 200 years. These people were salt of the earth, mostly just ordinary farmers and laborers. One common theme linking all the generations is that the men of my family were soldiers; they served in all our country's wars since the earliest times.

All my ancestors were Yankees. My family was fervently opposed to slavery, some being radicalized abolitionists who were part of the Underground Railroad. Many fought in the Civil War as volunteers. Two of my great-great-grandfathers were volunteer Union infantrymen. They marched with General Sherman across Tennessee, Georgia, the Carolinas and Virginia—suffering capture and imprisonment, hunger, illness and injury—finally making it all the way to the Grand Review in Washington, D.C.

Both my parents were born before man had achieved controlled, powered flight. Gas- and diesel-powered automobiles were still something of a novelty. My father, James Nasby Grey, was born in Monroe, Wisconsin, on March 15, 1896, almost seven years before Kitty Hawk. When WWI started, he joined the Army and was assigned to the Quartermaster Corps. While he was waiting in Cape May, New Jersey, for shipment to Europe, the war ended. He left the Army with the rank of Staff Sergeant.

My mother's name was Susan Cecilia Whitehouse. She was born in Richmond (Shawano County), Wisconsin, on February 23, 1902, nearly two years before Kitty Hawk. Her ancestors were among the very first pioneers in that part of Wisconsin. Her father, J. L. Whitehouse, was a prominent citizen of Langlade and — as the only white man fluent in the language of the Menominee Indians — was often called upon to interpret whenever one of that tribe had a scrape with the law. My maternal grandmother Mary weighed only ninety-five pounds, but used to hitch a team of horses by herself and deliver all the mail in Langlade. She bore ten children, all of whom survived to adulthood.

I do not remember ever asking my mother or father how they met, fell in love, got married, etc. But in conversations with my brothers, I learned that while Dad was working on a sheep ranch near Langlade and Mother was teaching in a nearby school, they somehow met and got married. Mother had not graduated from college, but had earned a teaching certificate at what in those days was called a "normal" school. Dad had only attended school through the third grade and dropped out. According to my brother Tom, J.L. and Mary Whitehouse disapproved of the marriage, but apparently could do nothing to prevent it.

My parents were married in the spring of 1922 and moved to Wisconsin Rapids (familiarly "Whiskey" Rapids), where Dad found work in the paper mill. Their first son was stillborn in August 1923. On one of my last visits home I could not locate the concrete grave marker Dad hand-made for him,

5

but we know that he was buried in the Forest Hill Cemetery on Spring Street. I obtained a copy of his death certificate while visiting for a Lincoln High School reunion in 2004.

One of the anomalies in my family is that ours is the only branch to spell our surname with an "e." With all my relatives and ancestors, it is spelled "Gray." There are two versions of how this came about, and I frankly don't know which is true. My brother Lyle tells a story that when Mother and Dad were courting, she would address love letters to him using the "e" spelling, apparently thinking it more sophisticated. I have never seen any of these letters, and expect none have survived. As the other story goes, when my parents were starting their married life together prohibition was the law of the land, and the acceptable residents of our town disapproved of alcohol.[1] There was just one other man in Whiskey Rapids with the same surname as us, Devere Gray, a man of ill repute (and no known relation to us) who ran an illicit gin joint in town. The version I heard was that Mother changed the spelling of our surname to prevent the townsfolk from making any erroneous connection between us and that no-good Devere. Whichever story is correct, it was definitely my mother who instigated the change of spelling from "Gray" to "Grey."[2]

---

[1] As children, Mother and her siblings were permitted to drink ginger ale, but if they referred to it by its other name of the era, ginger "beer," it was taken away from them, even though it contained no alcohol.

[2] Strict consistency with the spelling of names is a modern innovation. I once visited a family gravesite in a farm field near Pardeeville, Wisconsin, where eleven of my ancestors are buried together in a small plot. This plot contains grave markers with no fewer than five variant spellings of the same surname etched in stone, all these for members of the same immediate family.

Whiskey Rapids

I was born September 8, 1924, in a brick house located on 13th Street south of Grand Avenue, on the west side of the river in Wisconsin Rapids. While I was still an infant, our family relocated to another house on 16th Street, where we stayed until I was just over four years old. My brother Lyle was born in that house November 2, 1926. I heard a story later about my dad catching a "peeping Tom" looking through the windows of a neighbor's house across the street from our house there. Dad alerted the neighbor about it, and it was apparently not the first time it had happened. The next time this voyeur came around, the neighbor was ready with a brand new axe handle he had recently purchased: he snuck up behind him and struck him hard across the back of the neck, knocking him out. There was no investigation, and after the peeping Tom came to, he never came back.

We moved again, to a house on Two-Mile Avenue,[3] which became our permanent residence. Tom was born at that house December 9, 1933. The dimensions of our house started out 16 by 20 feet, very small by any standards. It offered little protection from the elements in either the extreme cold of winter or the extreme heat and humidity of summer. Our bathroom was a simple outhouse, also terribly uncomfortable during those Wisconsin winters. Our only source of warmth during the winter was a small, wood-burning stove where

---

[3] Everyone living in this neighborhood called it either Two-Mile or Sand Hill.

Mother also did all her cooking. We had a hand pump for well water, no electricity and no phone. We had one tub that was used for bathing and washing clothes.

Around 1935, Dad decided we needed a larger house. He dug a 20- by 26-foot earthen cellar and built a foundation, jacked up the house, set it on beams, rotated it 90 degrees, moved it over onto the new foundation and built out the house to fit the new foundation dimensions. It was still pretty small. Inside, the floor was made of pine boards full of knotholes, many of which had been punched out. Dad chewed plug tobacco and used to spit through the knotholes in the floor, normally with amazing accuracy even from a good distance. But I can remember being down in the cellar and looking up and seeing hundreds of frozen, black tobacco-juice stalactites hanging from the rims of those knotholes where he hadn't quite hit the center of the hole.

In January 1936, the Bonus Act[4] was passed, and as a WWI veteran Dad received a bond worth $600, which he redeemed immediately. He used the money to try to start a pig farm. The elementary school my brothers and I attended was next door, and the pigs used to make an awful racket screaming, which disrupted the classes. My teacher always glared at me when this happened, because he knew the sound was coming from my place.

Mother and Dad's families both had a vague Methodist connection, and Mother had a Bible she sometimes read, but my brothers and I were not baptized,[5] we never attended church, and we did not receive any religious training. The only instruction I ever remember getting from my father was, "Heaven and hell are right here on Earth, and you're dead a long time."

---

[4] Congress passed the Adjusted Compensation Bonus Act over FDR's veto.
[5] To humor my Mother, I allowed myself to be baptized much later ("Just in case...") on one of my home leaves after I had been serving in the Air Force for a while.

On the other hand, there were two religious cultures I do remember being raised to specifically distrust, namely Jews and Catholics. I never personally developed any prejudice or animosity toward them, but the attitude was extremely typical and prevalent in Midwestern Protestant America back then, and undoubtedly still is, though to a lesser degree than in the past. I cannot remember why our family would have nothing to do with the Catholics.[6] But there was a Jewish family with the surname "Bocanner" that had recently emigrated from Russia to the United States. The story was that they had arrived here penniless, but quickly became one of the most prosperous families in town, possibly with the patronage of another local Jewish family, the Garbers. When I was in high school, I remember that Bocanner's daughter was beautiful and one of the best-dressed kids in school. I, on the other hand, wore the same shirt every day for two years of high school, which itself was used and well-worn by the time it was handed down to me. I never had adequate shoes or clothing growing up, especially for the Wisconsin winters, and frequently got frostbite and chilblains on my feet. For the non-Jewish residents of Wisconsin Rapids struggling in the depression economy, the Bocanner family's sudden wealth automatically aroused envy and suspicion. In the early '30s, Dad was working for a business owned by Garber. Garber's company cut up old car bodies, fenders and other scrap metal and shipped it to Japan around the time that the Japanese Empire was ramping up armaments production for its (ultimately unsuccessful) conquest of Asia and the Pacific. When WWII hit, Garber was vilified as something of a traitor who profited by supplying raw materials to the enemy for its war machine, materials that were converted to weapons that were used against us in WWII.

---

[6] All three of my own kids ended up marrying Catholics, two Irish- and one Brazilian.

9

Survival in the Great Depression

The single thing that stands out in recollections of my childhood was absolute poverty. There was never enough food, and our clothes were hand-me-downs donated from neighbors or relatives. Often, breakfast, lunch and dinner consisted of bacon grease sandwiches on graham flour bread—sometimes not even that. I have a memory of my mother going to the welfare agency for money to be able to buy a small turkey or a chicken for our Thanksgiving and Christmas dinners.

Dad taught me to handle a single-shot .22 rifle at about seven or eight years of age, and I used to go across the dirt road by our house into Thalackers' woods to shoot rabbits or squirrels for their meat.[7] Of dire necessity, I became an expert marksman and could shoot any squirrel through the eye with one shot at a distance of up to fifty feet. The rabbits we hunted typically hid in oak or pine trees that were either rotted-out or had an opening down by the roots. On occasion, I and Dean Corey (or some other friend hunting with me that day) would spot a rabbit ducking into its tree-burrow before we could get a shot at it. We knew these rabbits crept up into the deepest reach of the hollowed-out tree trunk when frightened. One of us would break off a flexible tree branch to use as a crude measuring device while the other went to fetch an axe. We

---

[7] I must have been ten years old before I learned meat came from any other animals besides rodents.

would insert the stick into the rabbit's hole and push it up into the burrow until it hit the end. That would tell us how deep the hole went. Then all we had to do was cut into the tree trunk with the axe at approximately the right elevation until we had an opening large enough to reach in and grab the rabbit by the throat and choke it. As soon as the rabbit stopped moving and we knew it was dead, we just let it drop, then reached in through the opening at the bottom of the tree and pulled it out. It may seem like a lot of bother to go to, but we preferred it to shooting them. In 1932, rifle cartridges cost about two cents apiece, a lot of money to us back then.[8]

I learned to fish at an early age, also. I would cut a tree limb for a pole, dig for some worms, then walk a couple miles down the road to Nepco[9] Lake and catch some bluegills, sun fish or perch. I brought these small fish home and cleaned them, and Mother cooked them for me. These activities helped us survive, but they also gave me pleasure. Throughout all my adult life, I continued to hunt and fish recreationally, even though it was no longer a vital necessity.

My Dad was brilliant really, but a frustrated man whose potential could never be realized in any useful or profitable way due to his lack of education[10] and "snake-bit" luck.[11] He was a common laborer, and when he was working seemed to always get the most difficult, physically strenuous jobs. Dad always had a junk yard, lots of old torn-down cars, places where I could really get dirty and have fun. For the sort of work he did Dad always needed a vehicle for hauling, but

---

[8] The bounty on crows was five cents, but that's how much a shotgun shell cost, so the deal was no better than break-even.

[9] Nekoosa Paper Company.

[10] Dad was virtually illiterate, although he did have an old tattered copy of Walter Scott's *Ivanhoe* which he read and re-read. There was something about that book that really captivated him.

[11] The superstition in my family of a curse ensuring that we Gray/Grey men will never be rich.

we could never afford to buy an actual truck. So he would take an old Chevy or Whippet sedan, cut off the back behind the driver seat, build a flatbed over the rear section with beams and boards, and seal up the back behind the front seats, thereby converting it into an improvised hauling vehicle. They all had temperamental crank ignitions in the front, and it usually took two people to start the motor. They were especially difficult to get started in the winter, and I remember Dad would sometimes pass an oil torch under the engine to "defrost" it before trying to get it to start. Our vehicles always had a huge dent in the front fender where Dad would strike the crank after several unsuccessful attempts to start the motor.

After he bought the Forty[12] in about 1936, Dad built a saw mill from scratch. We would bring back logs we had felled at the Forty on our homemade truck, and he and Mother would saw the logs into lumber or make them into firewood. The Roche-a-Cri Creek runs through the Forty. Dad built an A-frame bridge across it that supported the weight of our vehicle with a full load of logs. The Forty provided sustenance for our family for many years. Dad did other odd jobs as a laborer sometimes. I used to help him pry rocks out of a quarry nearby our house, which we would load onto the truck and haul someplace. Then we would build foundations, cellars or fireplaces, some of which I know are still standing and in service today.

Once when I was about fourteen, Dad asked me to take my friend Dean Corey down to the Forty in one of his converted trucks to pick up a load of wood and bring it back. This was in the dead of winter, two feet of snow and freezing cold. The axle had already been broken on this particular

---

[12] The "Forty" was actually a plot of 42 acres of densely forested area about twenty-two miles south of Wisconsin Rapids, which Dad purchased for $100. I sold that tract later (c. 1975) for $50,000.

12

truck once when we were hauling a load of rocks, and Dad had soldered it back together. That fix had been strong enough for it to hold without cargo, but not enough to support a full load. On the return trip, we made it only to within about a half mile from the road when the axle broke at the solder joint. The truck got stuck and wouldn't move. We walked up to the road, followed it to Highway 13, and then walked about three miles more to the Big Flats Store. We stayed there long enough to just thaw out a little, and then set off again hitchhiking back to town. There was little traffic on that route, but we finally got a ride, and I brought the bad news back to my Dad.

There was another time we were at the Forty with another truck, this one with dual rear wheels. Dad was driving it very slowly, and I was following behind it on foot with a double-bladed axe. As I watched the truck rolling before me, I kept seeing a leaf that was stuck to one of the tires going round and round. I don't know why that bothered me, but I felt the urge to remove the leaf from the tire. I impulsively tried to use the axe blade to scrape it off when it came around. When I did this, however, the tire caught hold of the axe and pulled it up into the wooden platform above, forcing the blade to cut deep into the tire and flatten it. Dad was angry, but we were able to drive the truck back on just the one wheel on that side. The damaged tire was bald and should have long since been replaced, but we just glued a boot inside the tire and kept driving on it. That's how we did it back then, and I remember that fix lasted a surprisingly long time.

My Dad had an explosive temper over which he had no control. I once saw him throw a drunken man bodily into a car, saying, "This is how we handle you Chicago sonsabitches

13

around here." Dad could whip himself into a rage from a calm sitting position just by getting started talking about something that bothered him. I wasn't there, but I'm certain that this must have been how it happened that day in 1946 when he was sitting in the front room of our house, tried to stand, fell to a kneeling position with his head on the couch, and left this world. He's been dead a long time.

They say child abuse gets passed down through generations in families, and I have it from my cousin, Jean Carman (née Hill),[13] that Dad's own father, Thaddeus Eli Gray, was not only a child beater, but an alcoholic and a wife beater as well. Dad was not an alcoholic; in fact, I only saw him drink once. But frequently when Dad went into one of his rages he whipped me, usually with a heavy leather strap or belt. The beatings were severe, and I would suffer lacerations in my skin that bled and formed scabs before they healed. Because I was the oldest, I suffered the brunt of his anger. I don't remember him ever beating Lyle, who was sickly as a young child. I remember Dad used to carry him a lot, and in the early years he was excused from doing as much work.[14]

Something happened that may have caused Dad's abuse to eventually stop. My mother told my son, Jimmy, that once when Dad was beating me, she took a butcher knife, pointed it at his chest, and in all seriousness threatened to kill him if he didn't put down the belt. Later in life, when I had my own children, I never touched them in anger, instead leaving all the disciplining to my wife because I was afraid I might hit them too hard.

Growing up, I had a favorite uncle who was like a second father to me. He had an odd given name, Togo, after the Imperial Japanese Fleet Admiral Marquis Tōgō

---

[13] Jean and my son Jimmy are the family's unofficial "archivists."
[14] Lyle's nickname was "Neversweat," for never working hard enough to work up a sweat. But in fairness, Lyle did do a lot of hard work in the woods and on construction projects.

14

Heihachirō.[15] Uncle Togo lived in Portage, Wisconsin, with his wife (Aunt) Laura, and his children Dave, Dale, Jerry, Phyllis and Tom. He encouraged me and helped me gain confidence in myself during my growing up years. He let me drive his car places, and he took us to the lake to go swimming. I have many happy memories of him. My family occasionally drove to Portage to visit them. It is hard to believe that we had to plan, make sacrifices and save money just to make a seventy-five-mile trip to Portage to visit Togo. Sometimes we had to postpone trips for a year or two because we just couldn't afford it. Longer trips, for example to visit Mother's family up in Shawano, were extremely rare. Nowadays we travel longer distances just to go out to dinner and never think of the distance or cost.

---

[15] At the time of Uncle Togo's birth (1905), the Russo-Japanese War was a cause célèbre in America, partly because U.S. President (and my distant cousin) Theodore Roosevelt had mediated the peace that ended the war (Treaty of Portsmouth). Tōgō Heihachirō had gained international renown for his naval victories in that war.

Primary Education

By about five years of age my mother already had me pretty well versed in the numbers, addition and subtraction. I could also read the newspaper. By that time, I vividly remember being able to swear like a trooper, which I learned from my dad. Because he always had real problems working for anyone else, he mostly ran his own businesses. But I remember when he was working for Garber and brought home his paltry paycheck (our annual income in those days was about $300) I would take it from him and check the figures. I was always able to determine that he had been cheated out of two or three dollars. Mother always said to just forget about it, because it was money and Dad's work meant we could eat.

I remember really looking forward to starting school as I approached five years of age. In those days there was no kindergarten; children started their education in first grade. The rule was a child had to be five years old by September 1 to start school when the academic year began, but I would not be five until a week after the cutoff. My mother and I went to speak with the principal at Two-Mile School, Miss Cheatle, in the days just prior to the start of the 1929-30 school year. My mother pointed out how close my birthday was to the cutoff and requested that an exception be granted so that I could start school that year, to which Miss Cheatle agreed.

The schoolhouse was a large, two-story brick building with a basement. The toilets were in the basement, along with some storage areas and other rooms that were used for band practice, etc. The toilets were primitive by today's standards, but a luxury for me, being enclosed in private booths with closing doors. Underneath all the construction was a massive septic tank, which had to be pumped out periodically when it became full. The two classrooms were located on the top floor with a hallway down the middle. Grades one through four were on one side and grades five through eight were on the other side. There was one teacher for each classroom, and the upper grades teacher was also the principal. The teacher sat in the front on one side near a row of chairs in the front of the room. Each grade had from eight to twelve students, and when a particular grade was receiving a lesson, those students would move to the chairs in the front of the room, while students from the other grades studied at their desks.

Outside the building was our playground, which had a little merry-go-round. We played in these areas during recesses, and when it was time to return to class one of the teachers (or else some student the teacher chose) would go to the front of the school to pull the rope and ring the bell hanging in a belfry on the top of the schoolhouse. That bell is all that remains from our wonderful schoolhouse. It now hangs in a little monument at the site where the school was. Sometime in the 1980s, a bank bought the school property and the adjacent lot where our house had stood until that time. They leveled everything and built a bank there. Today, a couple of streets in my old neighborhood bear the surnames of some of my childhood companions whose families were the first ever to reside in those places. For example, there is Sweat Avenue (the kids we knew from that family were nicknamed "Toad," and "Tubby"), Corey Avenue (from my friend Dean's family), and Thalacker Avenue. Other than that, there's really nothing left to show who we were or how we lived.

I have fond memories from the eight years I spent at the Two-Mile school. I earned good grades and learned to play the clarinet while there. One incident that I will never forget happened when I was in the seventh or eighth grade. I had been doing something like throwing paper wads and the principal caught me. By this time, the principal was a man named Mr. Brockman. He came up to me and some other students who were also involved, scolded us and hit me and a couple of other students in the shoulder with his fist. I reported this to my dad when I got home, and he immediately stormed over to the schoolhouse and confronted Mr. Brockman. He told Brockman that if he ever touched me again that he would throw him right through the window. Brockman never touched me or any other student again.

It was at Two-Mile that I met Dorothy Sering. We got along quite well, were friends throughout our childhood, and later dated a little. We were both good spellers, and in our last spelling contest together she came in first and I second.

The summer before I started high school (at age thirteen), I got a job setting pins at the bowling alley. I could earn a nickel a game, a lot of money in those days. It was a dangerous job because you had to sit up on a small bench-like seat and avoid being struck by flying pins when the bowling balls crashed into them. Then you had to pick up the ball, place it in the ball return, pick up the pins and place them in the rack, and then get back on the bench. We were allowed to play for free when there were no customers, and I became a pretty decent bowler.

Lincoln High School is located on the south side of Wisconsin Rapids, about three miles from our house. I walked, rode a bicycle or hitched a ride to get to and from high school. In the wintertime it was quite an experience, especially when the snow drifts were six feet high along the edges of the road where the snowplows had pushed the snow. Dad thought I had had enough education, and wanted me to quit school and go to work with him. But Mother wouldn't hear of it, and so I stayed in school. I enjoyed high school, and graduated with about a B+ average.

Our town had a lot of German immigrants, many of whom had not become naturalized American citizens. These German families were typically very supportive of Adolf Hitler and what the Nazis were up to over in Europe, and toward the end of my high school years, in 1940 and '41, I remember the rest of us having a lot of arguments and conflicts with these Germans. In fairness, there were also some families in which one or both of the parents had become naturalized, who supported initially the British and later the American side of the war.

I haven't been to every one of my high school reunions, but did enjoy traveling back home for quite a few of them. I did not attend our 70th reunion in 2011, but I did speak to the classmate organizing the event. There were 114 kids in our graduating class; the organizer told me he had been able to contact only fifteen, one of whom (who had RSVP'd in the affirmative) had died the week before.

Early Interest in Aviation

I remember my first plane ride as though it happened yesterday. Dad took an interest in a wide variety of building projects and was good at most of them. Because of his natural mechanical abilities, pilots would sometimes ask him to go down to the airport[16] near our house and work on their planes, and I would accompany him on those jobs.

When I was four years old, Dad arranged for Mother, Lyle and me to get a ride in the front seat of a Waco[17] with a radial engine. This was a wooden frame, canvas biplane with an open dual cockpit. When the pilot (a neighbor of ours named Oppy Webb) started the engine, it made so much noise that little Lyle became frightened and started crying. So my dad took Lyle off the plane, and just Mother and I went on the flight. I remember we flew over Nepco Lake, and the flight lasted about fifteen minutes.

When I was ten and Lyle eight, there was a time that Mother and Dad left with Tom for Lake Delton, where Dad had some work to do on airplanes. Lyle and I didn't know they would not be coming home, but this became apparent as evening approached. We were hungry and I didn't know what to do, so I took from the cellar one of the jars of peaches Mother had canned and we both ate them for dinner. Later I

---

[16] The airport was Alexander Field – South Wood County Airport.

[17] Waco Aircraft Company was an aircraft manufacturer located in Troy, Ohio. Between 1919 and 1947, the company produced a wide range of civilian biplanes.

took the empty jar and lid and buried them in the sand floor of the cellar, thinking that my mother would have gotten angry if she knew I took the peaches.

The next morning I heard a new airplane fly by in the direction of our airport. I just had to go see what it was, so I got Lyle to operate the throttle and the brake while I turned the crank to start Dad's truck, then drove us both down to the airport. When we were getting ready to come back, Don McKercher[18] asked if we needed any help getting the car started, but I just said, "No." We got back before Mother and Dad returned. She found out about the peaches, but wasn't mad at me. They never found out about our little joyride, however (at least not until later).

As I grew older, I became increasingly fascinated with planes and flying, and would often walk about a mile and a half down the dirt road to the airport to shoot the breeze with the pilots. I would offer to do any odd job I could think of to get rides, like sweep out the hangar or wash the planes. By at least the age of ten, and long before the war had started, I had definitely decided to make the Air Force my career. The U.S. Army Air Force (it was not yet its own branch of the service but a division of the army) required two years of college to join the flying program. I had good grades, but did not have any money for college. But my father's sister in Madison, Aunt Mildred, had offered to help me enroll at the University of Wisconsin campus there, which I planned to do after graduating high school. That was the plan at least, right up until Pearl Harbor and the outbreak of the war.

---

[18] Don came from a wealthy family that owned a feed store in town. He was one of the barnstormer pilots that hung around the airport a lot. One day, after drinking with a group of friends, he stuck a loaded .45 pistol in his mouth and pulled the trigger. We never learned why he committed suicide.

From 1937 to 1941, while I was attending high school, Hitler was taking over one neighboring country after another, and we heard a lot about that in school. We were not hearing that much yet about the atrocities the Japanese were committing at the same time on the other side of the world. December 7th, 1941, was a typical winter Sunday, wind howling, snow three feet deep and 30 degrees below zero. Dad had removed the battery from the truck and brought it inside to power the radio. We were listening to "Heinie and His Grenadiers" playing their German oompah music on WLS Chicago (one of just two stations we received, the other being KMOX in St. Louis). It was around noon Wisconsin time when the program was interrupted by President Roosevelt announcing the attack on Pearl Harbor.

Part Two: Air Force Years

World War II

Basic Training

That announcement had a big effect on my plans. The Army Air Force dropped the college requirement for cadet training, and I postponed all plans for going to college. I had graduated from high school at age sixteen, but the USAAF had a minimum age requirement of eighteen. My mother would not allow me to join the Royal Canadian Air Force (the RCAF would take you at just age seventeen). So I would have to wait. During this period I took several odd jobs to make some money. First I worked for the Nepco Forestry Service planting trees (a job that earned me enough to buy my first car), then for the Preway Products Company making stoves. I joined the AAF Aviation Cadet Program on September 22, 1942, while still employed at Preway, and I continued working there until I was called to active duty.

I received orders by mail to report to the Army Air Force Aviation Cadet center in Decatur, Illinois, on March 15, 1943. Upon reporting there we were all grouped alphabetically and assigned to places on the train. There were no sleeping cars, but seats for two that faced one another. I remember that the other three in my seating area were George Gobel,[19] Jack Graden, and Gerry Green. George was an

---

[19] George Gobel (1919-1991) is best-known for his regular appearance on the popular TV game show "Hollywood Squares" (1965-1981). He wound

entertainer at the radio station WLS in Chicago, and I was already acquainted with his humor and singing. He sang and played the guitar, keeping us entertained for the next three days and two nights that it took us to get to the San Antonio Aviation Cadet Center[20] in Texas. I cannot remember too much else about the journey except that we were very tired with no sleep for three days. We catnapped as much as we could. I do remember that we stopped right in the middle of Jonesboro, Arkansas, at an intersection where several old cars and horse-drawn wagons were waiting for the train to move on. I had never been out of Wisconsin before, and everything was new to me. I had never seen a Negro[21] before, but now saw several standing there waiting for the train to pass. They could see it was a troop train, and everyone was cheering and waving at us, and we waved back. In this blessed time in our nation's history, the country was totally united from top to bottom and end to end in support of the war effort and race didn't divide people the way it does now. The words of the famous Admiral Yamamoto, who led the attack on Pearl Harbor--"We may have awakened a sleeping giant," —were indeed prophetic.

We proceeded on to Texas where, after leaving the train, we were taken by truck to the base. Again we were lined up alphabetically and issued uniforms, underwear, socks and everything else we would need to wear. We just discarded whatever civilian clothes we had, because wearing them would be prohibited for many years. It was well after the war

---

up spending the whole war in Oklahoma, and would boast that as long as he was there "the Japanese never got past Tulsa."

[20] Now Lackland Air Force Base.

[21] This is the term everyone used back then to refer to black Americans, including Negroes themselves. It was not then considered a racist epithet as some regard it today, but a neutral term with no intended or perceived negative connotation.

ended that we could wear civvies[22] while on active duty. With all my basic needs provided for, my $50 monthly salary was plenty. I even had enough to loan money to Gerry Green to help him pay off the engagement ring he had purchased for his girlfriend just before he left home in Oak Park, Illinois. On our first leave after graduation, Gerry and I went back there together and I met his girlfriend, her sister and family.

The basic training, indoctrination and testing lasted about three months. In the first six weeks, we never left the base. Our days began at 5:30 a.m. with Reveille and ended with a bed check and Taps at 10 p.m. The first activity was to move immediately to the field for fifteen minutes of intense exercises, then to the shower and then the mess hall. The exercises were a breeze for me as was everything else. Jack Graden was from Hollywood and had been a workout enthusiast all his life. He had a marvelous physique and he got me interested in working out at the gym. We did that each Saturday and Sunday together for at least an hour. It was there that I was able to press 150 pounds and do ten deep knee bends with 200 pounds on the bar. (I stayed with the workouts regularly, was still able to press 150 pounds into the 1950s, and continued the workouts at the gym at Elks Lodge #6 in Sacramento until the mid-1960s when it moved to South Sacramento.) The food was much better than I had been used to at home. I will always remember the sign in the mess hall which read, "Take all you want, but eat all you take." It was still the Depression, we were in a world war, and we could afford to waste nothing in those days.

There were lots of academics and testing, and some additional exercises they called "psycho-motor skills" tests. From these tests they were able to determine whether a cadet was qualified to enter one of the flying programs. I was informed that I had passed all the tests to be a pilot (I perhaps

---

[22] An old colloquial term used by military personnel for civilian clothing.

26

did too well on the mathematics), but because they needed navigators to fill crew quotas I would be sent to navigation school instead of pilot school. What a letdown! My dream of becoming a pilot would have to wait. Several guys flunked the physical exams and were sent to non-flying units. This had happened to my best friend from high school, Bob ("Stoney") Cahoun. Stoney was a little older than I and had begun cadet training a few months before I did. He flunked his flying physical, and transferred into the paratroopers. I never saw him again after he left Wisconsin Rapids. Stoney took part in the pre-D-Day invasion behind German lines and was killed in combat about ten days into that campaign.

After six weeks of this intense exercise and discipline training which included short-arm inspections in the middle of the night by upperclassmen, we were allowed to have our first open post. That meant we could go off the base for the weekend, provided of course that we had not committed any disciplinary infractions (for which the penalty was to walk tours all weekend long in the parade grounds with full combat gear and a rifle). One of the first things that I noticed on my trips to San Antonio was a sign stuck in the ground in front of one of the old hotels there (either the Lamar or the Gunter) that read, "Dogs and Soldiers Not Allowed." The sign was taken down, but we were told that it had been there since long before WWII and didn't apply to us.

In order to make our life more pleasant and to give the local debutantes the feeling they were helping out the war effort, some San Antonio girls would come out to the base to dance with us. It was carefully controlled; the girls would all be restricted to one side of the room and the cadets on the other side. A whistle would blow and a number of cadets equal to the number of girls would meet at the middle of the dance floor and dance to whatever was playing. Cadets were required to maintain at least six inches of daylight between them and the girl at all times. If this was violated someone in authority would step in and separate them. It was fun and resulted in some good connections for some of our guys, but not for me.

There were a lot of cadets in training. During one of our many weekend parades we were assembled into large formations that spelled out the words "Hi Mom" and photographed. Prints of these photos were made into post cards, and we were all given copies to send to our mothers. I sent one to Mother, and I know she enjoyed it very much.

The tour at the Cadet Center lasted a total of twelve weeks. After that, all those of us headed for navigation or bombardier school had to go first to Aerial Gunnery School. The guys going to pilot school did not have to go to gunnery school. I departed for gunnery school around June 15, 1943.

Aerial Gunnery School

Aerial Gunnery School was located at Harlingen Army Airfield,[23] close to Brownsville, Texas, near the Mexican border and close to Matamoros. I had a good time at this place in spite of the intense heat. Since part of the training was conducted in T-6[24] airplanes, we began drawing flying pay (my pay rose by fifty percent, to $75 a month).

We fired all kinds of guns including the .45 automatic, the twelve-gauge shotgun and the .30- and .50-caliber machine guns. The twelve-gauge shotguns we fired at skeet targets. With the .50-calibers, we trained on the ground in turrets built to simulate those in actual airplanes. We had to become real familiar with those guns because they were the standard equipment on the B-17s we would be flying. We practiced on the .30-calibers while airborne. They were mounted in the rear cockpit of T-6s, and we would fire at tow targets.[25]

I had a real scare one day while out practicing over the Gulf of Mexico just off the Texas coast near Punta Gorda Island. The pilot I had that day was a real hot rock. After I had finished firing and signaled to him that the ammo was gone, he abruptly whipped the airplane upside down and made a steep descent and a pullout. Although there was a heavy strap connecting me to the plane, I had to hang on with both hands

---

[23] Now Harlingen Air Force Base.

[24] North American T-6 "Terrible Texan," a single (propeller) engine advanced trainer aircraft.

[25] Targets pulled by other aircraft, in this instance other T-6s.

while the plane was upside down to keep from falling out through the open cockpit. Since I was just a cadet and the pilot was an officer, I couldn't even complain about it to higher-ups.

Before I arrived at Harlingen I had never drunk whiskey, had sampled beer but had not yet developed a taste for it, and I did not smoke. All that changed during my stay at Harlingen. We were allowed to go off base on the weekends. Matamoros was a typical border town, lots of bars and crawling with prostitutes. We had been given so many lectures and graphic presentations about venereal disease that nobody I knew even considered taking on one of those prostitutes.

Clark Gable had attended the Harlingen school sometime before I got there. He went on to Europe and flew combat as a gunner. He was promoted to major, the only gunner I ever heard of who was an officer (none of the gunners in my group were ever promoted beyond the rank of staff sergeant). Gable was already a celebrity and had some pull, obviously.

In order to graduate from Harlingen we had to demonstrate a certain amount of proficiency in firing the weapons, but the most difficult thing we were required to do was to field strip[26] a .50-caliber machine gun and put it back together while blindfolded and wearing mittens. I had a great time at this school, and now that we knew how to handle the

---

[26] Field strip means to take a weapon completely apart, piece by piece, and then reassemble it.

guns we were ready to proceed to navigator school. We left Harlingen about mid-August for the Hondo Army Airfield[27] Navigator School located about forty miles west of San Antonio, Texas.

[27] Now Hondo Municipal Airport.

Navigator Training

I remember less about Hondo than any of the other AAF schools I ever attended. The only thing that stands out in my memory is the interest I developed there in astronomy. This was obviously way before anything like satellites or GPS existed; the way we determined our position and direction back then was pretty much the same as eighteenth-century sailors – we used compasses, clocks and the stars. Stars and constellations were critical for celestial navigation, and we had to study and be able to recognize them. At one time, I had memorized the names and positions of eighty-eight different stars. My favorite constellation was Orion the Hunter, whose hunting dog contains Sirius, the brightest star in our night sky.

We flew a lot and I became really airsick a couple of times. We used the compass cover to burp in and then hoped it did not tip over during turbulence because then we would have to clean up the entire airplane. I remember our graduation flight to Biggs AAF[28] in El Paso, Texas. While we were waiting to board the plane back for Hondo, I observed several female pilots as they were getting ready to board their planes and fly them. These women were USAAF officers and their crews, whose duties included ferrying aircraft from one base to another. They were obviously not allowed to fly combat missions. Neither were they permitted to become

---

[28] The USAF ceased operation of this base and delivered it back to U.S. Army control in 1966. It remains an Army airfield to this day (actually the Army's largest), connected to Ft. Bliss.

instructor pilots. At the time I was definitely not happy to be stuck flying as a navigator while they were letting women pilot airplanes! I later became the father of two daughters, and my views moderated and are in now more in step with the modern times. But in 1943 the idea of a female pilot to me seemed radical and just a plain bad idea. The USAAF discontinued this program in December 1945.

I passed everything with flying colors and graduated a second lieutenant on January 15, 1944. Like many guys, I was somewhat worried about the prospect of graduating with the rank of warrant officer instead of second lieutenant. I never knew how they determined who would make lieutenant and who would be WOs. I crossed my fingers when the orders were published and was elated when I found out I had made second lieutenant. And I remember the sadness on the faces of those who were made WOs. It is customary still, and was then, that when you graduate and make officer, you give one dollar to the first enlisted man to salute you. I remember doing this, and the airmen who saluted all the new officers made a good bit of money that day.

I was given a thirty-day leave after graduation and went to Wisconsin Rapids by train. I changed trains in Chicago to the

Milwaukee Road which went through Portage, Wisconsin. The train always stopped there long enough for me to walk over to the Friendly[29] and have a Heilman's Old Style.[30] I would always run into a relative of mine whenever I stopped there. When the whistle blew, I would run back (less than half a block) to the station and get back on the train. I would get off the Milwaukee Railroad at Babcock (a stop with no buildings or people) and wait for another train to come along that would take me to Wisconsin Rapids.

Everyone was supportive of the Military during WWII and when I came home for the first time in my "Pinks and Greens,"[31] the reactions were unbelievable. I had gone from being a tough, Two-Mile neighbor kid to an officer in the Air Force in just ten months. Most of the boys my age had joined up, but few had become officers. And there I was, a new second lieutenant. Mother and Dad were very proud of me. Dad never said much but I could tell by his behavior. Although I was still just nineteen years old, Dad took me down to Fred Siegel's bar. I ordered a beer at the bar, and Fred said, "Jack, I know you are not old enough to have a beer, but if you're old enough to wear that uniform, you're old enough to have a beer."

Most of the guys my age were already off to the war. Dorothy Sering had joined the WAVES[32] but I didn't know where she was at the time. Prior to my leaving to enter the service, she and I had gone on a double date with a friend named Chuck and his date. Chuck liked Dorothy and I was

---

[29] A tavern in Portage, Wisconsin that belonged for a time to my cousins. It is still in operation today with the same name.

[30] A favorite local beer.

[31] Popular nickname for a winter service uniform worn by the USAAF. It consisted of taupe-colored trousers ("pinks") worn with a dark olive drab coat ("greens").

[32] "Women Accepted for Volunteer Emergency Service," a division of the U.S. Navy that consisted only of women during WWII.

attracted to his date, so we traded dates. I only had the one date with his girlfriend, but Chuck and Dorothy got married when she got back from the war. Dorothy's brother Herbert went into the Army and got a leg blown off by stepping on a land mine while escorting a group of captured Nazi soldiers somewhere in Germany. I was able to see Dorothy once while home on leave. She passed away many years ago, but I have kept in touch with Herb, who is still alive and well and still gets around quite well on his artificial leg.

Tampa

When I left Wisconsin Rapids after leave in mid-February 1944, everyone knew I was soon to be deployed in combat situations. My mother gave me a Bible when I left and marked some passages for me to read. I took it with me on all my combat missions in Europe and I still have it. My first assignment was to a B-25[33] unit in Columbia, South Carolina.[34] I reported to that unit and after about a week I was told that everything had changed and I was to go to a B-17 unit at MacDill Field[35] in Tampa, Florida. Several guys were with me in this transfer and we had been in Columbia just long enough to get acquainted with Tybee Beach and meet some of the local talent, consisting of several lovely southern belles.

I arrived at MacDill about March 1, 1944, and was assigned to the crew that I would be with until I returned from Europe in January 1945. The training was very interesting – we got as high as 16,000 feet, and at that altitude you could see the entire southern half of Florida. The B-17s were equipped with machine guns that we fired at tow targets. The technical part of the training was fun but I think the greatest part was the way the crew bonded together to form a unified team. We would protect each other against anything and everything. We enjoyed the training and flying

---

[33] North American B-25, a medium bomber that won fame in the April 1942 Doolittle Raid on Japan.
[34] Columbia Army Air Base, now Columbia Metropolitan Airport.
[35] Now MacDill Air Force Base.

together. Tampa offered a lot of enjoyable diversions, and the locals were very supportive of the troops.

It was during my training at Tampa that I met a girl named Vicki Ankerson, who became my steady girlfriend for a time. She was working as a bookkeeper at a bank. She was cute and petite, and really my first love. I cannot remember how we met, but she and her family were very good to me and frequently invited me to their home for dinner. One of Vicki's brothers was stationed in England, and her mother always reminded me to look him up when I got over there. Vicki and I went to the beach at St. Petersburg on weekends and got sunburned. Crew training continued until about May 20, 1944. When it was time for me to go, there were some tearful goodbyes. I promised to look up Vicki's brother, but was never able to find him after I arrived in England.

Combat Tour

The Boeing B-17 was a four-propeller engine heavy bomber used for daylight precision strategic bombing against German targets. It could fly at high altitudes, had a long range, was massively destructive, and could often make it back to base despite extensive damage. It was called the "Flying Fortress" because it had nine machine guns positioned all over the aircraft and could defend itself against fighter attacks from any direction. These planes were flown by a crew of ten men, consisting of a pilot, co-pilot, navigator, bombardier, engineer, radio operator, two waist gunners, a ball turret gunner and a tail gunner. The engineer also operated the top turret guns and the bombardier the nose turret guns.

B-17s could carry a bomb load of up to five thousand pounds. The mission planners decided what kind and number of bombs would be loaded onto our planes for each mission. We carried lots of smaller bombs (one hundred to two hundred and fifty pounds each) if our bombing was intended to cover a wide area. Larger bombs (one thousand to two thousand pounds each) were for specific industrial or infrastructure targets, like railyards, bridges and factories. We used incendiary bombs when we wanted whatever we bombed to ignite into a huge, spreading fire. Almost half of the 1.5 million tons of bombs we dropped on Germany in the war were delivered by these planes.

Because almost all able-bodied men had to go to the war, only women were available to work in the factories that built all the ships, planes, tanks, munitions, and other equipment that we needed. Until this need arose from the emergency of the war, few American women had ever worked at any outside jobs before, especially not industrial jobs. This experience is where the term "Rosie the Riveter" comes from. The wartime production arrangements did a lot to accelerate the feminist movement in America after the war. We picked up our brand-new B-17 at the factory in Marietta, Georgia, around May 26, 1944, and headed for Europe. Near the pilot's seat we found a little typewritten message left there by one of the women who had built our B-17 for us. In her note she said she was happy we were flying an aircraft that she helped build, wishing us success on our missions, survival and a safe return.

We spent the night in Bangor, Maine,[36] and then proceeded the next day to Gander, Newfoundland,[37] for fuel. From there

---

[36] At Godfrey Army Airfield, now Bangor Air National Guard Base.

[37] RCAF Station Gander was a strategic post for the RAF Air Ferry Command during WWII; 20,000 American- and Canadian-built aircraft stopped here en route to Europe. Today it has joint military and civil use,

we flew all night to our first landing in Europe at Nutts Corner,[38] Ireland, arriving at daylight, May 28. The U.S. military had a facility at this base for installing guns and other equipment onto the B-17s and otherwise preparing the planes for combat (the planes having previously been stripped of any excess weight to conserve fuel during the journey from Newfoundland). After food and sleep we were taken to a base at Stone, England, for more training. At that latitude and season it doesn't get dark until after 10 p.m., and from our location at Stone we could sit out at night and watch the Luftwaffe dropping bombs on London, and the glow of all the explosions and fires.

The Eighth Air Force consisted of three bombardment divisions, the 1st, 2nd and 3rd. Mine was the 1st Division, which was made up of several heavy bombardment wings and one fighter wing. My wing was the 1st, and it consisted of four heavy bombardment groups, one of which was the 381st. My crew and I were assigned to this Group and arrived at Ridgewell about June 22. Here we received some ground training in what we needed to do while on combat missions,

and is shared by Canadian Forces Base Gander and Gander International Airport.

[38] RAF Nutts Corner was a Royal Air Force station in County Antrim near Belfast. It was originally a civil airfield, then a military airfield and later Northern Ireland's main civil airport until the 1960s. Today it is no longer in use.

and my crew was assigned to the 535th Bomb Squadron[39] (a bomb group usually has four squadrons). After a two-hour training mission on June 27, our combat missions began the next day.

I kept a diary of my combat missions, recording some brief comments immediately after the completion of each mission and the debriefings. The complete diary is included as an appendix to this book. Many things happened during the missions that I might have included in the original diary, but in order to observe security precautions I cut everything to a bare minimum. The narrative that follows provides more context and detail helpful to understanding what we were really doing over there:

B-17s flew in formations of diamonds nested within diamonds. Four aircraft would fly in a diamond formation, which in turn would occupy the points of another diamond formation of those four sets of four B-17s each, which completed one squadron (sixteen planes). These squadrons were arranged in diamond formations with other squadrons; the lead squadron flew at a slightly higher altitude than the two squadrons flanking it, which in turn flew slightly higher than the last squadron in the formation (sixty-four planes, completing a group). Many, many groups would be arranged in such formations for a mission. You might imagine that organizing that many planes required careful, detailed

---

[39] The 381st Bomb Group was comprised of the 532nd through 535th Bomb Squadrons.

planning. The planes took off one right after the other from dozens of bases in England and once airborne, gradually, painstakingly assembled themselves into their places in those massive formations until practically the whole Eighth Air Force might be flying in unison. Sometimes as many as two thousand planes flew in a single formation, filling up the whole sky.

The allies' Normandy invasion had begun on June 6, 1944 ("D-Day"), just three weeks before my first mission. By that time, the American, British and Canadian armies had completed a massive build-up of ground forces on the beachheads and were preparing to "break out" into northern France. Because most of the ground military action was concentrated there, many of my first bombing missions were actually against targets in France.

Northern Europe had been having the worst summer weather it had in years, which worked very much against us throughout Operation Overlord.[40] On June 28 my crew and I flew a plane called "Touch the Button Nell II"[41] to bomb some German oil dumps[42] and marshalling yards.[43] On the return trip we had to land at Ashfield because of bad weather at our base. The hydraulic system in our left wheel failed, and a pilot of our squadron had to come and pick us up in another fort[44] ("Stage Door Canteen"). The next day we took off for another mission at 5 a.m., but couldn't find our formation and had to abort. On July 4, weather again was a problem for us, as we flew a ship called "Tomahawk Warrior" to bomb a bridge at

---

[40] Code name for the Battle of Normandy, the allies' ground invasion of German-occupied Europe.
[41] B-17 flight crews were permitted to name their ships and paint a kind of "logo" on the nose of the plane.
[42] Crude oil storage facilities.
[43] Or railyards, places where train engines and carriages are stored while not in use or assembled into trains.
[44] B-17.

Tours, France. This was the first mission that our whole crew got to fly together. We maintained an altitude above ten thousand feet and were on oxygen for six hours on that mission.[45] One of our engines almost quit. We watched another ship from our squadron next to us feather its number-four engine, salvo its bombs and drop out of the formation. This plane (commanded by a friend named Bobrof) and its crew, was declared MIA four days later. The whole continent was completely overcast, we couldn't find our target, and we flew home with both of our 2,000-pound bombs still aboard.

Although buzz bombs[46] were not considered to be of major military significance, they had been more than a nuisance to Londoners, with all the destruction of lives and property they had caused. Prime Minister Churchill persuaded General Eisenhower to prioritize taking out the Germans' buzz bomb

---

[45] Above 15,000 feet the air is so thin that you need to breathe from an oxygen mask to avoid passing out from oxygen deprivation. Modern airliners overcome this problem for passengers by pressurizing air in the cabin.

[46] These Fieseler Fi 103, or "V-1s" were pulse jet-powered guided missiles (precursors to today's cruise missiles), which the Luftwaffe fired into southern England from launch ramps located in Calais and Holland on the other side of the English channel. During the Blitz, the Germans fired more than eight thousand buzz bombs at England, randomly killing 23,000 civilians and damaging or destroying over one million buildings and houses, mostly in and around London.

launch sites. My third and fourth missions targeted these sites. On July 6, we flew the "Feather Merchant" to bomb sites at Nouvelle-Église, and on July 8 we took "Me and My Gal" to bomb sites at Pas-de-Calais. We encountered very heavy flak on the second of the two missions. In late August my crew and I would take part in a mission to bomb the factory in Leipzig where the buzz bombs were actually manufactured. One objective on that flight was to try and draw out a new fighter plane[47] the Germans had developed. We didn't encounter any, but did see a German fighter explode over Leipzig. We saw twenty unidentified fighters take off, but they attacked the wing behind us and left us alone. One of our waist gunners was injured by flak.

After the first couple of missions I flew, my crew was assigned its own B-17, which we named "Hell's Angel."[48] When it wasn't being repaired, we flew this plane on many of our subsequent missions.

On July 13 and 16, respectively, we hit our first targets inside Germany, both of which were in Munich. At about nine hours total flying time each, these missions were about twice as long as any of our previous ones. Munich was a heavily defended city, being a major hub of industrial operations that supplied the Nazi war machine. On the 13th, we destroyed

---

[47] The Messerschmitt Me-262 Schwalbe.

[48] Somewhat confusingly, there were other crews that separately came up with the same name for their respective ships, which was the case with Hell's Angel. This was obviously before the motorcycle club with a similar name got started.

some more railyards; on the 16th, our target was actually BMW.[49] Today this company is best known for building luxury cars and motorcycles; few Americans know that it began its life as an aircraft engine maker and was supplying engines for Luftwaffe fighter aircraft during the war. On both these missions, we sustained major damage to our plane from flak bursts. One piece blew a hole through our Plexiglas nose cone and scattered glass all around. German fighters came up to attack, but because we had a formation of B-24s[50] behind us, they left us alone and went after the B-24s, which were much easier to shoot down.[51] On July 31 we paid our third and final visit to the Munich area, again targeting BMW.

On July 18th we took off in Hell's Angel for a mission, but she blew an exhaust stack on takeoff, forcing us to feather one engine and return to base. The plane we transferred to happened to be the very same one we had flown over to Nutts Corner from Maine. We flew to Peenemünde, on the other side of the Danish peninsula, to destroy a hydrogen peroxide factory and experimentation center. Each ship in our formation dropped thirty-eight 100-pound bombs and hit the

---

[49] "Bayerische Motoren Werke AG," or "Bavarian Motor Works."

[50] Consolidated B-24 Liberator, an American heavy bomber.

[51] Back at base, I used to jokingly say I preferred to have a B-24 escort instead of fighters, because if they had a choice the Germans would go after them instead of us.

target dead on, as we could see smoke from the ground fires rise all the way up to 15,000 feet. The Russian army was active near this part of Germany, and I heard from American crews who had to emergency land in territories they controlled that the Russian hosts were out of control and offered the Americans an unbelievable program of hospitality that I cannot go into here. We returned to Peenemünde in Hell's Angel on August 4, with good bombing results. On this mission as we were just airborne, we watched one of the ships from our group (532nd Sq.) catch fire shortly after takeoff. We counted nine parachutes before the plane hit the ground and blew up. On our return, we learned that the tail gunner (Harold Norris) did not make it out of the plane.

During our 2002 reunion in England, we were joined in Cambridge by a Dr. Vernon Williams and his class from the Abilene Christian University in Abilene, Texas. It turns out that Harold Norris was Dr. Williams' uncle. Williams was there to try and obtain additional information about the crash, find and examine the site and recover some artifacts if possible. In addition to that, his class sang for us at our wreath-laying ceremony at our cemetery in Cambridge. Dr. Williams recorded interviews from several of the 381st members to be included in a project he was working on, which he intended to preserve on DVD so that 50 years from now, students studying history can get the facts from the people who were actually there. He conducted more interviews at our Houston convention in 2003. It felt strange to be talking to the nephew of an individual killed in a crash that I had witnessed nearly 60 years previously.

To support the continuing effort to win air superiority and eventually air supremacy, on July 19 we flew a mission to Augsburg (near Munich) where the Messerschmitt Company built jet-propelled aircraft. Our target was a factory and airfield. This was the first time we could see the target plainly, and we hit it dead center.

46

By late July, the American and British armies were still making very slow progress gaining ground in France after the Normandy invasion. General Bradley[52] hatched a plan called "Operation Cobra" to punch through German defenses, which called for strategic air support from the Eighth Air Force. His army had just taken over a town called St. Lô; on my ninth and tenth missions (July 24 & 25) we were sent to saturation-bomb[53] German tank and artillery positions there. Unfortunately, miscommunication and disagreement between Bradley and the air marshals led to some American deaths by friendly fire, but our bombs did unbelievable damage to the enemy. Operation Cobra became a turning point in the war, allowing General Patton[54] and his Third Army to break out of Normandy and launch his invasion of France. The United States would allow use of heavy bombardment again to support ground troops, but sparingly, because there seemed to be no way to totally eliminate friendly-fire casualties on the ground.

In August we flew a couple of missions to France on a ship named "In Like Errol,"[55] dropping bombs on fuel and ammunition dumps near Mulhouse (near the tri-border with Switzerland and Germany) and Paris. Flak defenses were intensifying on these missions as the Germans began fighting us more desperately. On my fifteenth mission (August 9) a piece of flak blew through the nose under my table, piercing my glove and cutting my left hand. It had been slowed by passing through several solid barriers before hitting me. The wound was superficial; nothing that I thought merited putting in for a Purple Heart.

---

[52] Lt. Gen. Omar N. Bradley, commander of the U.S. 1st Army.
[53] In modern vernacular, "carpet-bombing."
[54] Brig. Gen. George S. Patton, commander of the U.S. 3rd Army.
[55] A play on the expression "in like Flynn," combined with the Hollywood actor Errol Flynn.

By early August, Operation Cobra had been quite successful, and the British and American armies had encircled and trapped Field Marshal Günther von Kluge's fifth and seventh Panzer armies in the Falaise Gap. This was because Hitler insisted on counterattacking instead of withdrawing. Our mission on August 17 was to destroy a major road junction at Rouen, to prevent the remnants of von Kluge's army from retreating. We flew a plane called "Egg Haid." The flak was intense and accurate, and in one of the ships in our squadron, the navigator was killed and the engineer injured from flak bursts.

On August 26th, the date of my nineteenth mission, I was promoted to first lieutenant and made squadron navigator for the 535th, which meant my plane would normally be the wing lead ship on missions from that point forward.

On August 27, our crew took off on "Minnie the Mermaid" with the target destination of an airfield six miles south of Berlin. The weather was bad, and we had only gotten halfway to our destination when we were ordered to deviate and take a target of opportunity at Emden Harbor. We had some really awful luck on this flight. When we opened the bombay doors, the motor caught fire. After much difficulty we were able to extinguish that fire, but then the VHF radio caught fire, and our number-one engine was hit, quit, and started throwing oil. We had to feather the propeller, and because of the loss of one engine we began losing altitude. We had to drop out of formation and almost hit the lead ship's bombs (but we were able to release our bomb load with the rest of the group). A piece of flak came through the nose making a hole the size of a baseball, but it missed me and Mac.[56]

By this time we had lost our formation and were flying by ourselves. Metts[57] turned back towards England and we headed for home. We got more flak bursts as we passed close to the coast north of Hamburg, and it really looked like we were going to have to ditch the plane and bail out. I remember Mac and me looking down at the terrain below us and discussing as we prepared to jump whether we were more likely to fall on dry land or in the water. As we continued to head towards England, a battered P-38[58] approached and moved into close formation with us. One of its engines was feathered (so it was flying on just one engine). We flew that formation all the way back to England. As we approached the coast, the English shot flak up ahead of us to warn us that we could not fly over that area. By that time we had fallen to an altitude of only five hundred feet. We deviated a bit and were somehow able to make it back to Ridgewell.

The P-38 left us for his base. We got shot up pretty good on a lot of our missions, but this was the only one that I really thought we would have to bail out. Many of the planes

---

[56] Melvin McIntyre, bombardier of my crew.

[57] Floyd Metts, pilot of my crew.

[58] Lockheed P-38 "Lightning," a WWII fighter aircraft, both unusual in design (twin booms and a single, central nacelle) and extremely versatile (was used for dive-bombing, level bombing, ground strafing, photo reconnaissance, and long-range escort). The Luftwaffe hated this plane, calling it the "forked-tail devil."

in our group sustained heavy damage on this particular mission, and one came back with one dead and four wounded.

On September 12, we flew our first mission to Czechoslovakia, where I got a real close look at some Me-109s[59] that came up to attack us. On the remainder of my missions, the targets were inside Germany. Through September and October we bombed depots, oil dumps and railyards in Hamburg, Essen, Ludwigshafen, Kassel, Magdeburg, Cologne and Münster. Over Hamm our tail gunner was hit in the back by flak but his flak suit stopped it. The flak piece had blown through two cans of ammunition before it hit him. We were sent again to a target in Brüx, on October 8, but because of weather we instead bombed a secondary target at Zwickau.

I didn't fly on November 6, but our squadron was sent out to destroy an oil refinery in Hamburg. One of the ships of our squadron ("Chug-a-Lug IV") commanded by Lt. Levitoff was hit by a flak burst over the astrodome. A friend of mine was

---

[59] Messerschmitt Bf-109, or Me-109, the Luftwaffe's ubiquitous and versatile fighter, used as an interceptor, bomber escort, fighter-bomber, and for ground attack and reconnaissance. It flew in all weather conditions, day and night. The Nazis produced 34,000 of these planes during WWII.

flying next to him and told me he saw the co-pilot slump down in his seat, apparently unconscious. Later he counted six chutes. Poor weather conditions made November of 1944 a slow month for us operationally. The only mission I flew was on November 21, to a synthetic oil plant at Merseburg, aboard the "Alamo."

When a ship exploded in mid-air, there was no chance of survival of any of the crew members. But if a ship was disabled to the point that it could no longer fly, there could be time for some or all of the crew to try to bail out of the plane. Crewmen who were injured or already dead, or who for some reason got stuck and couldn't get out, remained aboard and went down with the ship. Whenever we saw a plane drop out of formation and go into a death spiral, we always watched to see if any of our guys made it out. From a distance, we could do this by counting parachutes as they opened. We were always looking for ten, because then we knew the whole crew had made it out and at least had a chance of surviving. The number of chutes we counted went into a report on our return and debrief at the end of each mission. We could always tell which plane and crew was lost, but we didn't always find out what happened to them. The chutes didn't always work, or got hung up in trees, etc. If an airman made landfall in a forest, he could hide, try to get help and escape to England. Many were captured by the Nazis and executed or held as POWs. Not everyone survived captivity; those who did were freed at the end of the war.

One of our bomb group who attended our 2010 convention told the story about how all ten of his crew bailed out safely when his ship was lost, but he somehow got separated from the rest of his crew. In the place where he landed he was surrounded by German soldiers, who immediately took him prisoner. He was able to see the rest of his crew land in a farm field a few hundred yards away, where they were captured by a group of German farmers. One of his captors spoke English and said to him, "You will never see your crew members alive again." He said he didn't know what that meant at first. But then, he watched as the farmers murdered each member of his crew one by one, running them through with pitchforks, the only weapon available to them.[60] Others of my group were luckier, landing in a spot of earth controlled by our side, or landing in the Channel and getting rescued by a patrol boat or some other means. In July 2011, I chanced to meet up with an ex-navigator from one of the ships in my squadron, James Long (at a veterans' convention in Woodland, California. I had not seen him since August 8, 1944, when his plane was shot down). He parachuted out a mile behind the lines controlled by the Canadians and made it to safety. I know so many people with stories like these, each one unique and fascinating.

In intelligence briefings, we were informed that Nazi submarines were patrolling New York Harbor and the Chesapeake, Potomac, and St. Lawrence Rivers, waiting to launch missile strikes on American cities. We were also told that the Nazi and Japanese governments had reached a secret accord to divide the United States at the end of the war at the Mississippi River, with the Eastern half going to the Nazi empire, and the Western half to the Japanese empire.

---

[60] Firearms possession was prohibited to German civilians under the Nazi regime.

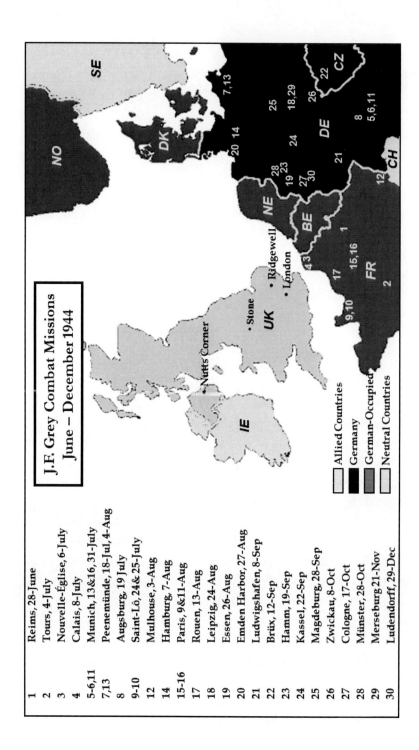

J.F. Grey Combat Missions
June – December 1944

1	Reims, 28-June
2	Tours, 4-July
3	Nouvelle-Église, 6-July
4	Calais, 8-July
5-6,11	Munich, 13&16, 31-July
7,13	Peenemünde, 18-Jul, 4-Aug
8	Augsburg, 19 July
9-10	Saint-Lô, 24 & 25-July
12	Mulhouse, 3-Aug
14	Hamburg, 7-Aug
15-16	Paris, 9 & 11-Aug
17	Rouen, 13-Aug
18	Leipzig, 24-Aug
19	Essen, 26-Aug
20	Emden Harbor, 27-Aug
21	Ludwigshafen, 8-Sep
22	Brüx, 12-Sep
23	Hamm, 19-Sep
24	Kassel, 22-Sep
25	Magdeburg, 28-Sep
26	Zwickau, 8-Oct
27	Cologne, 17-Oct
28	Münster, 28-Oct
29	Merseburg, 21-Nov
30	Ludendorff, 29-Dec

53

Our original crew stayed close, and before I was made squadron navigator, we took all our three-day passes together, usually in London but quite often in Southend-on-Sea, which is located on the coast about forty miles east of London. We liked to go there because the buzz bombs (which could carry only enough fuel to get about as far as London) never fell around Southend. The Brits called these devices "doodlebugs." The devices made a loud noise like a one-cylinder engine, which you heard as they buzzed overhead. If the noise stopped, it meant its motor had run out of fuel and the engine had just quit. That was a terrifying moment, because it was then you knew the bomb was about to fall somewhere near you and explode.

There was one night that a group of us got a terrible scare while walking along the street on the north side of the Savoy Hotel in London. We heard a buzz bomb coming and the engine quit when it was right overhead. We waited for the explosion: it fell right in front of the Savoy, blowing a bus over onto its side, and generally causing a lot of damage. The hotel windows were shattered from the blast, and huge shards of broken glass came raining down on us. Luckily, none of us were hurt, but we decided we'd be safer back at the base that night, and we hurried to the train station to catch the next train back to Ridgewell.

We knew that our base was just about out of range of the buzz bombs, and it was therefore unlikely that one would drop right around us. There was only one occasion that we heard a buzz bomb at our base and got into the bomb shelter. It was the only time we had to use that shelter, and one guy was so panicked he jumped in without looking, landing on another guy and nearly breaking his back. We heard the engine quit and the explosion, which was about a half mile away. It hit a farm house and cut it in half.

Our planes had designated parking spots, which were scattered among the farmhouses and fields in the area. Often a plane would be assigned to a spot quite close to a house, and in those cases the families residing there adopted the plane and its crew as their own. They regularly invited us to tea, meals and other visits. When we got ready to take off for a mission they cheered and waved to us. Then they would spend the hours of anxious hand-wringing and worry, waiting to see if "their" plane and crew would make it back. It was heartbreaking to watch the faces of the families, especially the children, when their crews did not return. Those who did make it home alive were always treated to more cheering and celebration.

For the most part, our relations with RAF[61] servicemen were pretty good. They were permitted to wear their hair long and sport facial hair, whereas we Americans had regulation crew cuts and were clean shaven. Some Brits condescendingly alleged that this American practice was necessary because of pandemic head lice infestations from the primitive sanitary/hygienic conditions in the "Colonies." The fact that British imperial power had eroded so much that they needed us Colonials to come to their defense naturally produced a bit

---

[61] Royal Air Force.

of resentment mixed with appreciation for our being there. They had already been in the fight for over two years by the time the United States entered the war,[62] and by 1944 it had taken its toll. They suffered intense shortages of just about everything, while we were coming in fresh, bringing plenty of money and supplies. Some playfully complained to our faces, "You Yanks are overpaid, oversexed, and over here," to which our comeback was always, "Yeah, well, you Limeys are underpaid, undersexed, and under Eisenhower."

English civilians did appreciate us being there and fighting for them. One time a family invited me to dinner and to spend the night at their home. They had a sixteen-year-old daughter whom, I was made to understand during dinner, they were offering to spend the night with me. I couldn't believe this was their custom, but I eventually got that they were serious (other U.S. servicemen I knew had similar experiences). She joined me in bed, but I could not allow myself to take advantage of her. I was nineteen at the time.

We really enjoyed dating the local girls, who were a lot more amorous than English women are typically given credit for. I remember one telling me that she had "messed around," but naïve as I was, I did not know for sure what she meant. I thought at the time that she had to be kidding, because she could not have been more than fifteen. Prostitution was not prohibited in Britain, or at least none of the laws prohibiting it were ever enforced. Once, while enjoying a three-day pass on a cold winter night in London, we encountered a girl named Silvia whom we had seen many times before. She was dressed in a long fur coat. I complimented her on her coat, and she stood and opened it to me, revealing she was wearing

---

[62] Britain had been at war with Germany since September, 1939. The U.S. declaration of war on Germany came only after the Japanese attack on Pearl Harbor in December, 1941.

absolutely nothing underneath, and asked me, "Well, what do you think of this, Yank?"

On many occasions we had dances, and a number of English guests would attend. We were treated to live performances by entertainers like the Glenn Miller Orchestra (who I thought was the greatest). The maintenance people would pull some flatbed trailers together in front of one of the hangars for a makeshift stage, and this was where the bands would set up and play. We danced on the concrete taxiway in front of the aircraft hangars. We stayed up late for some of those dances and got very little sleep before having to rise at three o'clock in the morning to prepare for a mission. Some guys were still drunk when they boarded their planes, and found it difficult to get going. But after a few minutes on 100 percent oxygen, they perked right up. After returning from the mission, they would go directly to bed for a short nap. Then it was right back to the club for more drinking and partying. We were tough in those days. And every time we came flying back from a mission, as soon as we got below 12,000 feet, the crew would shout at me, "Hey Rooster,[63] play us some music." I would tune the Bird Dog[64] in to BBC London, which would usually be playing Tommy Dorsey's "Opus One."[65]

Celebrities came to visit and entertain us from time to time. I remember one time when a pilot named Gene Demegalski and I were walking from the flight line to the hut we lived in. We were wearing our bomber jackets with our aircraft symbols on them, mine with the same "Hell's Angel" as the nose art on my ship. Just then, a staff car pulled up alongside us, with some people wanting to talk. We were

---

[63] The nickname they gave me because of my red hair.

[64] Servicemen's vernacular term for a radio compass, or radio direction finder. It is a navigation device that points to the source of a radio signal.

[65] "Opus One" was the theme song of British Broadcasting Corporation radio during the war.

amazed to see that it was Bing Crosby, Bob Hope and Marilyn Maxwell. We had a nice chat with them, and then they drove on to wherever they were headed. In those times, most Hollywood people were very supportive of the troops and war effort, much in contrast with recent times starting with the Vietnam War and Jane Fonda (whose hateful actions against the United States cannot be considered anything but treasonous).

I flew with my original crew for the first eighteen missions before being made squadron navigator for the 535th. Being a navigator was not so bad, I thought, but I still wanted to be a pilot. On Nov. 17, 1944, I was promoted to captain (at age 20, the youngest in my bomb group, and just ten months and two days after receiving my commission as second lieutenant). After that I only flew lead missions, with several different lead pilots. One was Gene Demegalski ("Deme"), and I flew most of my last twelve missions with him. With the promotion came changes in my responsibilities. A lot of the work assigned to me I had to do on the ground, so I did not fly as often as the others, and flew only lead missions. The number of missions I was required to fly to complete my combat tour was also reduced from thirty-five to thirty. We always had a squadron commander or the wing commander flying with us and he would be in command of sometimes as many as 1,200 airplanes that were following us on the mission. One of the responsibilities I had was to train another officer to take over as squadron navigator when I completed my tour, so I could leave and come back to the United States. The officer I trained and to whom I turned over my responsibilities was Lieutenant Bud Tabor. When Bud finished his tour alive and returned home, we were briefly stationed together at Ellington Field in Houston.

The Battle of the Bulge was going on during most of December 1944, and the weather was so bad in England that we couldn't fly (that's the whole reason the Battle of the Bulge happened – it was because the air forces couldn't fly). Because Deme and I had some vacation time coming and we were grounded anyway, we decided to spend a week in Scotland. Our train arrived in Edinburgh a few days before Christmas. The train station was located well below Princess Street, and there was a long, steep staircase to climb. I found a young Scotch boy to carry my heavy B-4 bag up the steps. He could tell by our uniforms we were American servicemen. I remember as we were going up the steps, he asked me, "Do you like the Limeys?" After a short pause, he answered his own question, declaring, "I don't like the Limeys." I couldn't tell whether he was serious or not, but I suppose he was. The Scots and English had been united for over two hundred years, but after so many centuries of war, there are Scots who still refer to the English as the "Auld Enemy." We visited Edinburgh Castle and had our pictures taken wearing Black Watch Regiment uniforms. I remember the views at the castle were breathtaking. It snowed heavily during our entire visit. A shipload of American army nurses were also in Edinburgh the same time as we were. They had just arrived after a three-week sea voyage. We all had a very enjoyable Christmas in Edinburgh, the Battle of the Bulge turned around, and Deme and I got back in time to fly our last mission on December 28, 1944.

Our objective was to destroy the Ludendorff rail bridge (famously referred to as "The Bridge at Remagen"). The allied air forces had bombed all the bridges crossing the Rhine to cripple German mobility on the Western Front. At one point in the war, the Ludendorff Bridge was the last Rhine bridge still standing; Americans captured it from the Germans in

March 1945 in our final drive into Germany's heartland. My thirtieth mission was a nice one to finish on. My assembly timing was perfect. The Luftwaffe's resistance had been steadily dwindling to almost nothing, and there were no flak or fighters.

Between 1936 and 1945, Boeing manufactured 12,731 B-17s. Of these, 4,754 (more than a third) were lost in the war. Today there are only about thirty complete models left in existence, only a dozen of which can still fly. We just lost one more this year, as an antique B-17 crash landed and burned at an air show in Illinois.[66] In WWII, B-17 crews suffered a high casualty rate (of about 38 percent). Some 250,000 Americans were assigned to B-17 crews in WWII. Of these, 30,099 were killed in combat, another 15,401 were injured, and another 49,065 were captured or went missing in action for a total of 94,565 casualties. My own bomb group lost 134 planes in combat, and 1,340 men out of 8,223 (or one in every six) were killed, taken prisoner or went MIA.

The 381st still exists today, but it has been deactivated and reactivated twice, and its mission has evolved over the years. During the Cold War, it ceased to be a heavy bombardment group and was transformed into a strategic missile wing. During this phase it maintained and operated Titan II ICBM

---

[66] The "Liberty Belle," operated by the Liberty Foundation of Oklahoma, crash-landed on June 13, 2011, in a field near Chicago. I had been a passenger aboard this very plane when it visited air shows on the West Coast.

missiles at McConnell AFB in Wichita, Kansas. Today, it provides training for space and ICBM operations and air-launched missiles at Vandenberg AFB.

Since 1978, the war-time 381st has gathered for annual reunions, each year at a different (usually major metropolitan) venue. Back in the 1980s we would get as many as 200 members at these events. In 1982, we organized the reunion in Ridgewell, visiting several of our old haunts in England, as well as several cities in Germany. One of the German cities we visited was Nuremberg, where some relatives of my late wife Hilda's (on her mother's side) lived. They very graciously hosted us for dinner at their home, and their son, who spoke English, was able to translate for us (although Hilda still had some German she remembered from her growing up years). One of our most enjoyable reunions was in Boston in 1987, which coincided with the Independence Day celebrations that year. At our 2010 reunion in Nashville we had 30 members in attendance. Of the original ten members of my crew, just our pilot, Floyd Metts (age 91), and I are still living. Floyd had come up from his home in Oxford, Mississippi, at my urging (he had stayed away from all of them until then), and that was the first time I had laid eyes on him since the war. His wife had passed away a couple years before, and his son was with him at the convention. Floyd and I had kept in touch regularly over the years, but it was just so good to see him again in person. It is impossible to explain or understand unless you've experienced it yourself, but to serve in a combat crew produces a much stronger relationship and bond than a man has even with members of his own blood kin.

The United States had over 16 million people in the armed services during WWII, 400,000 of whom didn't survive the war. As of this publication, there are fewer than two million of us WWII veterans left above ground, and we are currently dying off at the rate of almost 1,000 per day. People aren't supposed to like war, but I loved World War II. The camaraderie, the rush of the dangerous situations we sometimes faced, the knowledge that we were fortunate enough to be thrown right into the middle of what was certainly the most important event in human history and experiencing it firsthand, the fact that we were as loved and supported as we were by everyone around us as well as back home. We were young, strong, brave, and there to destroy the worst evil ever to hit the human race, and the outcome was a total victory. The war rescued me from the wretched poverty of my boyhood, which I left behind and traded for a life of traveling the world in great style. The convergence of all these incredible factors made the war a thrilling, beautiful experience for me, and the fondest memories of my twenty-two excellent years of service in the Air Force were from my year with the 381st Bomb Group.

Top: Me at age four with my younger brother Lyle, taken at our house on 16th Street in Wisconsin Rapids, just before moving to Two-Mile.
Bottom: Me at six months with my parents. Taken near my maternal grandparents' home on the Wolf River in Langlade, Wisconsin.

Left to right: Brothers Lyle, Tom and me standing in the doorway of our childhood home in Wisconsin Rapids, Wisconsin.

The old Two-Mile schoolhouse in Wisconsin Rapids, 1936.

The Two-Mile School Band, taken in 1936. I am the clarinetist, second from left.

The Cast of "Eyes of Love," produced by the Two-Mile Parent Teacher Association, 1936. I am second from left; my friend Dean Corey is standing next to the actress done up in blackface, and Dorothy Sering is dressed in the bridal gown.

The Lincoln High School "Red Raiders" Varsity Football Team in 1939. My best friend Robert "Stoney" Cahoun and I are standing in the back row, eighth and ninth from the left, respectively (End and Guard – "End of the bench, and Guard the water").

Me with some Whiskey Rapids yokels, at the City Service gas station near my home. To my right is Milt Sullivan; in the front row, left to right, are Roy Crutch, Len Verjinski, and Lloyd Thalacker, all friends from my teen years.

My friend Dean Corey on improvised snow skis. In winter we used to tow each other behind a truck and see how fast we could go.

The Portage relatives in the 1970s. Front row: Aunt Laura, Uncle Togo; Back Row, left to right: David, Dale, Phyllis, Gerry and Tom.

Me standing next to Lloyd Thalacker, in front of the "Forty" in 1979.

The U.S. Army Air Force at Alexander Field on its dedication day, July 26, 1928, the place where I took my first flight.

Me with my children and grandchildren inside the old hangar at Alexander Field, August 2004.

Top: Dorothy ("Dotty") Sering in her Navy WAVE uniform.
Bottom: Herb Sering, Dotty's brother.

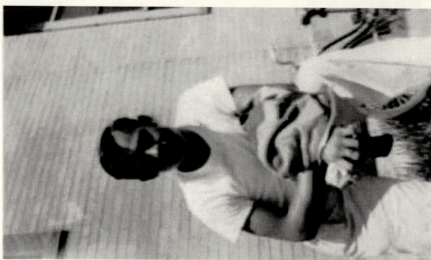

Top: Me in cadet uniform, taken at the Aviation Cadet Center, San Antonio, Texas, 1943. Bottom: Stoney Cahoun as a high school senior. He was assigned to an airborne unit that took part in the D-Day invasion and was killed in action shortly thereafter.

72

Top: Cadets Jack Graden and me at a gin mill in Matamoros, Mexico, during aerial gunnery training, Harlingen Texas, June 1943.
Bottom: Me in clothing worn for aerial gunnery training.

In the chow line at cadet school, where a sign was hung that read, "Take all you want, but eat all you take."

Thirty-day leave from Hondo Navigation School before my next assignment in Columbia, South Carolina, January 1944. Left to right are James N. Grey, Thomas L. Grey, me, Susan C. Grey and Lyle Z. Grey.

Me (on left) and fellow serviceman out for a stroll in a rainstorm in Tampa, Florida, 1944.

Vicki Ankerson, me, Floyd Metts and a girlfriend at the beach in St. Petersburg, Florida, spring 1944.

The "Friendly" tavern in Portage in August 2004, which belonged to my family and is where I frequently stopped for a quick beer whenever en route to or from home by train, is still standing. Photo is me with daughters Barbara and Susan and grandkids Ian and Carolyn (son Jimmy took the photo).

76

The crew of "Hells Angel" and their B-17 Flying Fortress.
Back Row: Felix Wojcik (waist gunner), Melvin R. McIntyre (bombardier), Floyd H. Metts (pilot), Kenny Lingenfelter (co-pilot), me (navigator); Front Row: William W. McClaren (engineer), Claude A. Curtis (radio operator), Edwin J. Bond (tail gunner), Omar L. Godfrey (waist gunner). Not appearing in photo was Leon S. Bucy (ball turret gunner).

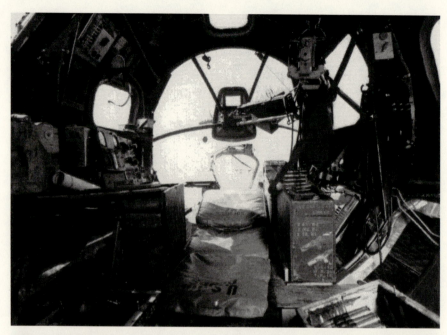

B-17 fuselage interior views: Top: Facing forward. My station was at the table in the foreground on the left; Bottom: Facing rearward.

Every crew member carried two photos like these into combat in case his plane was shot down and he survived. We were to use these to identify ourselves to the French Underground, who tried to help American airmen elude capture.

The 381st Bomb Group lining up for takeoff on a bombing mission, from its base at Ridgewell, England.

Some missions had thousands of B-17's flying in formation.

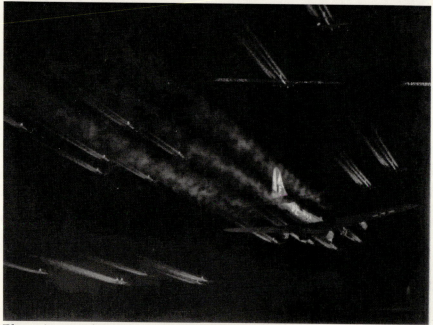

Planes in same formation, but at higher altitudes leaving contrails.

Same formation under heavy flak barrage.

Damage to our ship from a mission flown on Nov. 10, 1944. The crew's bombardier was killed on this mission.

Me and "Hells Angel" crewmembers on leave in London, July 28, 1944: (left to right) me (navigator), Ken Lingenfelter (co-pilot), Claude Curtis (radio operator).

Me in the traditional costume of the Scottish Black Watch. Taken at Castle Edinburgh, Christmas week, 1944.

Me standing outside the Mercury Hotel, West Berlin. Taken during the 381st Bomb Squadron reunion in Europe, 1982.

Also taken during the 1982 reunion, my wife Hilda (on left) with other members and guests, at "Le Compte de Flanders" pub, Amsterdam.

381st Bomb Group survivors visiting the monument erected to their memory at the site of their base in Ridgewell, England. This was the main stop for our 2002 annual reunion and European tour.

Me with WWII comrade Floyd Metts at our 2010 bomb group reunion in Nashville, Tennessee. It was the first time we had seen each other since the war.

381st Bomb Group survivors posing with the crew of the B-17 Flying Fortress "Texas Ranger" while visiting the Air Force Academy in Colorado Springs for our 2011 reunion.

Homecoming I

After completing my combat tour, I was loaded onto a nice C-54[67] and taken back to the United States via the Azores and Bermuda, to Bolling Field[68] in Washington. I remember as we banked over the Washington Monument, I noticed a pentagram on the very top of it. This feature is only visible if you look directly down onto it from above.

The Azores Islands are one of the most beautiful places I have ever visited, and in my Air Force career I had several occasions to stay there. I became very fond of the Portuguese wines available there, especially a champagne with the label "Monte Crasto," after the wine-growing region where it was produced. I really loved that champagne, and I remember one time in the mid-1950s while I was stationed at March AFB, my brother Tom (who was then also a USAF pilot) picked up a case of it while making a special refueling stop in the Azores on his way back from Germany in a C-124.[69] He knew I liked it and so flew the plane out to March just to deliver it to me. (This may not have been a proper way to use government assets, but we could get away with things like that back then.) I was given a thirty-day leave in Wisconsin Rapids with more of those rail trips (all travel was by train in those days), with a whistle stop at the Friendly in Portage, of course. During my visit at home, I allowed my dad to read my combat mission

---

diary. He was only able to get through about half of it. It seemed to emotionally overwhelm him, and he had to put it down and stop reading. I got the feeling he had worried about me while I was in Europe, and reading the diary graphically reminded him of the dangerous situations I had been in. I had been sending about $100 a month to my parents over the time I had been in the service, which was for them to use if they needed it, or to save for me for later if they didn't need it, and I had accumulated about $2,500 in savings. I remember asking Dad what he thought I should do with the money, and he advised me to buy land. I did end up using some of it to buy a couple of acres adjacent to our house, which I held onto for about three years before tripling my money on it (so it was good advice!). After this visit, it was on to a plush hotel in Miami Beach for six weeks of R&R. Good duty. SUPER good duty. The troops returning from combat tours were treated royally, and the entire country was united in proud support of its military.

Houston

My next four assignments were short and involved a lot of moving around the country. The first was at Ellington Field,[70] near Houston, Texas. The second was at Lubbock Army Airfield[71] in Lubbock, Texas. The third was at Columbus AAF,[72] in Columbus, Mississippi and the fourth was at Mather Field,[73] in Sacramento, California.

I left Florida about mid-March 1945. I was traveling with a serviceman and his wife who had just been reunited after his return from combat. They had a car, and we were all on our way to Ellington Field in Houston. I had talked them into driving through Tampa so I could call on Vicki. We were halfway to Tampa when we had a very minor auto accident. We handled it with the other driver to everyone's satisfaction, and resumed our journey to Tampa, but had not gotten very far when a sheriff car came up fast behind us with its siren blaring and lights flashing, and pulled us over. The deputy said we had left the scene of an accident and he escorted us to the jail in Tampa. I called Vicki and when she asked me where I was, I had to tell her I was in jail. I had not been driving so I

---

[70] Now Ellington Airport, a joint civil-military airport located in Houston, Texas.

[71] Now Reese Air Force Base.

[72] Now Columbus Air Force Base.

[73] What later became Mather AFB, this base was closed in 1993 as a result of the Base Realignment and Closure Act (BRAC), and reopened in 1995 as Sacramento Mather Airport.

had no real problem. After some short negotiations we were allowed to leave. The deputy was a petty and stupid individual who thought he had nabbed some real criminals, and the sheriff quickly straightened him out about how to deal properly with veterans returning home from the war.

We spent a couple of days in Tampa seeing Vicki and her family, and I found out that Vicki had a sister who lived in Galveston, Texas. Galveston is close to Houston and I promised that I would go there and look up her sister.

Quarters were not available for me at Ellington so I found a place to stay in town. There were three of us staying in a home owned by a woman whom we all called "Mom Livesay." She had a 1938 four-door Ford that she let us drive, and a very nice home. We loved it there. She introduced us to an illicit casino in Galveston that was built on a pier on the Gulf of Mexico. There were exit doors that opened out over the water, and we were instructed to jump out into the water and swim or wade back to the beach in case there was a police raid. The water was shallow and you could walk out a long ways before encountering deep water. We visited the casino several times but never got raided.

I had been in contact by phone and letters with Vicki in Tampa and she had asked me to go visit her sister and husband in Galveston. I did visit them and they were also great people. Vicki decided to take a vacation in Galveston so we could be together. When she got there I borrowed Mom Livesay's Ford and headed there to meet her. I was in for a surprise, because Vicki had somehow gotten it in her head that we were to be married right then and there, and had even informed some of her friends and family of that. Perhaps I had misled her in some way without intending, but I don't remember even thinking about getting married – I am sure she would have made a wonderful wife, but I simply wasn't ready. We met, had dinner and a wonderful date on the beach at Galveston, but she was terribly upset that we were not

91

going to get married right away, and the relationship ended. I did not talk to her again until the fall of 1951. While at pilot school in Bainbridge, Georgia, Hilda and I took a drive one day to Tampa, and we drove past Vicki's house. There she was, married to someone else and with two babies. We had a nice chat. She seemed happy. That was the last time I saw or heard from Vicki.

Bud Tabor finished his tour at Ridgewell and after his R&R was transferred to Ellington also. We were able to spend a lot of quality time with the abundance of talent in the Houston area. The U.S. government really had no definite plan for us returnees, and they kept moving us around with no real career plan for anyone. We would report to Ellington Field every day, listen to some lectures and then take off for a bar somewhere. Bud and I were transferred from Houston shortly before V-E Day (May 1945). I was transferred to Lubbock.

Lubbock

I arrived at Lubbock unhappily, because I had really found a home I liked in Houston and did not want to leave there. Lubbock turned out to be okay after I had been there awhile. I was made squadron adjutant. I went to work for some people who had never seen a shot fired in anger, and had been elevated to higher ranks than they deserved. They were envious of my DFC[74] and Air Medals[75], and they were in general hard to get along with.

There were several good things that came out of that assignment, however. I met a lot of great people in town. The base was scheduled to be closed in the fall and everything was winding down. We had to find a place to live in Lubbock because the base officers' quarters, or BOQ, were already closed. Three of us found a house to rent in downtown Lubbock (except for the base commander, we would be the last three officers to close the base). One roommate, Bill ("Trapper") Denning, had a '39 Ford convertible and we all used it. My other roommate was the motor pool officer, a fact that turned out to be pretty useful for our social activities: Lubbock was in a completely dry county,[76] so to buy booze

---

[74] Distinguished Flying Cross, awarded for heroism or extraordinary achievement during aerial flight.

[75] Also awarded for heroism or meritorious service during aerial flight.

[76] Lubbock has since gone from "dry" to "moist," meaning alcohol sales are permitted but not on the Sabbath. Twenty-six Texas counties remain completely dry to this day, forty-four are "wet," and the remaining 184 are moist, like Lubbock.

we would take one of the base ambulances to Amarillo and pick up a couple cases of liquor. We knew the local law enforcement wouldn't pull over and inspect a military vehicle. On the other hand, there was one time we had transferred our supply of booze to Trapper Denning's car, and some police saw us taking out a bottle and confiscated our whole stash. I eventually bought my own car, a '41 Mercury station wagon, light blue with a light wood body and red leather upholstery. I had fourteen people in that car one time, driving to a party at Texas Tech.

One of the highlights of the Lubbock tour was a trip to Mines Field in Los Angeles, which is now the LAX Airport. The base commander, then-Colonel Howell Estes, decided to take a B-17 and fly to Los Angeles. As it was a publicity trip, he took Charlie Guy, the editor of the *Lubbock Avalanche Journal* along to show him the Grand Canyon. He needed a navigator for the trip and I was the only navigator stationed there. Estes was a West Point grad, pompous as heck but a reasonably decent guy. He went on to become a three-star general (his son also became a three-star general, and his grandson a general). We flew the B-17 to L.A. and spent a few days there. The trip was described in several articles in that paper. Mines Field at the time was a small airport with one runway and very few small buildings. Two-engine C-47s[77] ("Gooney Birds," as we affectionately called them) were the airplanes used for civil aviation there.

We had our own Army Air Force football team in Lubbock. One of the Majors had been a football coach as a civilian, and he became our coach. Our team was never very good. We scrimmaged with the varsity team at Texas Tech and played poorly. The only game I remember well was the day we played against the V-12 cadets[78] at the University of

[77] Douglas C-47 "Skytrain" (or "Dakota").
[78] V-12 Navy College Training Program.

New Mexico. I played right tackle on defense and I can still see the quarterback's expression as I smeared him for a loss of yards. We also lost that game, but it was fun just being a part of it.

The War had ended in Europe, but the Japanese were still fighting. As people were transferred out, those of us left kept getting assigned different jobs. I was put in charge of supply. We had about three hundred prisoners of war there, all Italians who were pretty happy to be there. They lived in a barracks, had good food, and many of them didn't want to go back to Italy when the war ended. I spent many hours with one of them as he tried to teach me some of the Italian language.

The higher-ups decided that we would have a paper drive that would cover the entire city of Lubbock. The POWs were to pick up the paper that was put out by the residents and load it on the trucks we brought. Everything went well and we collected a lot of paper. I took an open jeep to patrol the section of Lubbock I was responsible for, and had brought a black master sergeant with me to help supervise the work.[79] We were on the street just east of the Texas Tech complex and it was lunch time. There were several restaurants there so I stopped at one and said to the sergeant, "Let's get something to eat." He replied, "I can't go in there." I didn't understand

---

[79] The services weren't racially integrated until 1947. I had this master sergeant with me to supervise the black troops who were participating in that day's tasks.

so I repeated, "We are both hungry, let's eat." "I can't go in there," he explained, "because blacks are not allowed to go to certain restaurants." When I finally understood what was going on, I really couldn't believe it. That was the first time I became aware there was such a thing as segregation in America.[80] I asked him if he knew anyplace nearby where he was allowed where I would also be allowed, and we went to a restaurant he recommended. I was the only white person there.

Another real interesting part of the Lubbock assignment was the fact that I learned to fly as a pilot and enjoyed flying my girlfriends around on weekends in a Piper J-3 "Cub."[81] My friends and I had met a woman whom we thought to be a little older than ourselves, perhaps around thirty-three years old. She was personable, owned a couple of clothing stores and two Piper Cubs. She had said that if I learned how to fly, she would let me fly her airplanes.

I found out I could get lessons at the airport at Tahoka, Texas, a small town not far from Lubbock. I went to meet the flight instructor and signed up to take flying lessons with him. I soloed in the Piper Cub after just two hours and ten minutes of instruction, and from that day until the day we left

---

[80] As I mentioned earlier, I had never even seen a Negro before entering the service; none had ever lived in Central Wisconsin where I was from. We weren't raised to hate or look down on blacks, and we never practiced segregation with Indians (the only non-white residents of my town). One of my good boyhood friends was a Menominee Indian named Carson Sine.
[81] A small, basic aircraft produced between 1937 and 1947. For its simplicity, affordability and popularity, it was known as the "Model T" of airplanes.

Lubbock, I would get together with this woman and other friends to fly her planes. We would take the airplanes, fly to a nice big field a short distance out of town, and proceed to fly our girlfriends around. The lady who owned the planes would take one of them up to three thousand feet or so, do a spin right over us and then land, and then we would fly. We never had any accidents but there were a few close calls. I remember one time in particular when an Air Force pilot named Jack and his girlfriend Peno took off in one of the planes. As they were coming in for their first landing, he pulled the throttle back to reduce power and the engine quit. They were not going fast enough for the relative wind to keep the propeller spinning and it just stopped. I can still see that plane coming in with the prop not turning. Luckily, he glided in for a perfect landing, but that was the last time Jack and his girlfriend flew the Cub. Those days flying the Piper Cub in Lubbock turned out to be a good warm-up for real pilot school, which would come later.

We celebrated the end of the war in Japan along with everyone else. The streets of downtown Lubbock were jammed with people. We had the top down on Trapper Denning's Ford, and we were sitting on top of the back seat while parading through town. Everyone had fully supported the war effort and we were all glad it was finally over. President Truman made many really stupid decisions during his presidency, but dropping the atomic bombs on Hiroshima and Nagasaki was not one of them. That really ended the war and saved around 400,000 American lives because Japan did not have to be invaded.

Now that the war was over, the time came to close the base (since as I mentioned, it was one of the bases on the closure list). As officer in charge of supply and maintenance it became my primary responsibility to oversee its closure. The Italian POWs were sent home and almost everyone had been transferred out. There were just four of us officers and some

97

airmen left. I arranged for all the remaining furniture and office equipment to be sold, and we secured permission to burn all the remaining tires and oil, something that would never be allowed today. There were several 50-gallon drums of oil and other flammable liquids. I had a trencher dig a shallow, flat-bottom hole and pile the dirt around the edges to create a ditch where I could place the tires and pour in the fuel and oil. I had the tires and other debris piled in there, poured in the liquids and set the whole thing on fire. The fire was intense, the smoke thick and black. The smoke rose several thousand feet and the west wind carried the smoke all over the city of Lubbock, which caused much concern among the locals. I had been granted permission to do it so the controversy was over quickly, but it was an event I will always remember.

The base was closed, and I caught a ride on a C-47 to San Angelo AAF[82] where I turned in the money I had collected from the sale of the remaining property. I had over $10,000 in cash in the side pocket of my B-4 bag and I left it sitting in the BOQ room over the weekend. I turned it all in to the finance office on Monday. Nobody ever needed to worry about theft back in those days. I was transferred to Columbus, Mississippi, around November 1945.

---

[82] Originally Carr Field, it was renamed Mathis Field, and is today a public airport (also known as the San Angelo Regional Airport).

Japan Occupation

Columbus, Mississippi

I arrived at Columbus in the fall of '45, when it was still warm enough to swim at the base pool. We had practically nothing to do there, and I don't remember much about the place. I did meet some nice folks, however. I remember the Thompson sisters who had just returned from active duty in the Navy (they were WAVES). None of the women in the services in those days were allowed to go to combat and these two had stateside duty. Columbus was in a dry county, and we had to go to the woods to meet up with revenuers[83] to get some bottles of really bad moonshine. I had my '41 Merc station wagon and I got along well with those folks alright.

I think it was about March of '46 that I transferred from Columbus to Mather. In the early summer I took a thirty-day leave and spent a vacation in Wisconsin Rapids. I remember my dad had a great time driving my '41 Merc with Mother to White Lake to visit Grandpa Whitehouse. It was a thrill for anyone from our humble, Two-Mile status to have a decent car to drive. I saw both my Grandpa Whitehouse and my

---

[83] This term applied to federal agents responsible for enforcing alcohol prohibitions, but was also applied cynically to the bootleggers themselves, the implication being that the federal enforcers were in cahoots with the bootleggers. Widespread corruption was universally understood to be commonplace in the enforcement of alcohol blue laws.

father for the last time on that trip. I remember paying a visit to Woodlawn City cemetery in Shawano with Grandpa Whitehouse where Grandma is buried, and watching him tapping his cane around the ground beside her where he would ultimately wind up. He was a wonderful guy and I thought the world of him. Sometime in the late summer of 1946, he traveled to Wisconsin Rapids to visit my mother and dad. I had left a fifth of Canadian Club with them so that I would have it there on my next leave. Neither of my folks drank anything and I knew it would be safe with them. Well, Grandpa found it and drank it all in one day. He was known to imbibe. He told my mother, "Tell Jack that he really buys good whiskey."

First Marriage

On the trip to Sacramento, I remember stopping for the night in Needles, California, and waking up the next morning to discover I had a flat tire on the Merc. All the tires were worn slick, but that's the way us guys who couldn't afford tires drove them. I got it fixed and drove on. California at that time was known as the land of the "fruits and nuts." I had never been to California before and I was looking anxiously forward to what was going to happen to me there. One of the first impressions that sticks in my memory was the trees. Driving down Capitol Avenue was like traveling through a tunnel of trees, so dense was the canopy overhead. The only lights on in downtown Sacramento after 6 p.m. were at Hart's Café on K Street, Buddy Baer's bar on L Street and the Senator Hotel.[84] Everything closed by 9 p.m. There was angular parking on K Street from 6th Street to 16th Street. Weinstock Hales was the biggest store in town. My short, first stay in Sacramento would have a profound effect on me that connected me to that town for the rest of my life.

There was only one very small building out by what is now Highway 50 to the north of Mather. The train stopped

---

[84] A Sacramento landmark situated directly across the street from the north-facing side of the State Capitol building, it hasn't had a bar or functioned as a hotel since the 1970s, when it was converted to an office building.

there to let people off and there were no buildings between Mather and Perkins Welding, which was located near 65th Street. My job was to fly on C-47 aircraft and teach returnee bombardiers navigation. This was pretty much all I had to do.

There was an active night life in spite of the fact that there were only about three places to go to meet girls. There were some wild places in Jackson but that was a bit of a drive. We spent most evenings at the Senator Hotel bar. We would go from there to Buddy Baer's, then to Hart's Café for food and then back to the BOQ. Buddy Baer was a brother to the boxer, Max Baer. They were both big guys. One night at the Senator Hotel, I met the entertainer Martha Raye,[85] a very friendly and fun lady. I might have had a date with her, but one of our other officers took her out. It was also at the Senator bar one night that I met one B. Gloria Niemi.[86] Gloria and her mother had come to the Senator bar to have a drink and pick someone up. I think Gloria was nineteen years old and her mother was thirty-nine or so. Another officer and I picked them up and went home with them. The mother (her name was Mabel Ricci) had a house on 26th Street between O and P Streets. We had more dates and spent more time at the house. Mabel had divorced Gloria's father and had remarried. Gloria's father was Finnish, I believe actually an immigrant from Finland. I never met him and we never talked about him. Gloria's mother was kind of a war-horse.

One day, after landing on return from a regular mission, one of my bosses told me that I had been transferred to a base near Salt Lake City, which was a staging area for troops being shipped to Japan. He also said that I should have been notified sooner and that I would have to leave right away. I loaded up the Merc and headed for Salt Lake City. I

---

[85] Besides being an Academy Award-winning film and TV entertainer, she became an officer and outstanding supporter of our military in the USO.
[86] First initial B. was for Bernice.

brought Gloria with me, and we spent a weekend together before she returned to Sacramento with an engagement ring. I was able to get back to Sacramento for a few weeks before leaving for Japan. We decided to get married before I left. We had heard that the American military was building dependent housing in Japan and we felt that we should get married. So we were married by a justice of the peace at the house on 26th Street on September 10, 1946. We had time for a two-day honeymoon trip to a ranch near Fort Bragg. The first night someone set off some dynamite outside our bedroom window.[87] It was far enough away not to do any damage, but it sure was loud.

Gloria came with me again to Salt Lake City to the staging area and spent a few days with me before driving the Merc back to Sacramento. I traveled with the troops by train to San Francisco to board a troop ship. We left for Japan on September 19.

I was halfway to Hawaii on that ship when on September 22, 1946, my father died of a massive heart attack. I found out about it from the Red Cross only after the ship docked in Hawaii. I was given an emergency leave and gathered all my belongings (in a foot locker and a B-4 bag) and boarded a C-54 from Hickam AAF[88] to Fairfield-Suisun Army Air Base,[89] and then caught a bus to Sacramento.

---

[87] Shivaree was a custom of making noise with pans, kettles, etc. to give a "mock" serenade to a newlywed couple outside their bedroom window. But in this case it was done with dynamite.

[88] Now Hickam Air Force Base.

[89] Now Travis Air Force Base.

I wanted to get to Wisconsin Rapids as quickly as possible but flying was not an option, so I purchased tickets for Gloria and myself on a sleeper train. It was an okay trip. I remember feeling anxious because Gloria was going to have to get used to an outdoor toilet, no running water and a lot of inconveniences that she was unaccustomed to. Her Finnish relatives in the Fort Bragg/Mendocino area had much more modern conveniences than my family.

We got home. I was okay until I got through the door. Then I nearly passed out. It was my first exposure to a death in the family, and it was overwhelming. You might suppose that because of all the harsh abuse I suffered as a young boy, I would not love my dad, but I did. I went into his bedroom and cried for over an hour. I was never that sad before over anything.

I finally got over the grief enough to carry on. Dad died with just $2.55 to his name and no insurance. The house was pretty much paid for and the only other asset was the Forty. Since the Forty was far away and represented only unpleasant memories of intense labor and hardship, no one wanted it. I don't remember exactly how, but it was mutually decided that I would inherit the Forty. I still have the $2.55 Dad had in his pocket when he died, consisting of two very old silver dollars and some other change. Mother was broke, and the three brothers agreed she would have to go back to teaching school. We made arrangements for her to go back to the normal school in Wisconsin Rapids and get a refresher course and get her teaching credential updated. I spent all the money I had to get her going and to provide food for everyone until Mother could start teaching. I was also completely broke then. Lyle had joined the Air Force and was still in at the time, but was about to be discharged. Tom was thirteen years old and still had to be taken care of along with Mother. She finished the normal school and got a teaching job in the Two-Mile area.

Gloria and I returned to California, stopping en route at Portage for a couple days. I remember that Jack Fields (one of Uncle Togo's best friends) saw Gloria and he said, "Let me get a good look at this blonde." Gloria was a natural blonde with long hair and green eyes, typically Finnish, really good-looking, so I was not surprised. Togo and Laura took good care of us as they always did. Somehow we got to Madison and spent some time with Aunt Mildred and Uncle John. After that we got on the train and headed back to California. I remember that as were walking beside the train the steam came shooting out like it always did from those steam engines, and we thought we were goners. I don't remember a lot about the trip back on the train until we got to Sacramento. We were both in the lower berth sleeping so soundly that the porter had both arms under the mattress shaking it and yelling, "LOWER FOUR!" as loud as he could to get us to wake up. We then had to get dressed in that cramped space and we barely made it off the train before it pulled out again.

I had to report to Fairfield-Suisun AAB and get back to Hawaii, but I had a couple more days to stay in Sacramento. By this time President Truman had decided to drastically reduce the size of the services. He had people assigned to categories one through eight depending on whether they were to be discharged right away or retained longer. All decisions were based on the manpower requirements for the occupation of Germany and Japan. While at Mather I found out that some of the guys who had conspired to place me on a slow boat to Japan (to keep from having to go themselves) were now looking at being booted out of the service and into unemployment. There was a lot of crying and whining over that, and I enjoyed every minute of it. I was happy to be shipping out to Japan and staying in the service. I had a very low priority getting on a plane for Hawaii, and did not arrive there until mid-November 1946.

Upon arrival in Hawaii I was placed on a ship loaded with about 1,700 troops headed for Japan. The ship was to go to Korea first and then to Yokohama. It was customary for the officers on a shipment like this to form a cadre to control the activities of the military on board, since the ship was run by Department of the Army civilians. The several Army officers aboard met to assign each officer duties to cover the basic functions. Partly because I was the only Air Force officer, and partly because I reported to the ship late due to my father's funeral, I got stuck with the dreaded job of provost marshal. This meant I was responsible for the security and proper deportment of the military personnel. I did not know at the time but I found out soon enough what those Army officers knew: that many of the troops were criminal convicts who had been offered a choice of either jail or the Army and had chosen the latter. That element caused a lot of problems on the voyage. Many of the airmen on board were blacks, and just as before in Lubbock, I found that the easiest (really the only) way to maintain discipline among these troops was by appointing black master sergeants as supervisors, which I did. This voyage started out badly and got even worse when we were still about two days' voyage from our initial destination of Inchon, Korea. At that time the crew tried to change boilers (for a steamship this is like switching engines), and the engine

106

quit. We were dead in the water for three days and two nights before another ship arrived from Korea to get us. We had to all go over the side to get from one ship to the other. We had been on the East China Sea those three days without food, toilets or other essentials, and the troops were extremely unhappy.

We survived that ordeal. After getting on board the other ship, we found it to be in much better shape than the first one. The two-day trip was uneventful as I recall. We arrived in Inchon in the morning and I remember it to be one of the coldest days of my life. I had on a full Pinks & Greens uniform, sweater, trench coat, scarf and hat, but I still froze. I was broke and had to hitchhike to get to Seoul. I was able to get a ride in a weapons carrier. As we drove along, I looked out and saw a lot of natives walking around or riding bikes, and I wondered how they could stand the cold. I saw women who appeared to be wearing only a heavy coat and pants, and some of them were nursing babies. Their coats were open and their bare breasts were exposed. The cold was bitter. The war had devastated Korea and its people. The Japanese had killed at least 6 million of them and made more than 600,000 female Koreans into "comfort girls" or sex slaves for the Japanese military.

Itazuke

I finally got to Seoul and borrowed some money from the Red Cross. Now I could pay for my food in the Officers Club. We used neither Korean nor American money, but instead some kind of red, white and blue scrip in the same denominations as our real money. After getting back to the ship I got warm and never left it until we reached Yokohama. I had no knowledge about Japan, so I did not know which part of the country to try to get stationed. After some time in processing, I was sent to Itazuke Air Base[90] in Fukuoka, Japan, on that country's southernmost island of Kyushu. I was made a supply officer and worked in an office that was located in a large warehouse. Capt. Paul Blake was my boss. He was an older guy (everyone was older than me in those days) and he had his family there, a real nice wife and a couple of young sons. He had me over to his house many times for dinner. They began to build homes for the occupation forces and the houses were built to American standards. By that I mean basically that the walls were made out of wood and not paper like the Japanese houses.

Japanese locals worked in the warehouses for us, and the language barrier made it difficult to manage them. The biggest problem was that the workers were stealing uniforms and other items from our warehouses. We posted signs in the area printed in both Japanese and English that said, "Anyone seen in this area will be shot without warning." Despite these

---

[90] Now Fukuoka Airport, a civilian international and domestic airport.

warnings, the thievery got so bad that we decided to set a trap one night, waiting inside the warehouse in the darkness to see if anyone would attempt another break-in. Sure enough, a thief came along, and we shot him dead. I think he was a Korean. We left him there where he fell, and the next morning the workers were forced to step over his dead body as they came in to start their shifts. Our translator explained to all of them as they walked past the dead thief that the same thing would happen to anyone else trying to steal from us. We had no further problems with stealing.

Our airmen weren't supposed to fraternize with the Japanese women, but lots of them did anyway. They would load up at the BX[91] on candy bars, liquor and clothing items, take them to their "corbitos,"[92] and fraternize. The Army Air Force wanted to try to protect their airmen from going too far in their relationships with the natives, and all company-grade officers had to occasionally perform the additional duty of V.D. patrol officer.[93] When I was assigned this duty, I would take an MP[94] with me, both of us armed with .45 caliber automatics, and go around the residential sectors looking for G.I.s breaking the rules. If caught, offenders were subject to administrative discipline, which any one of them would have

---

[91] Base Exchange (on-base retail store).
[92] Japanese girlfriend.
[93] "venereal disease patrol officer."
[94] Military policeman.

definitely wanted to avoid. On one occasion, we found a G.I. with a girl. He heard us coming, jumped up and burst out the back through the house's paper walls and into the rice paddies. He left his shoes, all his BX purchases, and a very wide-eyed, surprised-looking Japanese girl. When the MP and I stopped laughing, we went looking for him, but we never found him.

I was on flying status as a navigator and had to get in my flying time in a couple different kinds of aircraft. There was a need for good aerial maps of Japan and we flew in C-45s[95] equipped with cameras, photographing all of Honshu and farther north all the way to Kokura. The other aircraft that I got my time in was the P-61 ("Black Widow").[96] I made these flights between the southern end of the Korean peninsula and Vladivostok, Russia. We would cover that area to observe the shipping activity. Whenever we would see a ship we would buzz it and take photos of it. I can remember on the first pass there would be lots of people on the deck, but on the second pass when we took the pictures, there would be no one on deck. We never got shot at during these exercises but we were ready. Our Russian war allies and "friends" were obviously up to something they didn't want us to know about. The P-61 had four 20-millimeter cannons. We had a grand time flying to an island we used for target practice and firing those big guns!

---

[95] Beechcraft C-45 "Expeditor," a twin-engine trainer/utility aircraft, better known as the Model 18 "Twin Beech."
[96] Northrop P-61 "Black Widow," a twin-boom night fighter, and the first US military aircraft to be equipped with radar.

The occupation of Japan had been going on long enough by the time I got there that the average Japanese no longer harbored great anger towards us. Their leaders had indoctrinated them with all kinds of fears about our intentions, but they had come to realize we were actually not out to kill them all. During the first part of my tour there, around Christmas of 1946, several of the officers assigned to Itazuke Air Base were invited to attend a dinner at a small, traditional Japanese restaurant/hotel located in Kurume. We all took our jeeps and drove down there. I recall that they served pork chops and vegetables which we had been forbidden to eat. There were several reasons for this: first, they used only human fertilizer[97] and from this we could contract cholera; second, the meat was assumed to be contaminated; finally, we were under orders not to deprive any of the natives of their own food supply. The room was typical, no chairs, a soft tatami floor covering, a long low table with a hole in the floor with a hibachi fire going so we could warm our feet as we sat on the floor to eat. Japanese buildings had no heating or air conditioning and even the exterior walls were made of paper.

Shoes had to be taken off at the door, so there we sat shivering as the food began to fill the table. I don't remember

---

[97] It is a fact that fertilizer from human waste was used in agriculture back then throughout Japan, although I have no idea if this is still practiced there. Everywhere you went in the countryside, you could see cans sitting next to the canals which the farm workers used to relieve themselves. Servicemen used to call these cans "honey buckets."

the names of our hosts, but I do remember that they ran the tire industry (cartel) in Japan. Some spoke a little English but most of the evening was spent smiling and nodding. Each of us had our own waitress. Each was dressed in their native kimono and each one kneeled directly behind the person they were serving. I remember making the worst faux pas of the evening. Everyone smoked cigarettes[98] in those days and I thought those tiny shallow glasses with some sort of warm liquid in them would make a fine ashtray and a good place to put out a cigarette. When I did this, my waitress made a quick move to remove that small glass with the cigarette butt and get me another one. I was then told that there was hot sake in those glasses and I was supposed to drink it.

There was an officers' club in town that we went to regularly, plus a Quonset-type building[99] that housed an officers' club on base. I began exploring the territory on weekends and there was one trip I will never forget. I was driving a weapons carrier, which is like a big open pick-up truck, and had a couple with me. Art was a first lieutenant who had been stationed there long enough that his wife was already there with him. They had not been married too long and they drank a lot. We were sight-seeing somewhere between Itazuke and Kurume when we came across a building that we thought could be a small hotel. We stopped there and it was a hotel complete with a "hotsi" bath.[100] We had been drinking and we three decided to try the hotsi bath.

---

[98] Cigarettes cost a nickel a pack in those days and we all said we would quit smoking if they raised the price to a dime a pack.

[99] A lightweight prefabricated structure of corrugated galvanized steel having a semicircular cross section.

[100] The correct Japanese term is "sentō" baths. U.S. servicemen heard Japanese referring to them by what sounded like "hotsi" and came to the erroneous conclusion that this was a Japanese word when it was actually the Japanese attempting to say in English that the baths were "hot", but mispronouncing the word.

I had heard about these places but had never seen one. It is really more of an indoor pool filled with extremely hot water, than a bath per se. The procedure is, you take a bath first and then get into the pool. They introduce live steam into the pool regularly to keep the water hot. There were stools to sit on, soap and towels with which to bathe. Art and his wife were checked into one room and I into another where we could hang our clothes and change into a big thick kimono. I stripped and put on the kimono as did Art and his wife. We met in the hotsi bath room and after some embarrassment at being naked in front of each other, we proceeded to bathe. We finished that and eased into the water. The water was extremely hot and it was deep enough to come up to our shoulders. We had been in the hotsi for some time and we were tired and ready to get out when a Japanese family came in to get in the hotsi bath. There was a man and wife and two small children. They bowed and hissed[101] at us and proceeded to take their baths. Art's wife had long blonde hair (which was fascinating to the Japanese). She absolutely would not get out of the pool naked in front of this family so we stayed in the hotsi until the family left. By that time we were so weak from the hot water that we could hardly climb out. We dried off and went back to our rooms. A bed had been prepared and we slept for a couple hours. The bed was a thick futon on the floor with heavy blankets on top. The pillow was a typical Japanese type, small, hard cylindrical and uncomfortable. We got up, dressed and went out to the weapons carrier for the trip back to Itazuke.

---

[101] We understood at the time that the peculiar custom of hissing (and spitting), together with the bowing gesture, was a sign of courtesy and respect. During my time there, all Japanese hissed when bowing to Americans, and even to each other. I have been told this custom no longer exists in Japan (they still bow, but no hissing); modern Japanese seem to have no memory or knowledge of it being a past practice.

113

There is another trip that I will never forget. We were on a levee-type road wide enough for just one vehicle, and a steep slope on each side that ended in rice paddies. The rice paddies had ridges in them and they were wet and mushy. I began wondering what I would do if a vehicle approached from the other direction, and about that time a truck appeared coming straight at us. I was not about to stop, and neither was the other driver. We looked at each other for a time and then we got out to make some motions at each other (the Japanese man in the other vehicle could speak no English). We decided to each get one wheel off to the right and try and get by. It worked for the other vehicle, but not for us, and we slid off the road into the rice paddy. I managed to keep the WC[102] from tipping over as we slid down the embankment; I leveled it off in the rice paddy and then became hopelessly stuck in the mud. It was getting dark now and we were wondering how we were ever going to get word to the base that we needed help. I threw the whiskey bottle as far away from the WC as I could, because I knew that would be a factor in any investigation that ensued. Some MPs finally showed up with two jeeps to take us back to the base. They wandered around and found the whiskey bottle I had tossed, but they couldn't prove it was ours. They put Art and his wife in one jeep and me in the other, and off we went. I was in the back seat with an MP on each side of me. We were talking, and the driver got distracted and was going too fast around a slight curve on the dirt road when he slipped to the right and hit a telephone pole

---

[102] Weapons Carrier.

with the right front of the jeep and caved it in. The damage was bad, but not so much that we could not continue to drive the jeep to the base. I then said to the MP in charge, "Now that you hit that telephone pole, you didn't have a wreck, and I didn't have a wreck, right?" The accident was never reported. The motor pool officer was a lieutenant friend by the name of Konechne. He and I took a truck with a winch, pulled the WC back into the road and drove it home. It was undamaged.

We went on maneuvers with the P-61s at a very small airstrip located near the Northeast part of the Island of Honshu. The strip was near the water and the runway consisted of dirt and some steel mesh. We had an old abandoned building to stay in, sleeping bags on the floor to sleep on, and the usual field kitchen for food preparation. We would go down each morning to greet the tiny fishing boats as they sailed back in from their morning excursions, and relieved them of all the good fresh shrimp and small fish we wanted to cook and eat. When the tide was out we would walk out on the rocks and pick up mussels and oysters. The mess sergeant cooked these up nicely, and we actually ate pretty well. We flew short reconnaissance missions and this temporary duty lasted about a week.

There was a hill nearby that was shaped like an inverted cone, which was about 2,500 feet to the top. It was heavily wooded with lots of brush. That's where Konechne and two others in his plane were killed. Konechne was not a pilot – he rode in the P-61 in the seat right behind the pilot (just as I did). As they were returning from a mission there was a ring of clouds around the top of this little mountain and the pilot must have thought that it would be fun to nip through that little cloud on his way to the base. They slammed into the ground about 100 feet from the top, disintegrated and burned up. Early the next morning, we started up the hill with our squadron commander, Major De La Rosa. Climbing hand over hand part of the way through dense brush, we made it to the crash site by about mid-afternoon. Although the head, hands and feet had been almost completely burned off, I could recognize Koneckne's body just from the shape of it. We (about four of us) had consumed the bottle of whiskey that the major had brought along. There were some local woodsmen who climbed the hill with us. They knew where the trails were, and they brought the bodies down on some small wooden sleds that they used to bring logs down the mountain. I was a navigator at the time and had never flown as a pilot. After I went to pilot school and began flying single engine jets, I had fun nipping little pieces out of clouds, but I always did it at altitudes well above the terrain.

Later, (probably August of 1947) Gloria and I started having problems that ended in divorce. We both were frustrated at the length of time it was taking the military to get a house built for us, and after possibly misinterpreting explanations I gave her about the delay in a letter, she filed for divorce. I then began doing everything I could so I could come home and try to save my short marriage. I was at the Red Cross every day to try and persuade them to help me get an emergency leave, and writing letters to Army Air Force Personnel. Finally after a couple months of bickering, I was granted an emergency leave and came to Sacramento. The trip was on a regular C-54; we stopped at Wake Island, Johnson Island and Hawaii before arriving at Fairfield-Suisun AAB.

I hired a young attorney named Tom McBride[103] and told him I wanted to contest the divorce. I wanted Gloria and me to try and reconcile our differences, get back together, and then travel back to Japan together and get into the dependent housing. We met for a half hour or so in the attorney's office but there was no changing her mind. She was more mature and better looking, I thought, then when I had left her in Sacramento about a year before. It was over. I got her to quitclaim the interest I had given her in the Forty, and she kept the '41 Merc Wagon (or she had already sold it, I can't remember which). Apart from that we had no other property to divide. I never spoke to or saw Gloria again after that, but I learned recently that she lived out the rest of her life in northern California until her death in 1990. She kept the last name Grey all those years, so I guess she never remarried.

I signed in to the Senator Hotel, very sick with tonsillitis, and went to bed. I had purchased a ticket to Chicago on United Airlines and was going to visit Mother, Tom, Lyle and his wife Phyllis before going back to Japan. I was very sick and I had the hotel physician come up to my room to check my tonsils. Doctors in those days usually assumed that if it was a serviceman, he must just be nursing a hangover, and they were not very caring. After checking me, this one decided to give me a big penicillin shot. I told him I

---

[103] Tom McBride went on to become a Federal District Judge.

had to catch an airline to Chicago the next day. I got the shot, caught the airplane and got myself to Wisconsin Rapids.

The airplane left from Sacramento Executive Airport. It was a C-47 which was the most common airliner United flew at that time. I was the only passenger on the flight to Denver and we had to circle (hover) as they called it, to wait for better weather in order to land. The stewardess and I were freezing in the cabin and we huddled together with blankets to keep warm. That was the only unusual incident on that flight. The stewardess was nice and accommodating. After the leave in Wisconsin, I took a train back to Chicago, making my usual stop at the Friendly. I got back to California and Fairfield-Suisun AFB. I had the lowest priority to get on a flight to Japan and by now it was late December 1947. I spent New Year's Eve at the party at the base officers' club, and I met some actresses who were part of an Army special service group that was on its way to Japan to put on plays to entertain the troops. Like me, they had been assigned a very low priority for getting an airplane. That was when I met Barbara Spencer. We had some drinks and danced. At the end of the evening, just when we were arranging to meet the next morning for breakfast, we all got the word that we had been assigned to a shipment that would leave the next morning.

During the leg to Hawaii Barbara and I became better acquainted. She got extremely airsick from the turbulence on approach into Hickam. We spent six weeks together in Hawaii awaiting our departure for Japan. We had an apartment on Waikiki Beach, which at that time had only two buildings along the entire stretch, the Moanna Hotel and the Royal Hawaiian. That was another time I ran completely out of money. After getting to Japan, we spent almost an entire year together. I arrived in Tokyo one day before Barbara, borrowed some money from the Red Cross and met her when she arrived. We spent a few pleasant days in Tokyo and I left for Itazuke. I asked Barbara to try and get herself assigned as far

118

south as possible so that we could be together more easily. She was able to get her troupe stationed at the army headquarters in Kokura, about forty miles from Itazuke. We spent a lot of time together, doing a lot of sight-seeing and traveling around Japan.

I really fell for Barbara and she for me, but her job came first. Although she never achieved any real fame in her career, Barbara had acted professionally in New York City, where she had been married briefly. She confided to me that her ex-husband, also an actor/entertainer, confessed to her one day that he was having affairs with other men. This experience had turned her totally off of marriage and the "responsibility" of having a husband. I was also eight years her junior, factors which taken together prevented our relationship from developing any further.

Years later, in July or August of 1949 when I was stationed at Mather AFB and living in Sacramento, I received a phone call at the base that someone in San Francisco had been trying to reach me. The message was from Barbara. I don't know how she had found out where I was, but I had to explain to her that I had been happily married for over a year, and that it would not be possible to see her. I figured that would be the last I would hear of Barbara, but I ran into her again one last time in London in 1958 while on temporary duty in England (I don't remember now if it was Lakenheath or Mildenhall). I was in London for a weekend and there she was, working at a USO office. We had a nice lunch at a restaurant in the Chelsea area.

Then in 1964, while inspecting the units at Fairchild AFB, Spokane, Washington, one of the staff said he was going to buy a "bottle" and go visit a woman he knew who was stationed there in the special service department. When I asked him who she was, he gave the name Barbara Spencer. I asked him to give her a hello and regards from me, but I didn't see her. Barbara's and my paths had crossed many times, but that one was really the last time we were in the same place at once. She was a great lady. As far as I know, she never remarried.

Hilda

In August of 1948 the Air Force[104] decided that they had to rebuild the runway at Kadena Air Base in Okinawa. They established an Engineer Aviation Battalion, and in order to set up the command structure they needed officers. The only qualification you had to have was to be single, as they did not want to disturb anyone who had brought their families to live with them. So my Itazuke tour ended, and I was transferred to Tachikawa Air Base[105] near Tokyo, where the battalion was being formed to go to Okinawa. One day while in the base commander's office I noticed a young woman, the commander's secretary, reading *Stars and Stripes*. She let me share her newspaper, and we read it together. I was very impressed by her. Her name was Hilda Marie Huegel. One of the incentives they gave us for the sudden uprooting and transfer to Okinawa was that we could have any assignment in Japan we wanted after the runway was completed. I thought for a second about Hilda (whom I had only just met) and said, "I'll take Tachikawa."

The battalion arrived in Okinawa in September 1948. I was made the headquarters company commander, and as such was responsible for the care, housing and feeding of the

---

[104] Now its own separate branch of service.

[105] Part of present-day Tachikawa Airfield, which started out as a Japanese Imperial Army Airfield. The U.S. occupied this base from Japan's surrender in 1945 until 1977, when it was returned to local control. Now it is used by Japan's Ground Self Defense Force.

troops. We only had one engineer (an air force officer - the Army there had none of their own), which was kind of unusual considering our mission was to build a runway. The 93rd Bomb Wing from Castle AFB[106] (near Merced, California) arrived for their ninety-day TDY[107] with 45 B-29s,[108] and I was fortunate to be able to get my flying time in with them. One of the pilots was Doug Frost, a friend that I had met at Aviation Cadet School in Texas.

Things were going pretty well when along came Typhoon Libby.[109] There were two days of wind from one direction, one calm day when the eye of the hurricane passed over us, then two more days of wind blowing the opposite direction. The palm trees would bend so much they were almost horizontal, but they came back afterwards. The props on the B-29s were turning up to 1,200 RPMs from the wind, and the crews had to keep turning the planes into the wind to keep them from blowing over. After sucking up all that sand and sea water, the engines on every single one of those B-29s had to be changed before they could fly again.

---

[106] Closed in 1995, it is now known as the Castle Airport Aviation and Development Center.

[107] U.S. military term for "temporary duty."

[108] Boeing B-29 Superfortress, a four-prop engine heavy bomber used in late WWII and the Korean War.

[109] Libby was a tropical cyclone that struck Okinawa in October of 1948. The storm lasted three days, had winds over 160 mph and caused incredible destruction.

The destruction was unbelievable. Four by eight feet sheets of plywood were flying through the air like paper. Our Quonset was safely anchored in concrete with steel cables. But when it was safe to go outside, we found that the winds had carried away the eight-seater outhouse that was located right behind our Quonset. Our buildings took a beating during the typhoon and the roofs blew off the dependent houses that had been built for the U.S. families that were going to live there. The roofs were supposed to be typhoon-proof. After the storm, it was surprising to see that the native shacks near the beach made from little else but grass were almost completely undamaged.

We finished the runway, and then we all transferred to the bases we had chosen for ourselves elsewhere in Japan. Barbara and I had a parting of ways and I started going out with Hilda. I got assigned to the supply division working for a real nice lieutenant colonel. I bought a maroon-colored, 1939 Plymouth coupe from one of the guys who was leaving to go home. I frequently loaned it to Hilda, who loved taking it to Tokyo for weekend shopping excursions with her girlfriends.

Before my assignment in Japan, I had experimented a little with golf at base courses, but I did not take it up as a serious pastime until Tachikawa. There, Hilda and I had access to the Kogenei Golf Course in Tokyo, which was operated by the U.S. Air Force and used for the recreation of the American military, and we played a lot of golf together there. In 1949, green fees for eighteen holes cost fifty cents, plus a pack of Lucky Strikes for the caddie. Then and now, Kogenei has been one of the most exclusive country club in Japan. As of this writing the green fees are about U.S. $350 for a round of eighteen holes during the week. Hilda gave up golf after Japan; without a caddie to select the right club for her, find her ball, and lug her clubs around, it wasn't as much fun for her. But I really fell in love with the sport, and stayed with it ever since.

Besides golf, Hilda and I went to see a lot of movies on the base, went dancing, and did a lot of traveling around northern Japan. When I met Hilda, I couldn't dance very well. But she was an excellent dancer and patiently taught me the steps. We visited Hirohito's palace in Tokyo, and we visited Osaka and Nagoya. Sometimes we caught a glimpse of General MacArthur[110] leaving the Dai Ichi building,[111] and amazedly watched every Japanese in the area (scores of them) holding long, low bows for him until he was out of sight.

Speculative accusations have been made that MacArthur demanded the Japanese perform this act of submission, but this is a revisionist lie. Before their defeat, the imperial government had brainwashed the Japanese citizenry into believing that the Americans were bloodthirsty savages who would kill all of them if we prevailed in the war. Most Japanese were unaware that the opposite was essentially true, considering how their military brutally murdered 20 million Chinese and 6 million Koreans (numerically dwarfing the Holocaust), along with so many other unspeakable atrocities. Japan still has not acknowledged its wartime crimes against humanity, and none of its leaders were ever prosecuted for those crimes (in contrast to the Nazi war criminals at Nuremberg).

Modern historians have revised and sanitized the story of Japan's acts in WWII, and most of that country now unfortunately lives in a state of proud denial about what really happened. Japanese school children today are taught that America was to blame for the war and it ended in a draw, when the plain fact is that Japan attacked us without

---

[110] MacArthur and his staff wrote the Japanese constitution that was implemented in 1946 and has been in force ever since.
[111] The Dai-Ichi Seimei Building (now called DN Tower 21) in Tokyo served as the Supreme Command of the Allied Powers (SCAP) and was MacArthur's Japanese headquarters during the occupation of Japan until it regained independence as a sovereign nation in 1952.

provocation, only to lose everything and surrender unconditionally on the deck of the USS Missouri four years later. One thing our occupation of Japan did accomplish, however, was to correct the Japanese people's perception of us. They were so relieved to discover what a noble, benevolent and forgiving people we really were, they came to love and respect the United States, and have been a fairly reliable ally ever since the war. The Japanese people who bowed to MacArthur did so because they deeply admired and respected the man. How do I know this? How can I make these claims? Because I was there.

Today, anyone with an ideological axe to grind has an easy time passing off as fact new interpretations of historical events which they themselves never witnessed firsthand. Add to this a shrewd, conscienceless, greedy lawyer to contrive some bogus victim scenario and a judiciary grossly indulgent of spurious, frivolous lawsuits, and you manage not only to rewrite history, but also to redistribute billions of dollars of other people's money and collect a percentage of the action. That is how in 1988, Japanese-Americans received $1.6 billion in reparation payments for the internment of other Japanese West Coast residents and Japanese-American citizens during the war, which government action was demagogued as "race prejudice, war hysteria, and a failure of political leadership."[112] But that was not true, at least not everywhere the program was implemented. I worked with a bank attorney during the 1970s who had spent his whole life in Sacramento,

---

[112] 100th Congress, Senate Bill 1009.

and who, during WWII, was directly involved in the local relocation operation. According to him, ethnically Japanese families were given the option of renouncing their Japanese citizenship[113] and any further allegiance to Emperor Hirohito. If they refused, they were interned. If they agreed, they were not required to relocate. Young men of service age who agreed to these terms actually joined the U.S. military, becoming what we called "Nisei."[114] The motives and goals for internment had nothing to do with racism. Rather, the program was created to protect ethnically-Japanese citizens and residents from race-based persecution. Americans were enraged with Japan over the Pearl Harbor attack and subsequent excesses committed by the Japanese military, and our Japanese-Americans and residents were extremely vulnerable to reprisals and general hostility. The internment camps undoubtedly prevented mass lynchings and arson attacks up and down the West Coast states. Not to mention the fact that we were at war with Japan. Should the U.S. government have simply allowed confessed Japan loyalists living among us to freely commit whatever acts of espionage and sabotage they wanted to? Clearly not. The internment camps were not only appropriate, but necessary, and the inconvenience it caused some people should be seen today rather as their own personal, patriotic contribution to the war effort, than any undue hardship, humiliation or injustice. We all had to make sacrifices to win that war, and theirs were less than most. The next big war is going to be between the civilized nations of the world and Islam (in fact it has already begun). When the fight comes to our territory on a major scale, it will be necessary to do the same thing with the

---

[113] Some naturalized U.S. citizens still kept their Japanese passports and a sort of dual citizenship status, although such status was never officially recognized by the U.S. government.
[114] After the Japanese term meaning a second-generation Japanese-American.

Islamists living among us as was done with the Japanese in WWII. Many of these immigrants are subversive jihadist moles awaiting activation by their offshore terrorist command. If we expect to survive, preserve our freedom and way of life, the United States and all other civilized countries will need to come to their senses, lose the suicidal insanity that is political correctness once and for all, and completely destroy this dangerous enemy.

In occupied Japan there were still some elements hostile to us, so we could never assume we were safe traveling around the Japanese countryside. Hilda and I got a scare one night when returning to the base at Tachikawa. It was around 10:30 p.m. and there was an 11 p.m. curfew for Department of Air Force Civilians. We ran out of gas in my '39 Plymouth coupe. It was a pitch-dark night with no moon. I was going to walk somewhere to try and get some gas but Hilda would not stay there by herself, so we just sat there. Suddenly we heard a noise – I opened the door and went outside and encountered an older Japanese man on a bicycle. I brought him around to the gas tank and through some pidgin Japanese and some motions he got the idea that we needed gas. He nodded, bowed, hissed, and left us. Remember gas was rationed and not generally available to the Japanese and to this day, I don't know how he did it, but he was back in ten minutes with a can of gas. I poured this into the tank, gave him a pack of

Lucky Strikes and after some more bowing he left us. We barely made it back to Tachi[115] before the curfew, but we did.

Over in Europe, Stalin began closing all the surface routes into Berlin from the American and British sectors, which led to our implementation of the Berlin airlift. The 317th Troop Carrier Wing stationed at Tachi was transferred to Germany to participate in that effort. They used C-54s. Another C-54 unit from Guam was sent to be part of the Berlin airlift, and the dependents from that unit were transferred from Guam to Tachi. One of my jobs was to prepare for these arrivals. When the ship arrived in Yokohama Bay with the families on board, my lieutenant colonel and I went out with the harbor pilot to board it. We had to climb a rope ladder from the pilot boat up to the portal on the side of the ship, while trying to carry the briefing materials we had with us. This got us and our sparkling Pinks and Greens soaked, but we made it and conducted the welcome briefing without further difficulty.

---

[115] Tachikawa.

Homecoming II

With Hilda an employee of the Department of Air Force Civilians, me in the Air Force, and the army running all the transportation, it took a lot of logistical coordination to get Hilda and me on the same ship to return to the United States. The Air Force had somehow broken its contract with the civilians and they were allowed to come home earlier than their originally scheduled return date. This is how Hilda and I were able to come home at the same time. My three-year tour was complete and I had some leeway. My time in Japan had been enough for me to become semi-fluent in the language, and certain common local expressions had crept into the everyday language a lot of Americans used with each other. For example, if you wanted to get someone's attention, you said, "Ah Don A," which translates to English as "By the way...," but was used more the way we would the expression, "Hey, you." I used it so often when I wanted to get Hilda's attention that it became my nickname for her, and during our entire marriage she was "Ah Don A," which also got shortened to "Ahno."

Hilda and I didn't return to Japan until November of 1989, when we made two short stops, just layovers really. The first was on a Space-A[116] leg en route to Korea to visit our daughter Susan, who was on active duty at Osan Air Base,

---

[116] Flying on military flights for personal reasons is allowed to active duty and retired military personnel, dependents on a space-available, or "Space-A" basis.

and we spent the night in Iwakuni.[117] The last was on the return trip, with another overnighter in Okinawa.

We boarded a ship sometime around mid-May 1949 and it took nearly two weeks to get home. We sailed under the Golden Gate Bridge and docked either in Alameda or San Francisco, I cannot remember which one for sure. Hilda went to Ohio and I went to Wisconsin. I had ordered a 1949 Pontiac convertible which had been sitting at the dealership for nearly two months before I got home. My high school classmate George Nimtz[118] was working at the dealership and said he could have sold the car to a hundred others before I got back to claim it. Here, bear in mind that all the U.S. automobile manufacturers had stopped making cars in 1942 in order to shift production to tanks and military vehicles until the war ended. After civilian vehicle production resumed, the first cars came out only in 1946 and because supply had been suppressed for so long, there were still wait lists as late as 1949. I had ordered the Pontiac in January of 1949 and the dealer didn't get it until March. It was beautiful, dark blue, with whitewall tires and all the extras you could get back then.

I had a thirty-day vacation, and after a short visit in Wisconsin Rapids I headed for Youngstown, Ohio, to meet Hilda's dad and family, bring her back to Wisconsin Rapids and get married. She had two brothers and three sisters. One sister, Anne, was married to a man named Jack Marsh. They had their own daughter, Jackie, and had also adopted Hilda's youngest brother, Jimmy, because Hilda's mother had died of cervical cancer shortly after Jimmy's birth. Hilda's father, Julius Huegel, accepted me, although I am sure he would have liked it better if I was of German descent. Both of Hilda's

---

[117] Marine Corps Air Station (MCAS) Iwakuni.
[118] George defeated me for the varsity tennis championship our senior year at Lincoln High in a grueling match that lasted from 2 p.m. to 11 p.m.

130

parents were immigrants from Siebenburgen (the German exonym for Transylvania) in present-day Romania. Julius was actually sort of proud that his daughter was going to marry a captain in the Air Force. He had served in the Austrian cavalry in WWI (ironically, fighting on the opposite side of my father, who as I mentioned was in the U.S. Army during that war) and had immigrated to America in 1920.

I brought Hilda back to Wisconsin Rapids and we got married on June 30, 1949. After our visit together in Youngstown, I drove Hilda back to Wisconsin Rapids. Since I had never belonged to any church, and Hilda had been raised a Lutheran, we decided to get married in the Lutheran church in town. The parson initially balked at this because we were not members of that particular church, and I was not a member of any church. I reminded him that I had been overseas protecting him while he remained comfortably ensconced at home in Wisconsin, and suggested that he relax his rules a little and just give us a break, which he ultimately consented to do. A lot of the Lutherans in Wisconsin were of German descent, and many of these had been Nazi sympathizers during the war. From his attitude, I had my suspicions about where the parson's loyalties lay.

With that hurdle overcome, the next one was to prepare my mother's hair so she could look proper at the wedding. Mother behaved very selfishly, and it embarrassed me. I thought Hilda was the one who really should have been especially taken care of, it being her wedding and all. But Hilda was a good sport and took care of my mother. By that point, our house had electricity and a telephone, but still no plumbing. The outhouse was a novelty for Hilda. Her family was not rich either, but was financially a lot better off than mine. Hilda took everything in stride, realizing we would be leaving there shortly after the wedding.

Lyle and his wife Phyllis were at our wedding. So were Dean and Betty Corey. We spent our wedding night at a motel

131

not far from the house and I remember we had one of the most severe lightning, hail and rainstorms that I have ever been in. I managed to sleep through it but Hilda was awake the whole time. I think the motel was called Motel Eight as it was located on Eighth Street South in Wisconsin Rapids.

Hilda was not a maverick exactly, but she did want to make up her own mind about things. I believe she left home to get away from relationships she didn't want to be part of any longer. Hilda had left for Japan with the Department of Air Force Civilians sometime in 1947. Prior to that, she had struck off on her own to live in New York City, staying with some German relatives while working for Western Union. She said that in that job she would wear roller skates and carry messages back and forth on them. She also worked at the Corn Exchange Bank in NYC and afterward at the Dollar Bank back in Youngstown (she had returned home when her mother died). Her banking experience would prove a major influence on our decisions and lives later on.

My next Air Force assignment was to be at Mather AFB near Sacramento, California, and that was our destination when we left Wisconsin Rapids for our honeymoon. Things did not start off well at all. I had foolishly made a promise to my mother to drive her to Oregon to visit her brother, Harlow, and she had arranged to visit him right after our wedding. This meant that she would be with us on the first part of our honeymoon. Mother also maneuvered herself into the front seat of the car, which was annoying and unpleasant for my new bride. Actually, having her there at all was extremely inconvenient and a bad decision on my part. We survived it, but I took a lot of heat about the fact that my mother came along on that trip, one which should have been just for the two of us. We made a couple of stops between Wisconsin and Astoria, Oregon. After dropping Mother with Harlow, Hilda and I drove down to Lake Shasta where we stayed for a couple of days before proceeding to Sacramento. I then checked in at Mather AFB to attend the Aerial Observer Bombardier (AOB) School.

Cold Warrior

Mather

The Air Force was sending all the navigators, bombardiers and radar operators through the AOB program so we would be "triple-headed" in preparation for the phasing in of the B-47s[119], which the Air Force planned to have in operation by the mid-'50s. We flew in the front of B-25s and dropped practice bombs on targets in the Marysville area, and did radar navigation training down the valley toward Modesto and Fresno. The school was okay but I still wanted pilot school.

Hilda and I rented an apartment in North Sacramento somewhere near Auburn Boulevard and Watt Avenue. A neighbor nearby us raised a large flock of guinea hens there, whose screaming was so loud and constant that we couldn't wait to find another place to live. Then we found a brand-new apartment building at 39th & J streets across from the Catholic church. We were the first tenants to occupy our apartment. The rent was $95 per month, and it was real cozy and nice. We bought a kitchen table and chair set, a nice sofa and chair, and a bedroom set. We added a table and some lamps. That was

---

[119] Boeing B-47 "Stratojet," a long-range, six-jet-engine medium bomber that could fly at high speeds and altitudes, designed especially for nuclear attacks against the Soviet Union.

all the furniture we had when I finished my coursework at the school. Because of Hilda's experience in banking and operating bookkeeping machines, she wanted to go to work while we were in Sacramento. We visited a Bank of America branch at 8th and J streets on a Thursday morning to ask if they needed any bookkeepers. They asked if she could start the next day, and she did. She worked there until we transferred.

Our married life was great except for one event that I thought could be the end of our marriage. We met some folks and began a modest social life. Hilda was already an enthusiastic bridge player and she wanted me to learn to play. We had not played bridge in Japan and I was a novice at it. One evening we were playing and I made an error. Hilda kept harping and correcting me to the point that I became very embarrassed. I had already gotten her point the first time. We quit the game for that night, went home, did not speak, went to bed and did not touch each other. The next morning we both got up and went to work without speaking. That evening I got home and as usual walked to the bus stop on J Street to meet her when she got off the bus. By that time we had both had time to think it over. I explained to her first that I did not want to ever lose her, but asked her to be more discreet issuing her bridge instruction because I could not stand being ridiculed in front of others. We hugged right there at the bus stop and cried a little, and that's the only time that we had a serious misunderstanding in our whole married life. We had other disagreements, but none that bad.

135

The location of our apartment was quite convenient. I would take 39th Street to Folsom Boulevard and from there went straight in to the base. Hilda would walk half a block to the bus station and get a ride to the bank. I would get home in time to put the car in the garage and walk to the bus stop and meet her. The owner of the apartment house was a gentleman named Joe Green. He was a member of Del Paso Country Club and took me there several times to play golf. Hilda and I got to know Sacramento pretty well during our time there. There were no freeways. Folsom Boulevard was a two-lane road, as was what is now Interstate 80. It had a mild climate, was quaint, homey, and most importantly of all, had two local Air Force bases, Mather and McClellan. Like so many Air Force retirees, we agreed that when I left the service we would return to Sacramento and make it our permanent home.[120] In April of 1950 I finished my training program at Radar Navigation School at Mather, and we were transferred to Barksdale AFB in Shreveport, LA.

---

[120] Having convenient access to base services (medical, retail, etc.) was important. Unfortunately, by 2001, both bases were eliminated under the Base Realignment and Closure Act (BRAC).

Start of the Korean War

When we left Mather in April 1950, we had a thirty-day leave (which I think we spent in Wisconsin; for the first several years of our marriage we always spent our vacations visiting relatives in either Wisconsin or Ohio[121]) and then reported in to Barksdale. I was on a B-29 crew there and was initially assigned to an air refueling squadron, providing aerial tanker support for the bombers.

A lot of great things happened to us at Barksdale, and I hope that I've recalled all the important ones here. We found a nice little house on a cul-de-sac in Bossier City, close to the base. I bought a small motorcycle so I could get to the base quickly. It also gave me the advantage of being able to ride it all over the flight line. It had a small engine and was driven by a fiber belt from the engine to a pulley attached to the rear wheel. Hilda was not able to get a job with a bank there, but she did get a job at a feed store. The neighbors got a thrill every morning when I gave her a ride to the bus on the front of the cycle. She would sit sideways on the top of the fuel tank with her legs sticking out straight (ladies all still only wore skirts in those days, as it was well before the days when women first started wearing pants). The neighbors, all friends in the Air Force, would hear my motorcycle's engine start, and they would open their doors and wave at us as they watched us drive off. It was a fun way to start the day.

---

[121] Most young couples nowadays seem to want to be on their own and not visit their mothers and fathers.

The Soviet Union had declared war against Japan just two days before Japan's unconditional surrender and the end of WWII. President Truman and his staff believed that our Russian "allies" should be rewarded for this outstanding show of solidarity, and just "gave" them North Korea. Many Americans disagreed with Truman's decision, but that's how it came down. For its part, the United States maintained a presence in South Korea to help it recover from the devastation caused by years of Japanese occupation. Sometime in May 1950, I was at home listening to the radio when I heard President Truman make an unbelievably uncomplimentary remark about Korea. I immediately found Hilda and told her, "Hilda, Truman just said, 'Who the hell needs Korea?'" I can remember this just as clearly as if it happened today.

Shortly after Truman's unofficial abandonment of Korea but before the outbreak of the Korean War on June 25, 1950, my crew was assigned to deliver a B-29 to the Tanker Unit at Burtonwood Airbase[122] in western England. We were to leave the plane there and fly back to Barksdale in another one. Our route would take us first to Bermuda, then the Azores, and finally England. After spending a day in Bermuda, we took off for the Azores. About two hours into that leg of our journey, our number-three engine went out and

---

[122] This base was established in 1940 and located near Warrington, Lancashire. It was used by the USAAF/USAF until 1959. The U.S. Army resumed use of the base in 1966 when the French withdrew from NATO, until it was closed in 1994. Everything there has been demolished, and a motorway now runs directly through it.

had to be feathered, and we were forced to turn around and fly back to Bermuda. There were flames and balls of fire coming out of the engine for about an hour, quite a harrowing experience (I hadn't been inside a plane that was on fire since my combat tour). It took several days for another engine and installation team to be flown in, but Bermuda's beaches are excellent after all, and we did just fine. Once our plane was fixed, we left again for the beautiful Azores and more Monte Crasto champagne.

Burtonwood is located on the Western side of England, not far from Manchester. We got there without further difficulty and delivered the plane. We were only supposed to be away for two weeks, but our plans changed abruptly when the Korean War broke out.

Second European Tour

We were then placed on alert status, and I had to remain in England for the rest of that year. I wondered to myself if the North Koreans had heard the same words from President Truman that I did, and if that is what inspired them to start their war against us. We stayed on pretty tight alert status for a couple months before things went back to normal. I had to stay and pull alert duty, and so could not return to Barksdale.

I was able to take a week of vacation in Copenhagen, Denmark, during this part of 1950. I stayed at the Angliterre Hotel right in the center of town. I traveled around the city and went on some tours. I remember taking a boat trip through the center of Copenhagen on the canals where the docent was explaining everything in four different languages. I also visited some beautiful old castles, and the world-famous Tivoli Gardens. And I remember seeing that beautiful statue of the Little Mermaid in Copenhagen harbor. The statue is close to the shore,[123] and it's not very far across the bay from there to the Swedish coast. The food and drink were very good in Copenhagen. I met and spoke with some Danes who told me that the Germans stole food from them after invading and taking over Denmark in the war. But they said that the Germans were never able to get their hands on everything, and there was still plenty for themselves.

---

[123] Due to vandalism and other destruction by tourists, Copenhagen officials have announced that the 100-year-old statue will be moved further out into the harbor.

Prior to this, Hilda and I had not been separated even for one night since we were married, and we were not happy about this unexpected, prolonged separation. After an $86 phone bill about two weeks into my stay in England, Hilda called to say that she and Peg were coming to England. Peg was the wife of George Martin, the radar operator on our crew, and we were all good friends. The girls had tickets on the "Liberte" (a French ocean liner) and Hilda gave me the dates. The Liberte sailed first to Bourdeaux and then to Southampton, where I met them. I got some time off, got reservations at the Dorchester Hotel in London, and met them at the ship. We stayed there one night and then we went to Burtonwood. We got food ration cards[124] for the four of us and rented spaces at the Hill Cliff Hydro Live-In Hotel in Burtonwood. We also rented a Woolsey four-door sedan. We gave the ration cards to the hotel management so they could buy food for us.

When not on alert, my crew and I did spend some time training. But there was plenty of free time, which we spent traveling and sightseeing all over England. I took Hilda to see all the important attractions, from Shakespeare to Stonehenge. I was grateful for the opportunity to show her the places I used to go on three-day passes to London during my combat assignment, like the Windmill Theater and the St. James Tavern in Soho. The Windmill never closed at any time during WWII, and there were occasions when the performers on stage and we in the audience could hear the Luftwaffe's buzz bombs screaming outside, not knowing where they would fall and wondering if we would get hit. The St. James Tavern had been in continuous operation for over 600 years, and it was a must-see attraction every time we got to London. An overnight stay at the Dorchester used to cost much less at

---

[124] Meat, eggs and other items were still in short supply in Britain five years after the end of WWII and still being rationed.

about £30 (US$45) then, versus £1500 (US$3,000) today. The Dorchester Hotel had been Eisenhower's headquarters during WWII. It is a beautiful, elegant and luxurious hotel. England was and still is a country where I could live very happily anywhere. When we were not traveling, we played bridge with Peg and George. By now I was getting pretty good at bridge, and Hilda and I were winning most of the time. We used to keep a running score – sometimes we would be many thousands of points ahead of them.

We spent some time at Blackpool, which is located on the western bay between England and Ireland. It is a lovely resort area and I have several pictures of the four of us at that resort. It would be impossible to recount all the great times we had there. We were in our second year of marriage and enjoying every moment of it. Eventually, our crew was split up and I was transferred to Mildenhall AFB[125] located on the other side of England. George and Peg stayed in Burtonwood. Hilda and I rented a very small two-door car (I can't remember what kind), packed our bags, put them in the back seat and left for Mildenhall. During the trip about four hours outside of Mildenhall, the frame broke on this little car in the rear and the body slid sideways causing the fender to scrape against the tire. I had to push the body back into position and stack the bags on the other side in back as much as possible to try and hold it there. We drove slowly and whenever the body would slip again, I would have to go back and straighten it.

---

[125] Royal Air Force Station Mildenhall, Suffolk, England.

Finally we got to Mildenhall. It was very cold and we had no place to stay. We went to a pub located inside the Bird in Hand Hotel to try and find a room. The hotel is located just outside the perimeter of Mildenhall AFB and was popular with all the airmen stationed there. We got acquainted with someone who said he had a girlfriend who had a place where we could spend the night, so we went there. In one room, there was a small electric heater that had to be fed shillings every few minutes to stay running. There was a huge bathtub in the bathroom adjacent to the room. We could only get about three inches of hot water from the geyser,[126] which didn't work very well at all. Can you picture two adults trying to get clean while freezing in a cold bathroom with no more than three inches of water that was getting cold in that big tub? We survived that experience and got a room at the Bird in Hand where we remained for the rest of our stay in England until Hilda returned to the States just after Thanksgiving. Our room was located right above the pub downstairs, where we were usually serenaded to sleep to the strains of "Goodnight, Irene" being sung loudly by euphoric Yank and British patrons.

While at Mildenhall we continued our traveling. It was a lot closer to London so we were able to spend more time there. We visited Westminster Abbcy, Tower of London, the palaces and every place else we could legally go. We rode bicycles a lot. I got rid of the rental car with the broken frame and hired another one. The cars we rented there of course had the steering wheel on the right side and were all set up for driving on the left (or "correct," as the British would say) side of the road. When we asked if we could rent a car with a heater they would just say, "Oh, we don't have anything as modern as that."

---

[126] An instantaneous, and often dangerous, hot water heater using hot steam.

143

A couple other things happened during my duty in England in 1950 that I should mention. In mid-1950 the Air Force decided to transfer a wing of our brand new jet fighters to Manston Air Base[127] in England. This base was located on the eastern coast of England across the Straits of Dover southeast of London. At that time there was no such thing as satellite pinpoint navigation. In order for the fighters to make it successfully from Iceland to Kinloss Air Base[128] (located on the northernmost tip of Scotland), the fighters needed a radio beacon to get from Iceland to Scotland. I was assigned to go on TDY from England as navigator on a B-17 that had been modified to provide ADF[129] navigation for the fighters. The B-17's pilot's name was Bob Boardman and he was a frustrated fighter pilot. We flew out of Aldergrove Air Base[130] in Ireland for about a week and then out of Prestwick Airport[131] in Scotland for about a week. Aldergrove is located in Belfast not far from Nutts Corner, Ireland, where I had made my first landing in the British Isles in May of 1944. Our mission from either base was to fly to a point about halfway between Iceland and Scotland, circle there, and transmit our beacon. When the last fighter had flown by, we would return to Aldergrove. That was the first time I was able to stay in an Irish version of a BOQ and enjoy the services of a "batman." We were instructed to leave our shoes outside the door when we went to bed, and when we rose the next morning, the batman would have seen to it that our shoes were shined and ready for us to use. The batman also cleaned the room, made the bed and did laundry if we asked.

---

[127] Formerly a Royal Air Force station, this base was used by the USAF (SAC) during the Cold War for its fighters and fighter-bombers.

[128] Royal Air Force Station Kinloss.

[129] Automatic Direction Finder.

[130] Royal Air Force Station Aldergrove.

[131] Now the Glasgow-Prestwick Airport, this former USAF base was previously a Royal Air Force facility.

Then-Princess Elizabeth, "heiress apparent" to the English throne,[132] came with her sister Princess Margaret to visit the base one day, and quite an elaborate reception was given for her. Prior to her visit, officers' wives were restricted to a sort of sewing room at the officers' club. They were not permitted in the bar area with the men, or anywhere else in the club, for that matter. This rule was lifted on the day the princesses arrived. How the servicemen's wives indulged their newfound privileges, traipsing around everywhere carrying pitchers of gin and orange juice and generally having a grand time! I had already met and spoken with Margaret once before at a London pub during the war, and did so again on that occasion.[133] I was close to and saw Elizabeth, but did not get to meet her in person. The servicemen's wives' freedoms were short-lived. As soon as the princesses left, the rule restricting women to the sewing room went immediately back into effect.

When we did get to visit Aldergrove, we were advised to not say we were Catholic (which wasn't a problem for me). The Anglo-Irishmen would get drunk on weekend nights at the pubs and then go out and throw empty bottles at statues around town to commemorate the Catholics being driven out

---

[132] Her rule of Britain and the Commonwealth Realms as Elizabeth II would begin about a year and a half later.

[133] She had been right there toasting the war effort and throwing her champagne glass into the fireplace along with all of us. Members of the royal family were much more in the habit in those days of fraternizing informally with commoners, ironically something no longer possible due to security risks.

of Northern Ireland by William, Prince of Orange. To digress a little, Hilda and I would take some great vacations with my brother Tom and his wife to England and Ireland. One coincided with a bomb group reunion in England in 1993. On this particular occasion, we rented a car and took it all over the island. Tom was well acquainted with some folks in both Northern Ireland and the Republic. We stayed with some friends of his in Belfast and did a lot of sightseeing there, traveling to Nutts Corner. Someone at the museum there said we were the only Yanks to have ever visited the place, which I found hard to believe. We drove to the north coast of Ireland and visited the famous Bushmill Distillery, where they have been making Irish whiskey since 1608. Northern Ireland is breathtakingly beautiful everywhere you go. We continued on to the Republic of Ireland, and while there visited the Waterford Crystal factory and some superb woolen mills. We stayed with a retired postal employee named Paddy Doyle (you can't get a more Irish name than that) at his home in a small town south of Dublin. I remember one morning Paddy asked me to look out his kitchen window, pointed to a tree some distance away and said that if you could see that tree, it wasn't raining too hard to play golf. On our last night we ate at a magnificent dinner house in Dublin, and bought a number of tickets for the Irish lottery,[134] promising each other that if we won we would never leave Ireland again. I could live very contentedly in that country, in spite of the generally rainy weather.

---

[134] Irish lottery winnings are completely exempt from any tax.

Back to 1950, Prestwick, Scotland, was another great place we stayed. We flew out of the municipal airport, lived in the Prestwick Airport Hotel and had a great time there. The airport is located near the town of Ayr. Residents of that town used to come out to the airport and paid a shilling to sit and watch the airplanes take off and land in a park-like setting. Everyone treated us royally at Prestwick. After all the jet fighters had passed by, we flew to the airbase in Kinloss. We met and talked to some of the pilots and after that our hastily-formed B-17 crew split up and we all went back to our respective bases in England. Bob Boardman and I got reacquainted some years later at Davis-Monthan Air Force Base in Tucson, Arizona and at the Cameron Park Country Club after he retired.

Hilda and I returned to Barksdale--she around Thanksgiving and I around Christmas--and I continued to serve as navigator on a B-29 air refueling crew. We stayed at Barksdale until I went to pilot school in September 1951. Several interesting things happened during the nine months we had left in Barksdale. Hilda went back to her job at the feed store and I resumed carrying her to the bus stop on my little motorcycle (to the sound of cheering neighbors). Sometime in the spring Hilda's sister Claire came to live with us. She found a job and she stayed almost until we left for pilot school. It seems like one or two of Hilda's relatives stayed with us for a while everywhere we were stationed.

During the summer we had many parties at the officers club, including pool parties. On one of those occasions I was responsible for taking care of the swimming pool. The weather was hot and the pool water had gotten too warm, I thought. I arranged for some ice to be delivered, backed the truck up to the pool, and dumped the ice in it. The chunks were about four feet square and we would swim and push the blocks around the pool like we were in a giant punchbowl. I have never heard of this being done before or since, but I can tell you, it worked – the pool was very refreshing. We took a small vacation in New Orleans during that time and we saw all the important attractions, like Antoine's and Louis Armstrong.

Bainbridge

I applied and was finally accepted for pilot school. A requirement at the time was that you had to start pilot school before turning twenty-seven, and I barely made it, starting school on September 1, 1951, and celebrating my twenty-seventh birthday just one week later. Basic pilot school was scheduled for September 1 at Bainbridge Air Base[135] in Georgia. The school was just being reopened and I would be in the first class. There was an operations officer back at Barksdale named Bill Miller whom I will never forget. He was a pilot who very typically looked down on navigators. In addition to that he was a congenital liar. The war in Korea was heating up pretty good and replacement crews were being sent over there from all the B-29 bases. One day Bill came up to me and said that all my crew members had volunteered to go to Korea and he expected me to volunteer. I knew this was a lie. I didn't know what Bill did before he got in the service and went to pilot school, but I did know that he had never heard a shot fired in anger. So I said to him, "Just as soon as you can show me a DFC and five Air Medals, then you can talk to me about volunteering for Korea." Meanwhile, I told him I was going to pilot school in September, and nothing was going to interfere with that. Bill was one of the worst kinds of jerks you sometimes meet in the service, unfortunately.

---

[135] Bainbridge Air Base was inactivated in 1961 and is now the Decatur County Industrial Air Park.

I have a lot of good memories of Barksdale in spite of the run-in with Bill Miller. Claire returned to Youngstown and we got ready to leave for Bainbridge. By this time I had traded that wonderful '49 Pontiac convertible for a new red, '51 Olds convertible. That was the beginning of a bad habit I developed--buying too many new cars before the ones I had were worn out. But we both liked convertibles at that time and I couldn't resist. Much later, when we started our family, we switched to mostly station wagons. After the kids were grown and gone, we moved into Lincoln Mark VIIs and Town Cars.

My orders came transferring me to basic pilot school at Bainbridge and I left Barksdale to look for a house (while Hilda stayed behind). I stopped at Jackson, Mississippi, and drove on the next day to Bainbridge. There was virtually no housing in Bainbridge and I finally had to rent half of a house from a woman who decided to make her home available to the soldiers. She rented the other side to a student officer second lieutenant named Ralph Pittman and his wife. Most of the student officers were just out of ROTC. With one of them, James R. "Red" Patton, an ROTC second lieutenant from Georgia Tech, I became really good friends. I went back and checked out of Barksdale, picked up Hilda and drove back to Bainbridge. We still didn't have a lot of furniture or other possessions, and the Air Force shipped everything for us.

Basic pilot school was a real satisfying experience for me overall. I had personality clashes with some, but it was generally fun. We used the T-6 for flight training. It was quite different than flying our girlfriends around the sky in Piper Cubs back in Tahoka, Texas. My primary instructor was a former Navy pilot who had flown PBYs[136] during the war, had left the service, spent some time unemployed and finally had come to Bainbridge for work when he heard the flying school was opening up. He was an okay pilot, but in the PBY, you never exceed 12 degrees of bank and three hundred feet a minute during a let-down. Because of this he was woefully inept at acrobatics, and acrobatics was what I most wanted to zero in on. We did get to go with other instructors; some were very good at acro and I was able to learn most of the maneuvers okay.

I learned to fly the T-6 pretty well, but it was difficult to land, and had a tendency to ground loop in the slightest crosswind during landings. You had to stay alert constantly. One night during solo landing practice I did a ground loop but it was not caused by wind. The civilian senior pilot in the tower that night was one of the supervisors who did not care for me. During takeoff I had a malfunction in that the tail wheel locked in the left turn position. I had no way of knowing until I made the next landing that the tail wheel was locked. You properly land the T-6 on the main wheels and then let the tail down slowly as the aircraft slows down. When the tail wheel hit the runway the aircraft started to turn left, I held it straight as long as I could, but when I could not hold it any longer, the aircraft made an abrupt 180-degree left-turn off the runway. Through my headset, I could hear this jerk in the tower say, "This guy is really confused." That comment irritated me no end. The flying safety pilot came out to investigate and when he discovered the tail wheel locked sideways and further discovered that I had not hit any

---

[136] Medium to heavy twin amphibious aircraft used for maritime patrol, water bomber, and search & rescue; "PB" denotes "patrol boat," and "Y" indicates Consolidated Aircraft Company as its manufacturer.

151

runway lights or damaged anything he commended me for my skillful piloting ability. There was a pilots' meeting the next morning and the flying safety guy went over everything. He was very complimentary to me, which really burned the instructor who had been in the tower.

There were about fifteen or so officer student pilots and the rest were cadets. Part of the discipline training for the cadets was to march everywhere they went, do a lot of saluting, that sort of thing. I had the pleasure of being the ranking student officer and I also outranked several of the military cadre that was running the school. I anticipated that we might have some trouble in this area, so before we went to the flight line for our first meeting with the military pilot I went to the administrative officer, a major and a real nice guy, and explained to him that it was not necessary to teach the students to become officers and it would be quite inconvenient for the officers to march to the flight line. I explained that many of us would drive right from where we lived to the line. The major agreed and the student officers never had to march anywhere. When we arrived at the flight line the first time, we were assembled in a group when out came this feisty little captain stating that we were supposed to be in a marching formation. He was really upset, but he got even more upset when I told him that we were already officers, his job was to teach us to fly, and we were not going to march anywhere. He took off on a dead run to the same major that I had spoken with, thinking he was going to bust me. But he came back in a heartbeat, and with a false smile on his face said, "You're right, you don't have to march anywhere." We never became friends, but we got along okay after that.

Red Patton and his wife Dottie were both from the Carrolton suburb of Atlanta, and they took us up there several times when Georgia Tech was playing football. Red would get us seats right with the players and we would all root for

152

Georgia Tech. We also spent weekends in Florida at the beaches. We spent very happy times around Pensacola and near Ft. Walton. There was a target out in the gulf about five miles from Ft. Walton where we used to drop 10,000-pound simulated A-bombs from the B-29s. The Gulf beaches are beautiful and we really enjoyed our times there.

I learned to do the barrel rolls and slow rolls real well. A barrel roll is really the most fun of all. Then came the instrument flying. Some guys were unable to catch on to it and washed out, but I liked the instrument part of it. I remember the final graduation flight with a really nice major who was the chief pilot of the school. The final check ride included all the basic instruments plus recovering from a spin while under the hood. [137]The check pilot[138] puts the plane in a spin and says, "You got it." You had to first stop the spin and then recover from it going straight down to straight and level flight. The major said afterwards that I would have no trouble with instrument flying.

A WWII ace by the name of Loveless, I think, came by one day to cultivate interest among us in going to advanced fighter pilot school. I was lucky to be one of the students allowed to go on a short flight on a modified two-seat P-51[139] and I loved it. I could remember those P-51s we had as escort during our

---

[137] For instrument pilot training, a hood would be slid under the canopy covering the back-seat cockpit, blocking all outside view.

[138] Instructor pilot checking out trainee pilots.

[139] North American P-51 "Mustang," a long-range, single seat fighter used in WWII.

flights over Germany in the B-17s. I tried to make a fighter approach and landing like I had seen in England and it worked pretty well. As much as I wanted to go to fighters, I was told that because of my previous navigator, radar operator, and bombardier training that I would have to go to multi-engine advanced flying school. We graduated from Bainbridge about February 15, 1951, and I transferred to the B-25 advanced pilot school at Vance AFB in Enid, Oklahoma.

Enid

We arrived at Enid in our '51 red Olds convertible and found a house to live in. The people were very friendly and appreciated the military being there. Most of the country was very patriotic in those years, except for California. Sacramento in particular only tolerated the military but never really supported them. These conditions haven't changed fifty years later.

Our house was okay and there were many student officer pilots living in the area. About halfway through the course, our next door neighbor, also a student pilot, contracted polio and died within a week. His name was Frost and he left his wife Polly and two little kids. We saw Polly several times at different bases around the country over the ensuing years.

In the early summer we got a leave and went to Ohio. After visiting the relatives there, we picked up Hilda's sister Anne's two kids and brought them back to Enid with us for the summer. Jackie Marsh was about seven and Jimmy was younger, but he was already riding a bike (which would cause us problems later). We drove back to Enid through the Black Hills and I remember that the kids enjoyed that trip. As I have said before, we usually had some of Hilda's relatives living with us wherever we were. On many occasions during our tour at Enid we would want to go out to the officers' club or someplace else, and when the babysitter arrived we could usually locate Jackie, but we would have to scour the neighborhood looking for Jimmy and his bike. We always eventually found him and gave him hell, and he would promise to do better next time (but he never did improve on that score).

We had the T-6 and the B-25 to fly at Enid. We all got checked out quickly in the T-6 because we were fully qualified in them from Basic Pilot School, and then took on the B-25. One time during formation training in the T-6, I was flying with an instructor who was teaching the others how to assemble into a formation. All of a sudden the instructor pilot grabbed the stick and pulled the plane up about a hundred feet. As I looked down to see why he had done that, another T-6 went sailing right through where we had been. We narrowly missed a mid-air collision. His alert reaction prevented the other T-6 from hitting ours. That aircraft was piloted by a second lieutenant student pilot named Joe Grainger. The instructor told Joe via radio to go back to Enid and land. Joe was washed out a few days later and left the school. The next (and last) time I heard of Joe was when I saw a picture of him in a newspaper kneeling down, blindfolded and about to be shot in the head by the communists. He was somewhere in the Far East just prior to the Vietnam War and had been captured. Joe was a nice guy from Massachusetts and had a nice wife.

Another interesting time in the T-6 was our night flight to Chicago's O'Hare Airport for a night navigation training mission. There were four airplanes, one with an instructor and we three students flying a loose formation, getting looser the darker it got. As we flew over this large lit-up area it was difficult to find the airport but we did and when it was my turn to land I got everything lined up and was on final approach when the inevitable happened: when you reduce power on the T-6 the generator puts out less power and all the lights get dim. Because of this I could not read the airspeed indicator. I quickly whipped out my flashlight, took a quick look at the airspeed, put the flashlight back and figured that if I did not change anything I should maintain that 70 mile per hour airspeed until roundout[140] and landing. It worked, but it was hairy all the way down the approach. We spent the weekend in Chicago and then flew back during the daylight hours.

The B-25 is a very noisy bird and I think half of my hearing loss came from flying them. One of the interesting things that happened to me during the B-25 flying came during one of the single-engine training days. The instructor's name was Dufield and to this day I have nothing but the greatest respect for those instructors, what with how they were able to sit patiently and watch students make errors that could kill them. Dufield cut the fuel supply to one of the engines and it quit. I went through the proper procedures quickly, feathered the engine and the last thing to do is to turn off the magnetos. I proceeded to turn of the magnetos to the feathered engine, but accidentally turned off the mags for the one engine that was running. For an instant, we were "gliding" (not something a B-25 is really designed to do). Reacting very quickly, I turned the mags back on for that engine and turned them off for the feathered engine. Dufield meanwhile, never changed expression. All he said was, "Gets

---

[140] An integral part of a landing. It follows descent (or glide path), and occurs just before flare and touchdown. Roundout involves raising the nose slightly so the plane doesn't plow into the ground and explode.

quiet, doesn't it?" That's all he needed to say. It never happened to me again.

The graduation flight for the B-25 took us to the Long Beach Airport where we landed and stayed over the weekend before returning to Enid. The instructor on that flight was Frank Kanick of Youngstown, Ohio (Hilda's home town). Coincidentally, his wife Audrey was one of Hilda's sister's childhood friends. We saw them a lot while we were stationed at Enid. The flight was rather routine, except for the fog we encountered on landing at Long Beach. We stopped in Arizona en route. After graduation we all went our separate ways and finished our careers. The Kanicks retired in Sacramento like ourselves, and we spent a lot of good times together. Frank is a few years older than I and is a member of the Order of Daedalians[141] in Sacramento. His health is not that great now but we still see each other occasionally at the Daedalian meetings.

Graduation was September 13, 1952, and I graduated first in my class. Because of this I was given my choice of Strategic Air Command ("SAC") bases available to me for my next assignment. Because of my prior navigator, radar operator and bombardier training, my choices were limited to the three SAC bases, one of which was March AFB in Riverside, California. I thought that that would be a good place to go. I had never been stationed there, but it was the only base available in California. That base would be our home for the next ten and a half years.

---

[141] A fraternal and professional order of American military pilots. The namesake of the order is Daedalus who, according to Greek mythology, was the first person to achieve heavier-than-air flight.

We took a thirty-day vacation and headed for Ohio while our few furniture and household goods were packed and shipped to California. The trunk of our Olds was full of personal articles and as we were heading east somewhere near Coffeeville, Kansas, we were involved in a wreck that could have been disastrous. We were going down this hill on a narrow two-lane road (Highway 40, I think) with deep ditches. In front of us was a black '40 Ford four-door sedan. We were going about 65 miles per hour, and we started slowing down as this car began to slow down in front of us. I honked the horn and started to pass the Ford when he suddenly stuck his arm out and indicated he was going to turn left onto a dirt road. I slammed on the brakes, knowing I wouldn't be able to stop. And since the ditches were too deep to take a chance I turned slightly to the right and slammed into the Ford with my right front fender hitting the car in the left rear end. It caved in our right front fender and bumper and we had to pry it out before we could drive any further. The driver of the Ford was partially drunk and had a young sixteen year-old girl with him. The sheriff arrived and some cowboys came up on horseback. It was obvious that they all were acquainted and wanted this handled quickly and to keep everyone happy. The sheriff was very courteous to Hilda and me. He could see that the accident was not my fault, but because he knew the other driver, he didn't want to cause him any trouble either. The Ford driver also had scars and scabs on his arms from another accident that he had caused recently. The sheriff helped us pry the fender back from the tire and sent us off. Some of the cowboys remarked that they really knew how to put those Oldsmobiles together, because the damage was relatively minor. That was the only wreck I have ever had. USAA[142] sent a guy to get a statement from me while we were in Ohio and we had the car fixed there. The rep who took my statement agreed the accident was not my fault, and my premium did not increase (at that time, I had been with USAA for only about a year). After the vacation in Ohio we went to Wisconsin to visit the relatives, and then took a nice return trip to the land of fruits and nuts.

---

[142] United Services Automobile Association, a provider of insurance, banking and investment services for U.S. military people since 1922.

Vindication

The Korean Armistice was signed on July 27, 1953. Our government had been trying to entice Korean pilots to defect in order to capture and evaluate a fully mission-capable Soviet MiG-15.[143] On September 23, a North Korean pilot named No Kum-Sok flew his MiG from North Korea to South Korea, landed at Kimpo Air Base[144] and defected. He told the Americans who took him captive, "I want to become an American."

I later met No Kum-Sok at a speaking engagement and book signing[145] at the Aerospace Museum of California (at the former McClellan AFB). At that event, he happened to be introduced by the very same pilot who was the first American to meet him at Kimpo when he defected (quite a coincidence indeed). No was in his early twenties when he delivered the MiG to us. One of the first things he wanted to do was to learn the English language (can you imagine this being a first priority for any new immigrants to the United States today?). During his speech he told us that in early June 1950, the Russians gathered all the North Korean military together and said this to them: "It appears that the United States is not going to support South Korea, so let's take it now," and they

---

[143] Mikoyan-Gurevich, or "MiG" 15, a Korean War-era Soviet swept-wing fighter aircraft.
[144] Now Gimpo International Airport, this was originally a military airstrip built by the Japanese. The U.S. took control of this base after the WWII.
[145] His book is entitled *A MiG-15 to Freedom* and is a very worthwhile read.

started the Korean War. Apparently the Russians had indeed heard the same message from President Truman that I had in that momentous radio broadcast. In my opinion, all it would have taken was for Truman to have shown an unequivocal commitment to our new Korean ally, and the war would never have been fought.

No Kum-Sok provided much first-hand, factual information about the Korean War, including information that was kept from the American public at the time, and is still not acknowledged by the U.S. government today. He confirmed, for example, something that we had suspected all along: that Russian and Chinese pilots were flying warplanes against us in aerial combat. He had lived in North Korea after the Japanese took over the country, and explained their takeover was brutal and absolute. He was also in the country when WWII ended and he got a chance to see first-hand how the Americans treated people after the end of WWII. He knew the communist propaganda demonizing the United States was all untrue, and after living under Russian control, he decided he was going to leave the country.

When the Americans finished examining the captured MiG-15, they offered to give it back to the Russians. But the Russians would not accept it because to do so would be to admit their direct involvement in the Korean War. The American authorities decided that No was sincere in his desire to become an American. He was awarded one hundred-thousand dollars for delivering it to us, and moved to the United States to begin his education, eventually becoming a professor at Embry-Riddle Aeronautical University in Daytona Beach, Florida. He became a naturalized U.S. citizen and changed his name to Kenneth Rowe, and he was later allowed to bring his family to the United States from North Korea. He currently resides in Florida and the MiG he flew to freedom is on display at Wright-Patterson AFB in Ohio.

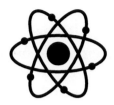

The Atom Bomb

I had been assigned initially to the 22nd Bomb Wing at March AFB, and during the signing-in process one of the first places I needed to go was wing operations to get my crew assignment. The officer who interviewed me, George Perbetsky, found out right away that I had only just graduated from pilot school and asked me how many hours of pilot time I had. I answered about 250 hours. He immediately stated that they couldn't use me in the 22nd because they were changing from B-29s to B-47s and could only use pilots with at least a thousand hours for these sophisticated six-jet-engine bombers.

After this conversation, I thought I had better go and check out the other bomb wing at March, which was the 320th. I learned that the 320th was also going to change to B-47s, but not for a year or more. They accepted me and said that I should try and get a thousand hours of pilot time within a year's time so that I could qualify to be on a B-47 crew when they made the switch. George Perbetsky retired in the Sacramento area. He and I belong to the same Daedalian chapter, and I regularly remind him jokingly about how he treated me back at March in 1952 (we are good friends now).

All during the Cold War, we trained regularly with atomic bombs aboard. My colleagues and I had all been to the atomic training at Kirtland AFB in New Mexico and our mission was to be prepared to drop atomic bombs on Russia if they attacked us. The prevailing theory guiding our national security policies at the time was "Mutual Assured Destruction" ("MAD"), between the United States and Russia. Under this theory, if the Soviets attacked us with nuclear weapons, we would reciprocate with a full-blown counter attack. The result would be the total destruction of both countries, along with the rest of planet Earth. Our training at Kirtland covered an understanding of all the components inside the weapons we carried, and everything we would need to know to make certain they detonated successfully. As we were handling radioactive devices regularly, we were exposed to minute amounts of radiation. Everyone on crews like mine wore dosimeters,[146] which would continuously record how many roentgens[147] of radiation we were exposed to. No crew members that I am aware of ever recorded very high radiation levels on their dosimeters.

Both the United States and the Soviet Union were continuously improving and developing ever-more sophisticated atomic weapons. It was sometime in 1954 that we were asked to provide an aircraft and crew to observe an atomic bomb test about ten miles east of Indian Springs, Nevada. The purpose was to fly through the cloud after the bomb was detonated and determine the amount of radiation in the cloud. Our B-29 crew left March AFB and went to Indian Springs[148] to prepare to take off on our mission. We were warned to look away when the bomb was about to go off, to protect our eyes from the intense light. We were about ten miles from the explosion on the ground when it happened, but the noise was unbelievably loud. Immediately after, we watched the mushroom cloud and massive ball of fire rising in the sky. My crew and I then received orders to board our B-29 and prepare for take-off. Our aircraft had been equipped

---

[146] A device worn on the person for measuring the quantity of ionizing radiation to which the person has been exposed.
[147] A unit of measure of the ions produced by x- or gamma radiation.
[148] Indian Springs AFB, now Creech AFB.

with Geiger counters located at the bombardier position. We took off and entered the cloud at about 8,000 feet, following it through Nevada, Arizona and into Mexico. The Geiger counters never clicked once and no radiation was detected, and we reported this information to our superiors.

Riverside

We purchased our first home at 3958 San Marcos Square in Magnolia Center for $11,200. It was a three-bedroom, one-bath home, built in what had once been an orange grove. We had two beautiful orange trees in the back yard. The two-car garage was a free-standing building not attached to the house. We were the first owners in this new tract, and we got to know a lot of the folks who bought homes there. Many of them were Air Force. George and Margaret Paulin bought the home next door, where Margaret still lives (George passed away some years ago). I remember when we moved in sometimes the bathroom plumbing failed. George and I would walk over to one of the vacant houses under construction in the neighborhood looking for reliable parts for the repairs we needed to do, and just traded them.

Hilda and I added a kidney-shaped pool after our first year, which required us to take out one of the orange trees. After one season with the other tree, we had it removed because of the leaves. I personally put in a cement block fence with some decorative wood on the top. We did all our own work in those days regardless of what it was. We decided that it would be nice if we had another bathroom so we had one added beside the master bedroom. This was also on the end of the patio so we could enter the bathroom from the pool/patio. It was kind of an unconventional design, but very practical. We had lots of pool parties, and before long Hilda's natural talents as a teacher became apparent as she started teaching neighborhood kids how to swim. Later on in our marriage, she taught kids to read, play piano and ride bikes. And wherever we were, we always had a pool and she always taught small kids to swim.

Hilda's brother Jimmy Marsh came to live with us again while he was in high school. He played in the band and wore a handsome green uniform. When he went back to Ohio, Hilda's sister Margie came to live with us. We sort of put her through nursing school at UCLA Med Center – she was tempted to quit a few times but Hilda wouldn't let her. She would come home on weekends with a couple of her friends so we always had people in the house. It was just a great life. Margie went on to get her PhD in psychology. I started night school at Riverside City College and got an associate in arts degree before we transferred to Omaha, Nebraska in 1962. I knew how important it was to have a college degree and had taken some Saturday and night classes at Sac State[149] in 1949 while we were stationed at Mather AFB in Sacramento.

Brother Lyle had gone through Two-Mile and Lincoln High just like me, and entered the Aviation Cadet Program in 1945. But the war ended before his training was through and the Cadet program was suspended, so at Lyle's expressed preference he was stationed at Madison Army Airfield.[150] He chose this assignment because it was closest to home and close to our favorite relatives in Portage. Lyle was discharged

---

[149] California State University, Sacramento (CSUS).
[150] Now Truax Field Air National Guard Base, in Madison, Wisconsin.

from the service in 1945, and was at home when Dad died. While working in Wisconsin Rapids, he met and began dating Phyllis Jones, a cute young lady from South Dakota who was staying with our relatives in Portage. They were married on May 3, 1947. They had a son, Lyle James, in 1950, but he did not survive infancy (he is buried in the Gray family plot at Pacific Cemetery, near Portage, Wisconsin). Lyle became a reservist when WWII ended and had been recalled to active duty at F. E. Warren Air Force Base[151] when the Korean War started. After the war ended he returned for a short time to Wisconsin, but he and Phyllis decided to move to California in mid-1953.

The first job Lyle was able to get in Southern California was delivering milk. After that he decided to try the insurance business, and he became very successful as an independent broker. They lived fairly close to us, just forty miles away, and we saw a lot of each other over the next ten years. Lyle and I never missed a Los Angeles Rams football home game. I would drive to Lyle's place in Garden Grove and from there we would go together to the Los Angeles Coliseum. In the mid-1950s our mother decided to move to California to be near us, and she found a place in Westminster, close to Garden Grove. She got a job as a school teacher there. Lyle and I played a lot of golf together at some beautiful courses in Southern California, such as Torrey Pines and Riviera Country Club. It was great to have Lyle and Phyllis close by. They had another son, but he also died in infancy and was buried in Westminster. In 1952 they had a daughter, Vicki, who now resides with her husband and son in Las Vegas,

---

[151] Converted to a USAF base after WWII, Francis E. Warren Air Force Base in Cheyenne, Wyoming, had previously been a U.S. Cavalry base (Fort Russell, since the 1860s), and had an illustrious history. It figured prominently in our wars against the Sioux Nation, the Spanish-American War, the Mexican Revolution and WWI, and was home to the famed Buffalo Soldiers.

Nevada. Hilda and I always thought that the loss of their first two children may have driven Lyle and Phyllis to spoil and dote on Vicki, to be overly indulgent and lenient with her. They have had problems in their relationship with Vicki over the years.

Fortunately for me there were plenty of assorted aircraft to fly at March AFB and I was able to get my thousand hours of pilot time in my first year there. There were T-6s and B-25s which I checked out in quickly, and C-45s which were easy to fly. The 320th still had B-29s and the base had a squadron of KC-97[152] tankers, and I managed to get some time in both those aircraft as well. I flew every weekend and took all the remaining T-6s on a flight to Randolph Field,[153] Texas (where we left them) and returned to March on a B-25. I think there were five T-6s in that formation.

Hilda had found a bank job, I think Bank of America again. My intense flying schedule was not without some difficulty and could have put a huge strain on my marriage. But Hilda understood that it was critical and urgent for me to get in this flying time in order to achieve what I wanted to in my flying career, and she never complained. She never complained about anything, really, and we had a beautiful relationship.

---

[152] Boeing KC-97 "Stratotanker," a tanker used for aerial refueling in the 1950s.
[153] Now Randolph Air Force Base.

It felt as though Hilda and I dated for the first ten years of our marriage (there were some changes when the kids started arriving). Hilda was the kind of wife who thought the husband deserved to be completely taken care of. She was very practical and thrifty, and if she had had her way, we would still be driving the '49 Pontiac. She thought we wasted too much money buying new cars every couple of years, and she was right. I know that she knew that I loved her with all my heart and soul.

Sometime in 1954 the 320th Bomb Wing began training the crews transitioning to the B-47s. The crew training was conducted at Pinecastle AFB, which was located in Orlando, Florida. Four of us bought a car and drove it to Florida to attend the training. That way, none of our wives would have to be without a car during our absence. In those days everyone seemed to have only one car, not like today. The B-47 training was fun. We were in Florida for about a month and did lots of flying. Pinecastle AFB was closed as a military facility some years later and is now Orlando International Airport. A lot of memorable things happened during the training. One was when we flew into a large flock of seagulls on one flight shortly after takeoff. None were sucked into an engine but when we landed there was blood everywhere on the leading edge of the nacelles and wings. I also got to spend some time flying the T-33[154] while there. When we returned to

---

[154] Lockheed T-33 Thunderbird, a jet trainer aircraft.

March AFB we were assigned to a more or less permanent crew. I was assigned to be copilot on a crew, Ed Bailey the aircraft commander and Ray Barrett the radar/navigator. Both of those guys were great and we had a fine relationship. I had been promoted to major in April of 1953 so all three of us were majors. We flew as a crew from late 1954 until I got my own crew.

Ed, Ray and I were like a family. We did everything together socially and as a crew. Over the next few years we had several ninety-day TDYs to different bases in England and Guam and we spent a lot of two-week TDYs at Eielson AFB in Fairbanks, Alaska, on alert. During this period the Cold War with Russia was hot and almost all of our training was geared toward how we would respond to an A-bomb attack by the Russians. One time we flew a mission for twenty-six hours straight, and I never left the pilot's seat for the entire flight. We flew all over the States, and we had to do three mid-air refuelings to accomplish this. I think they were trying to assess whether this type of a mission could be phased into the overall combat plan. We took no-doze pills ("bennies," we called them), to stay awake for that long.

On another mission we mounted a mock invasion of England and had to be at an altitude of 45,000 feet upon entry over English airspace. This altitude is about the limit of how high a B-47 can fly. It was tricky because the airplane was in a continuous stall,[155] with lots of shuddering and vibration. Another time we took off from England, flew a mission, and landed somewhere in North Africa. We spent the night there and left the next day for England. The shacks we stayed in were wood halfway up, then open the rest of the way up to a canvas roof. We were told to be watchful because the Arab natives could steal the pajamas right off you without waking you up. This place was close to the Mediterranean, we could see the beaches, and it was hot.

Ed was an excellent pilot. He was an instructor in every aircraft that he flew and I was very fortunate to have him as an AC.[156] I really learned a lot from flying with him, even doing the aerial refueling from the back seat. After Ed retired from the Air Force he got a job flying for an oil company in Pennsylvania. He somehow contracted diabetes. He had to quit flying, so he and Millie moved to Seattle and bought a beautiful home on Mercer Island. Hilda and I visited them there several times after we retired and moved to Sacramento in 1965. Ray moved to Florida. When he retired, Hilda and I visited him and Alice whenever we took one of our many vacations there. We met at MacDill AFB in Tampa, and really loved Florida. Ed died sometime around 1996, and Ray in 2005.

---

[155] In aviation, a stall refers to failure of lift for a plane in flight due to the lower density of air molecules passing over and beneath the wing. At higher altitudes, a plane loses lift and may stall at the same true airspeed at which it could safely fly at lower altitudes without risk of stall.
[156] Aircraft Commander.

In 1958 I got my own crew. George Harbaugh was my copilot and Anthony Simon Ching Chong was my radar/navigator. George was a lieutenant and Tony a major. George's home was in San Diego, and Hilda and I began spending a lot of time visiting there. He was an only child whose father was a doctor who had served in WWII. His family was quite wealthy and owned property in San Diego and in Mexico, where we would also go for weekends. I remember one time over the Fourth of July we visited there and did some water skiing. We spent a lot of time in Tijuana watching the bullfights and the horse races. Hilda was filming one of the bullfights on our movie camera when the matador was gored. As soon as the incident occurred, her reaction was to pull the camera from her face and stare at the awful scene with her mouth hanging open. All we had left to remember that scene was a home movie of Hilda's shoes.

We always enjoyed the horse races in Tijuana. One time prior to having our daughter Barbara we went to the races and bet on a horse named Pumptail. We were happy when Pumptail won and we won some money, but when driving back to the border we were right behind a truck and as the truck went through this traffic signal it was green for the truck but it changed to red. I could not see the signals because of the truck, and instantly a motorcycle cop was on us. He stopped us and took my driver's license and directed us to follow him. We thought to ourselves, "There go all our winnings." When we stopped I had to go in to see the sheriff. He said, "You pay the fine, Señor." The fine was two dollars and the sheriff took a huge roll of bills from his pocket, wrapped my two bucks around it and stuffed it back into his pocket and gave me back my driver's license. We saw firsthand the corruption that exists in Mexico. The sheriff obviously reported to no one and the fine money became his. I had also observed this type of corruption previously in Juarez so I was not surprised. We were just happy that they didn't take all our winnings from the races that day.

There was another time when Hilda's German father, Julius, and his wife Josephine were visiting from Ohio and we took them to the bullfights. Although he had owned a slaughterhouse and had been a butcher by trade, he was very upset to see animals treated so inhumanely. Come to think of it, there wasn't much about Mexico he agreed with. He commented that the food's presentation aspect made it appear "someone had already eaten it."

With Julius' financial help, one of Hilda's mother's sisters (nicknamed "Mitzi") moved to the United States with her husband Friederich ("Fritz") Galter in the mid-1950s and settled in La Porte, Indiana. We traveled to pay them a visit there, and when Hilda laid eyes on Mitzi for the very first time, she broke down in tears, crying, "Meine Mutter" ("my mother"), so close was the resemblance. Mitzi was about eleven years younger than Hilda's mother, and therefore had about the same age and appearance as Hilda's mother did at the time of her death in 1946 (and Hilda's last memory of her). Mitzi and Fritz had a tragic but fascinating story. They had been living in Brenndorf (Bod), Romania, when WWII broke out. Fritz was drafted into the German Army and was shipped off to the war. As time passed and the Soviets started getting the upper hand in the ground wars all over Eastern Europe, they moved in and took over Romania. They confiscated all the real estate and other property, and in early 1945 deported all the working-age German inhabitants of Siebenburgen to the USSR. [157] Mitzi was transported on a railroad cattle car to work in a Soviet slave labor camp. She was sentenced to work there for five years, but after three

---

[157] This was done under Secret Order 7161, which was part of a 1944 Soviet plan for extracting war reparations from captured German civilians through slave labor. Tens of thousands of ethnically-German Romanians were displaced under this rule.

years her weight fell to about eighty pounds. She would not have survived much longer, but a Russian nurse whom she had befriended somehow arranged for her to be sent to the Russian occupation zone (what became East Germany). From there she got more help and was able to escape to West Germany. She had been out of contact with her husband since the outset of the war, and had no idea whether he was alive or dead. Fritz had been captured by the British Army and remained in a POW camp until the war ended. When Mitzi got to West Germany, she found him working on a farm. Fritz passed away many years ago. Mitzi passed away in April of this year at 98 years of age.

We became acquainted with another couple who had escaped Eastern Europe, I believe with assistance from the same church group that helped Fritz and Mitzi get to the States. Hilda and I first met Cary and Yvette Bryan[158] in 1957 at our home in Riverside and we became very good friends with them over the years. They had come to America as refugees from the short-lived 1956 Hungarian Revolution. The Red Army had moved through all of Eastern Europe chasing Hitler's armies back into Germany, and by the end of WWII, like their Western allies, they had forces occupying every country they invaded. But unlike us, the Soviets intended not only to remain there indefinitely, but to forcibly spread their revolution to these shattered countries and make them slave

---

[158] They had changed their names from Carl and Maria Borbelas, to have more American-sounding names.

states to a new communist world empire. Due to its unfortunate geography, Hungary was one of those countries to be taken over in succession by both totalitarian systems in the last century. Living conditions in Hungary were already terrible because of the war and just deteriorated under Soviet dominion. In 1956, thousands of Hungarians took to the streets to demonstrate against the Soviet presence, but after only a few weeks the revolution was crushed. People who had played any role in the revolt were rightfully fearful of what the Soviets would do to them, and went into hiding or fled the country.

Cary and Yvette were members of the Budapest intelligentsia, both with engineering degrees, I believe. They had taken part in the failed revolution, and believing their lives were in danger, decided to flee the country. They had a five-year-old daughter, Andrea, whom they had to take along with them. I'll never forget the story Cary shared with us about walking through a minefield the Russians had laid with Andrea in his arms. As they made their way through, he told Andrea to try to get to a farmhouse and just wait there in case he was killed. Prior to this, Yvette told us that there was a morning back in Budapest (in 1955), when they were reading a newspaper article about the opening of a new theme park in Southern California called Disneyland. Cary had Andrea sitting on his lap, and showed her the pictures, saying, "One day we are going to take you there." At the time Yvette thought it was cruel to make such an impossible promise to their young daughter, but it came true after all.

Hilda helped them prepare resumes and begin looking for work. Yvette went to work for Lockheed, and Cary went to work for Hewlett-Packard. They became naturalized U.S. citizens and very successful, and live in a beautiful home in Saratoga. Andrea grew up to become an attorney and later a Superior Court Judge in Santa Clara County. Cary and Yvette have been retired for several years now.

176

Even if the Air Force was the ideal career choice for me, it definitely wasn't for everyone, and George Harbaugh was one of those people. In fact, officers were leaving in such huge numbers that D.C. legislators were coming out to exit interview some of the departing officers to try and figure out what was causing the exodus. When George decided to resign his commission, he was interviewed by Clare Booth Luce.[159] He told her that he did not think that his aircraft commander (me) was getting treated properly considering his time of service and war record, etc., and that he wasn't going to stay in and take a chance on getting the same shabby treatment. George got out of the service and took a job at Convair Astronautics in San Diego. His advocacy on my behalf did not result in a change in treatment of me. We stayed close until I transferred later to Omaha in 1962.

My new copilot was a first lieutenant named Andy Miller. He played the trumpet in a swing band and was a real nice guy. Chong left the service and I got a new navigator, but I cannot remember his name. He and Andy and I were the ones who had the emergency while en route to Alaska on one of our TDYs. We lost the operation of the forward auxiliary boost pump and were unable to transfer fuel from that tank. Because we were carrying an A-Bomb in the Bombay that weighed 10,000 pounds, our inability to transfer fuel from the forward aux caused a serious out-of-balance condition. In

---

[159] At the time, serving as a congresswoman in the U.S. House of Representatives.

177

order to counteract this condition we used all the fuel from the center main tank and kept as much as we could in the aft main tank. We were still nose-heavy but we managed a good safe landing at Eielson AFB.

In 1959 I had a commanding officer named Sam Byerley who would become a great and close friend for the rest of my life. Sam had joined the Air Force and started flying planes in 1939; he was a Colonel when I met him. From 1960-61, we were both working in operations at 15th Air Force Headquarters and we worked together for a couple of years. One of the many memorable experiences Sam and I had occurred when I was asked to fly Sam to Castle AFB for a conference. I scheduled a T-33 and off we went. It was raining when it came time to fly back to March. We were sitting in the airplane waiting for the instrument clearance. Because of the weather, we had the canopy down and the crew chief had placed the Form One[160] in one of the air inlets for the engine to keep it out of the rain until we were cleared for takeoff. The clearance came through; we started the engine and took off. When we landed at March, we looked for the Form One, but couldn't find it. It had been sucked through the jet engine, and

---

[160] Form One is a notebook with a metal backing in which all the pertinent information about the aircraft is kept, including the names of pilots who have flown it and dates, and the condition of the aircraft after each landing.

all that was left of it was the metal backing, which was discovered on the engine screen. I mentioned this to Sam the next day, but rather than chew me out as I expected he would, he just said, "Well, we found out what happened to the Form One, didn't we?"

Our paths crossed many times until I retired in 1964. He was easy to work with and for. I will never forget how he would say, "Call me if you need me, otherwise you can handle it yourself." He was a terrific leader who always backed up subordinates in their decisions. In 1962, Sam was transferred to Beale AFB in Marysville, California, and I would see him there while conducting inspections as part of the inspector general staff at SAC in Omaha, Nebraska. After this, Sam was transferred to Guam where he commanded the Air Force units engaged in the Vietnam War. By this time he was a major general, the rank he retired with when that war ended.

Brother Tom grew up in the same crushing poverty as Lyle and me, and he did the same kind of strenuous, hard work at Dad's saw mill. He attended the same schools Lyle and I did, graduating Lincoln High. He somehow grew to be much taller than Lyle or me. We only made it to 5 feet 10 inches each, but Tom made it to almost 6 feet 3 inches. After school he got some odd jobs wherever he could, including work at a service station.

In 1956 Tom married his first wife, Jane Frank. She was from Marshfield, a town about thirty miles northwest of Wisconsin Rapids. She was also a good friend of our mother's.

Tom joined the Air Force and attended the same pilot school that I did at Vance AFB (he was in Class 54F, which graduated just two years after mine, Class 52F). Tom became an excellent pilot and he had an extraordinary flying career. He flew the KB-50[161] and was stationed in Japan. He and Jane had two children together, a boy and a girl. Their first, Tommy Jr., was born in 1957, and their second, Kim, was born at a military base hospital in Japan in 1961 during their assignment there. When they returned to the States, they were able to visit us in Riverside.

It is quite uncommon for two brothers to get to fly the same military aircraft, but in 1958 or '59, Tom and I were able to take the same T-33 on a cross-country flight. We intended to fly from March AFB to Andrews AFB in Washington, D.C. Our first stop was at Biggs AFB near El Paso Texas, where we landed without problems. But when we took off again from there and attempted to raise the landing gear, the nose wheel locked in the right turn position and the gear would not retract. For this, we would need to land and have it repaired, but because of the nose wheel malfunction, there was a high risk of a major accident on landing.

The base personnel were alerted to the situation, and flame-retardant foam was spread on a portion of the runway we would be using. When we touched ground, the nose wheel shuddered somewhat but moved immediately into the proper position and the rest of the landing was uneventful. Because all this happened on a weekend day, we were unable to get the nose wheel inspection and sign-off handled quickly so we had to cancel our trip to Andrews. The airplane was repaired and we flew it back to March. I remember Tom remarking about the 90-degree banks and the other maneuvers I did in

---

[161] The Boeing KB-50 was used by Tactical Air Command as a refueling tanker, adapted from the B-50 "Superfortress" heavy bomber, a post-WWII revision of the B-29.

the T-33. Tom's experience had been in much larger airplanes that almost never exceed 12 degrees of bank.

On March 14 1961 an accident involving a B-52[162] occurred which I tried unsuccessfully to prevent. I was working the night shift in the command post on that date, and was in contact with the pilot prior to the accident. The aircraft was on a "Chrome Dome" mission, a USAF operation designed to counteract the threat of a Russian nuclear attack. B-52s armed with thermonuclear bombs were kept perpetually on station[163] in the vicinity of the North Pole. If the Russians attacked us, we would retaliate by giving our Chrome Dome aircraft the "go" code to head immediately over or around the pole to drop their nukes on designated Russian targets. This manner of détente between the U.S. and the Soviet Union was common and had been in place for years. On the night of the accident, one of our B-52s had a pressurization malfunction, prompting the pilot to descend to an altitude of 10,000 feet (the maximum altitude at which pressurization is not required) and headed for home base. The aircraft was flying very near the North Pole, and had a long way to go to get home. This situation became a real concern for me. At lower

---

[162] Boeing B-52 "Stratofortress," introduced in the 1950s. Production of the last models ceased around 1960, but the USAF currently plans to keep them in service until 2040.

[163] In close air support and air interdiction, the term "on station" refers to airborne aircraft that are in position to attack targets or to perform some other mission designated by the control agency, in this case 15th Air Force HQ Command.

altitudes, an aircraft's ground speed is much slower (and travel time therefore much longer). Jet engines also burn a lot more fuel at lower altitudes. The pilot/aircraft commander was also an instructor pilot and very well qualified. He and I discussed the fuel situation several times. He thought he had enough to get home.

Night shift duties in the command post included monitoring the activities of all the 15th Air Force aircraft on night operations. At the end of my shift, at 8:00 AM, I briefed the day shift crew coming in about the B-52 having problems, and advised that this particular flight should be followed very closely to ensure that the aircraft had enough fuel to get back to base. If it was determined that fuel would run out before the B-52 reached its destination, the command post was to launch an aerial tanker capable of delivering between 50,000 and 100,000 pounds of fuel in mid-air. I went home after giving my briefing and went to bed. At about 10:00 AM I got a call from 15th Air Force HQ and I had to go through everything again for General Olds and the operations staff. A KC-135[164] tanker had finally been launched and prepared to refuel the B-52. The B-52 got into refueling position and just as the boom was being lowered for insertion, the B-52 ran out of fuel, the engines lost power and the aircraft started down. The crew all ejected/bailed out successfully and the aircraft crashed. The nuclear bombs on board were in a safe condition and never were in danger of detonating. If they had launched the tanker just 5 to 10 minutes sooner, the aircraft and bombs would have been saved. The Refueling Squadron Commander who had been responsible for delaying the tanker launch was relieved of duty and replaced that day by General Olds, who also severely chastised many of the operations staff. His final comments about the incident were, "It looks like my

---

[164] Boeing KC-135 "Stratotanker," an aerial refueling aircraft.

Command Post people were the only ones who did everything right."

Uncle John and Aunt Mildred had visited us several times and we always enjoyed their company. They were the only rich relatives we hard scramblers from Two-Mile ever had. I think we subconsciously accepted them as substitute mother and father. Uncle John had a real responsible job with the Wisconsin state government. The capitol building in Madison had a big dome in the middle and four smaller domes, one located at the north, east, south and west corners. Uncle John's office took up almost all of one whole dome in one of the corners. He did some investing for the state and did some work in agriculture. They had three kids: James, the oldest, who became a chemical engineer at Du Pont; Jean, who was in medicine and I think the youngest kid; and John Jr., who went to West Point and eventually retired as a full colonel in the Army.

Uncle John died at a rather young age from prostate cancer. During the last visit to our house, I remember him saying that he did not want to become an "old fart." He must have been having some premonitions because about a week after they returned to Madison, he died. Aunt Mildred was born in 1893. In January 1993, my brother Lyle and I were planning to attend her 100th birthday. Her birthday was in January and she was living with her daughter Jean in Bloomfield, Michigan. We never made it to the birthday party because Aunt Mildred passed away about ten days prior.

Hilda and I had enjoyed the long courtship we had together without children, but by about mid-1958 we got to wondering if we were ever going to be able to have any kids, and whether maybe there was something wrong with us. We tried and tried but to no avail. And then Hilda got pregnant. She did not tell me right away, and it ended in a miscarriage. She did not tell me about that either, until much later. Hilda was old school German. It's hard to explain, but her background had instilled in her a unique kind of respect and regard for husbands.[165] She had this miscarriage one night, I knew she was not feeling well but I didn't appreciate that it was anything serious.

Hilda did eventually get a successful pregnancy, leading up to the happiest day of my life up to that point, when my daughter Barbara was born on October 28, 1960. During the pregnancy Hilda did everything correctly, took all the necessary vitamins, and looked absolutely great. The AFB hospital at March did not have facilities for childbirth, so we used a hospital in Riverside. Dr. Trotter was the delivering physician. I stayed in the labor room with Hilda and a neighbor lady who had a baby almost at exactly the same time as us. They sent me out of the labor room when the transition phase of labor began, and Barbara was born shortly after that. It had been a rather rocky trip, and she had to spend the first night in a glass box with oxygen pumped into it. She looked great though, and Dr. Trotter assured us that she was ok. We got home with Barbara after about three days and our lives changed dramatically. The total medical costs for Barbara's

---

[165] An example of this attitude was the way the second wife of Hilda's father Julius would refer to him in conversation as Mr. Huegel, not as "your dad," or "your father-in-law."

delivery and the hospitalization came to $25. We paid exactly the same amount when Jimmy was born a year and a half later.

Before Barbara, Hilda and I would have martinis each evening when I got home from work, and quite often we would have too many. Then we would go to a restaurant and eat luxuriously. Quite abruptly after Barbara came, we decided that we could not keep living the high life, so we quit the martinis. We didn't become teetotalers but we cut back significantly on the drinking.

I used to say I was surprised that Barbara ever learned to walk because I carried her everywhere we went. She was prone to carsickness though, and she did throw up a lot when we went driving with her. In March of 1960 when Hilda was pregnant with her, we visited Hawaii and did a lot of outrigger canoeing, and we both thought the motion from that may have made her susceptible to carsickness.

We loved Barbara so much. One time when she was about six months old we decided to go to see George and Betty Harbaugh in San Diego for the weekend and while there we would go to Tijuana for the afternoon. George and Betty had asked a real responsible couple if they would watch Barbara for that afternoon. When it was time to go, Hilda decided that she could not bear to leave Barbara with anybody for that long, so we did not go to T-town.

Barbara was a very happy baby and she caused us no trouble at all. It was fun for me when she would wake up hungry in the middle of the night. I would get her out of her bed, bring her to ours and Hilda would nurse her. When she was done I would either take Barbara back to her bed our let her finish out the night sleeping with us. I thought it was interesting that she never used a baby bottle, but went straight from breastfeeding to a cup. I could go on forever about the things Barbara did that made us so happy. Sometime in

September 1961, Hilda was pregnant again. Again we were extremely happy and we were hoping for a boy.

We wanted to give Barbara a present for her first birthday but did not know what to give her. Between the two of us, we were smoking about three packs of cigarettes a day so we decided that a great present we could give Barbara would be for both of us to quit smoking. Although we quit "cold turkey," I don't recall it being that difficult. Hilda never smoked again, but to my everlasting regret, I broke my end of the deal in the early 1970s and resumed smoking, a fact which adversely affected my relationship with my family because of the effect on my moods. I did not want Hilda or the kids to see me smoking, and stole away and stayed places where I could indulge my habit. As a result, I missed a lot of family time. When I was at home, I was often irritable and lost my temper more than I should have. I quit smoking for good on July 23, 1985.

Hilda also did everything correctly during the pregnancy with Jimmy, who arrived on April 16, 1962. While Hilda was in labor with Jimmy, I babysat Barbara. We barbequed a steak on our back patio, and I remember Barbara checking the steak with a bone-handled fork I still have, and still use whenever I barbeque. All kinds of wonderful things continued for us after Jimmy was born. Dr. Trotter was again the attending physician. Barbara liked the new baby, but she had to share the number-one position and that was a problem for her sometimes. We already had a bike with a seat located over the rear wheel so that we could ride the bike around with Barbara on the back. Now that we had a "boy for you and a girl for me," we bought another bike and we went riding around San Marcos square many times with our kids. We knew all the neighbors and they all were happy for us.

Omaha

When Jimmy was about three months old, I was transferred to
SAC Headquarters, in Omaha, Nebraska. By 1959 we had
already become a two-car family so we traveled there in both
vehicles. George Harbaugh had a '57 T-Bird, and I liked it so
much that I bought one for myself. Because Jimmy was so
small I built a bed for him that took up the complete rear seat
area of our other car, a '56 Olds convertible. This enabled him
to have a nice bed and an area where he could roll around
without getting hurt. When he got hungry we stopped and
Hilda nursed him. I drove the T- Bird and Hilda drove the
Olds. Several things happened during the trip. I had Barbara
with me at one point and I think we were somewhere in
Colorado. Predictably, she got carsick, and did so all over the
inside of my T-Bird. After I got it cleaned up I made her ride
in the Olds with her mother for the rest of the journey. I was
leading the caravan somewhere in Kansas and I noticed that
Hilda had dropped way back and out of sight. I stopped,
turned around and drove until I eventually found her pulled
over with a flat tire. It was in July, very hot, and I put on the
spare. We stopped at the next gas station and bought a
second-hand spare.

We arrived at Omaha and found a nice house located in
Bellevue, Nebraska, near the base. Our address was 1008
Durand Drive. We bought this house after selling the house in
Riverside. It was a three-bedroom two-bath unit with a full

basement. The two-car garage was located in the basement and it was quite nice. The winters were bitter cold with lots of wind. We had a pet dachshund, Mitzi, and with her being so low to the ground she had a tough time in the snow. She hated to go outside in the winter. The kids had a good time there in spite of the weather. Our backyard fence backed up to a high school football field and when they had games, we were able to watch.

I reported to the inspector general (IG) staff and that was to be my job for the next two years. It involved inspecting units all over the world and being away from home most of the time. Several of the senior officers were also poor leaders and difficult to get along with. I did not like the job and I tried to leave it after I had been there one year. But the Air Force said that I had to put in at least two years on the job. We did get to travel a lot. I was unable to take my full 30 days' annual vacation because of the workload. When we took off to inspect a unit somewhere we were only told what kinds of uniforms to bring and we found out where we were going after takeoff. This was kind of hard on families because we couldn't tell them where we were going and they couldn't find out until after we landed at our destination.

Our job was to give no-notice inspections to all the SAC bases worldwide. For instance, when we went to do our no-notice visit to the B-52 units at Guam, we would leave Hawaii on a clearance to the Philippines or Japan and then land unexpectedly at Guam. We visited all the SAC aircraft and missile units worldwide twice during the two years that I was on the IG team. This took us to Spain, Germany, Japan, Guam, England, Alaska, and all over the United States. Once when we were on an inspection trip in Texas we had just finished inspecting the B-58[166] unit at Carswell AFB[167] at Ft. Worth and were in the air and our way to the base at Austin,[168] Texas, when we were notified that President Kennedy had been shot in Dallas. Some believed that this might trigger the Cold War into a hot war and we waited for further instructions from SAC Headquarters. After a short time they said to proceed as scheduled, and we did. I was flying the single engine T-33 jet during this two-year period to get my flying time.

When we were not on inspection trips I worked at the inspector general's office in SAC Headquarters where we conducted briefings for the senior staff. This is where the generals seemed to take particular delight in trying to embarrass us lieutenant colonels. General LeMay had left and General Powers replaced him. Powers was a nice guy and whenever he was there during the briefings we did not have to suffer any crap from the other generals. The Cold War was real in those days and everything we did was a part of the effort to protect America from attack by the Russians. Communists had infiltrated all parts of the government and

---

[166] Convair B-58 "Hustler," a supersonic bomber.

[167] The USAF ceased to operate this base in 1994. It is now operated by the U.S. Navy, and has been renamed as the Naval Air Station Fort Worth Joint Reserve Base, Carswell Field.

[168] Bergstrom AFB (1942-1993), now Austin-Bergstrom International Airport.

the colleges. Stalinists were trying to take over the country from within. Senator McCarthy[169] was trying to identify and out these traitorous elements, while being discredited and ridiculed by the communist-friendly media. The United States survived this period, and the communists eventually lost the Cold War, but there are still some persistent communist agitators among us who are trying to undermine our government and way of life. Things are the same today, except that there is a new enemy in our midst, namely Muslims. They started infiltrating the country in 1979-1980. Now there are hundreds of mosques in the country with hundreds of thousands of Muslims. Many of them would kill all of us in a heartbeat if they could get away with it, and every time any charge is brought against one of them, the politically correct media moves to support them as does the ACLU and CAIR, the Council on Islamic Relations.

Besides briefings there was other work to do at SAC Headquarters. We spent a lot of time in the vast underground command post. In order to provide direction for the country in case of attack by the Russians, Headquarters had a special aircraft which would become an airborne command post. The president also had this same type of aircraft. It was a specially equipped KC-135 that remained airborne around the clock. When one landed, another would just be getting airborne. I had occasion to fly on this aircraft several times. A general was always on board as flight commander. We would provide

---

[169] U.S. Senator Joseph R. McCarthy, Republican from Wisconsin.

the operational support. The airborne command post was supposed to direct the retaliation of our missiles for any Russian attack in coordination with the president. We all had top secret crypto security clearances at that time.

One of the places I flew to accumulate flying time was Biggs Air Force Base in El Paso, Texas. We affectionately called this Juarez Air Force Base because of its proximity to that Mexican border town. We enjoyed crossing for a steak dinner and bringing back half-gallon bottles of Oso Negro gin and vodka. There was not much room to pack clothes and shaving kits in the T-33, so we carried a pod beneath the fuselage where we packed our clothes and the vodka and gin for the trip home. Occasionally while unloading the pod, we would suffer the embarrassment of a bottle falling on the ramp and splashing gin all over the concrete. I remember another incident while flying the T-bird. Another IG pilot was with me in the back seat and we were returning from Juarez AFB. The weather was bad and we did not have a lot of fuel left. We iced up on the descent and there was a lot of ice on the leading edge of the wing. The tower asked me to make a go around and I said we were low on fuel. The tower then asked me, "Are you declaring an emergency?" and I replied, "Only if we cannot land on this approach." So we were given permission to land. After landing we were able to get out and see how much ice we had picked up. Some of the ice broke off on touchdown but we still had some jagged icicles more than a foot long sticking out from the leading edge of the wing.

The most interesting inspection trips were the trips to Spain. We would file a clearance to Africa or Italy and then land at Zaragoza[170] and do the inspection. From there we would continue on to Morón Air Base[171] at Seville where we

---

[170] Zaragoza Air Base was a United States Air Forces in Europe (USAFE) base. Since 1994 it has been Zaragoza Airport, a civilian airport.
[171] This base remains a base for the USAFE today.

stayed at a beautiful garden hotel. On one trip there, we all went to a bullfight where we had seats close to the ring. It was raining slightly and the matadors were not the best in Spain. Near the end of one fight when the matador had stabbed the bull with the long sword and was not successful, he had to stab the bull again with a long straight sword that has a crossbar on it about six or eight inches from the tip. When this sword is inserted, about two feet of the blade and the handle are sticking out of the bull's neck close to the head. The bull swings his head violently trying to dislodge the sword. The sword can fly anywhere. This time, the sword came out and flew end over end right at me. It missed me and struck the officer sitting next to me. Fortunately, it landed flat and did not stick him, but his raincoat was covered in bull blood. He had been taking pictures at the time and did not even try to dodge that missile. Some attendants came running over, and when they saw that he had not been injured they just took the sword back into the ring.

We spent some quality time in Madrid and Frankfurt on the weekends. We stayed at the Von Steuben Hotel in Frankfurt and had a great time there. Of all the places I've visited in Europe, I think Spain is the most beautiful. The terrain is a lot like California in many places, and the oranges were far better than the ones we get in California or Florida.

I never wanted any other career but the United States Air Force. But like all good things, it had to come to an end. WWII was over, and an armistice ended the Korean conflict. The Cold War was real, but President Kennedy believed he could save the government some money by shrinking the size of the military. Probably because I was not a regular officer[172] and did not have a college degree, I was among the officers who were given a mandatory retirement date, in my case,

---

[172] Throughout my entire Air Force career, I was always in the Reserve Air Force.

May 1965 (which I was informed of in the spring of 1964). The requirements for retirement at that time were a minimum of twenty years' total duty, ten of which had to be active duty. We were called "Twenty-Tenners." We had supposed when Kennedy was first elected that all the officers who were Freemasons (I was acquainted with several) would be "twenty-tenned," because of Catholics' disdain for Masons.[173] Of course, he did not do anything like that.

Hilda and I had some quick decisions to make. We talked everything over, finally deciding that I should go into banking as a second career. She had been working for banks in New York City and in Youngstown, Ohio, long before we met. After we were married (but prior to starting our family), she worked at banks practically everywhere we were stationed. It was a safe job compared to everything else I had done up to that point, so I set my sites on banking.

I would need a bachelor's degree, but since I had been attending night school for the last 15 years, I almost had enough units for one. I had earned an associate in arts degree from Riverside City College with a major in psychology, plus some additional college courses. I went to the University of Nebraska, Omaha (UNO) to see what options there were, and discovered I was not the only military person inquiring about education. In fact, there were so many of us that colleges were launching new programs just to accommodate the flood of early retirees. It was called the "Bootstrap" Program, and it was designed to help retirees get a four-year college degree in the form of a bachelor of general education, or BGE. This program was a good fit and worked out perfectly for me. After evaluating my prior credits, they prepared a schedule that would allow me to graduate in six months, or a semester and a half. I majored in economics and minored in history.

---

[173] It seems trivial today, but Kennedy's election as the first non-Protestant president of the United States was a really big deal at the time.

The terms of my transfer to SAC Headquarters required that I stay at least one year before I could retire. I had already been there for over one year, and proposed to move up my retirement from the required May 1965 date to September 30, 1964, to which the Air Force agreed. School began on September 15 and I had an accumulated leave of two weeks, which allowed me to begin school on time. The goal Hilda and I set was for me to complete 22 years of service, get my BGE, return to Sacramento (the location we had already chosen for our retirement life), and start my second career, all before I turned 41 years old.

My retirement pay was $425 a month, obviously not enough to live on. We had saved a little money, and allowed ourselves to dissave each month just enough to keep our total monthly resources at the same level as when I left the service. Hilda was pregnant again, and the baby was due in late February 1965. With Hilda now 39 years old and me 40, this was an unexpected additional complexity to consider in our transition to civilian life.

Our house in Omaha had a full basement where we parked our two cars. Many times during the winter of 1964-65 I had to shovel three or four feet of snow out of the driveway before I could back the car out to go to school. Our basement also had a small room which Hilda converted into a study for me. I studied hard and tried to do the best I could. I managed to get straight As in economics and accounting, but just Bs and Cs in the other classes.

I remember a few incidents from my days at UNO that gave me my first insights into the warped, liberal mentality of American higher educators. The first related to the fact that Hilda and I had decided to purchase a 1965 Oldsmobile Vista Cruiser Station Wagon (the 60s equivalent of a "minivan"), to accommodate our expanding family. The subject of labor

194

unions came up in one of my classes,[174] and I made the comment that the car I had just bought for $2,600 had about the same amount of steel, iron, glass, rubber, upholstery and sheet metal as a new Dodge two-door sedan one of my uncles had bought in 1936 for $600, and the only factor that could explain the price differential was union labor. The hostile reaction I got from the professor made it seem I had just blasphemed before a Spanish Inquisitor, and it seemed for a moment he was going to throw me out of the classroom.

A second incident happened during mid-term exams in economics. I had scored a 98 percent on the first test, but I had overstudied for the mid-term and was so keyed up I couldn't even write my name on the test paper. I can't explain the anxiety, but it was intense and prevented me from answering questions I knew the answers to. I shared all this with the instructor, a Dr. Steele. He told me not to worry about it (I did fine on the final, and got a final grade of A).

A final incident was in anthropology class. I answered some of the text questions with facts right out of the textbook we used, but the professor teaching that class was expecting different answers for some reason I never understood. I asked him why he bothered to assign us to read the text if we weren't going to be allowed to use the information. He gave me a "C."

---

[174] I had been required to join a labor union when I worked for Preway, the stove manufacturing company.

Our third child, another daughter, was delivered on the same day as our Vista Cruiser, Feb. 26, 1965. We named her Susan after my mother, but gave her no middle name, figuring she could use Grey as her middle name when she got married (which she did by the way, twice). I picked up the car and took it to the hospital to get Hilda and Susan. It was cold and snowing, and I covered up the new baby very carefully and carried her to the car. The total hospital bill was $3.75. That was the charge for food for three days at $1.25 a day. After Susan was born, Hilda and I agreed that was all the children we needed.

I knew of other officers in the Air Force who, like me, were not West Point grads (that is to say, not regular officers, and commissioned initially either in the reserve or the Army of the United States, which was the designation in the early 1940s). Some of those men had been sent to a four-year college to obtain a degree while on active duty, and upon finishing college were assigned to operational Air Force units. I may have had two opportunities to do this myself. One was during my assignment at 15th Air Force Headquarters at March AFB. The Deputy Commander of the 15th AF was Maj. Gen. Joe Nazzaro, with whom I had become acquainted initially through work and also working out together at the gym. Nazzaro was the individual who had organized the 381st Bomb Group in Pyote,[175] Texas, and took the unit to England in 1943 to fly the group's first combat missions against the Germans. I got to the 381st in 1944 after he had already completed his tour and returned to the United States. But because of our mutual war-time records in the 381st, I believe I could have asked him to intercede on my behalf at Headquarters to get me into college and continue on for a full

---

[175] Pyote AAB turned out several heavy bomber groups (B-17 and B-29) during WWII. The base was decommissioned in 1963 and almost nothing remains of it today.

military career. The other opportunity would have been for me to contact my congressman in Wisconsin and ask him to intercede for me. Unfortunately, these ideas did not come to me until it was too late. Looking back it is a big regret I have, not to have thought and acted on it at the time.

We had several things to consider before making the move back to the land of fruits and nuts. We decided we would leave the '57 T-Bird in Omaha, and drive just one car to Sacramento. I took the car to Bekins Storage, figuring I would come and get it after we got settled in Sacramento. The charge for storage was $30 a month. The next thing we decided to do was to sell the house, although this proved later to be a mistake. We advertised the house through a Realtor and sold it at a loss of about $1,500. Had we kept it as a rental for just a couple of years, we could have sold it for a good profit.

About mid-April 1965, our household goods were loaded into a moving van in preparation for our move to California. We loaded the children, the dog, and our personal baggage into our new Olds VC and headed out. The way the back seats folded down allowed us to create a huge playpen for the children and dog (naturally, no cars were equipped with seat belts back then). Hilda could reach them by just turning around and kneeling in the passenger seat. It was a perfect vehicle for long-distance family trips.

Top: Me and friends in the V-J Day parade in Lubbock, Texas, 1945.
Bottom: Me seated on the hood of my wood-paneled, 1941 Mercury station wagon. It was a technical violation of regulations, but servicemen from this era who were stationed anywhere in Texas typically wore cowboy boots with their "Pinks and Greens" uniforms.

Laura Rudomski, me and one of Laura's friends taken during a leave in Wisconsin just after returning from combat tour.

One of the two Piper Cub J-3s in which I first learned to fly, Lubbock, Texas.

Col.Howell Estes, Lubbock Air Force Base Commander,Capt.Jim Grey, Charlie Guy, Editor of the Lubbock Avalanche Journal prepare for a trip to Mines Field (Now L A Metro Airport) September-1945

Sep. 1945 public relations flight from Lubbock, Texas, to Mines Field (now LAX), CA. Left to right: unidentified crewman, me, Col. Howell Estes (Lubbock AF Base Commander), Charlie Guy (editor, *Lubbock Avalanche Journal*), and another unidentified crew member. September 1945.

Top: Me aboard a C-45. I was the first to do aerial mapping of southern Japan, c. 1947.
Bottom: Lt. Konechne, friend who helped me out of a scrape with a vehicle mishap. Koneckne was later was killed in a P-61 crash while my unit was on maneuvers on Kiushu, summer 1947.

Me standing in front of a P-51, Itazuke, Japan, 1947.

In front of my Jeep near Itazuke, winter 1947.

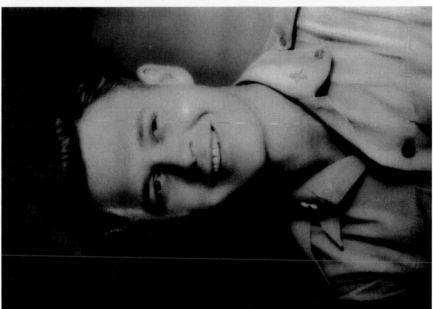

How we looked when we met...
Top: Hilda Marie Huegel, at age 20. Taken in her hometown of Youngstown, Ohio just prior to her move to Tachikawa, Japan.
Bottom: Capt. James F. Grey, Itazuke, Japan.

Top and Bottom: Hilda at Tachikawa AFB, Japan, spring 1949.

204

Me and Hilda dining with friends at a geisha house in Yokohama.

Me and then fiancée Hilda, taken in the grounds outside the "Ga-Jo-En" Hotel, Tokyo, May 1949.

Marriage at the Lutheran church in Wisconsin Rapids, June 3, 1949. Left to right: Lyle Z. Grey (brother and best man at the ceremony), me, Hilda, and my mother, Susan C. Grey (as matron of honor).

206

Walking in front of the old Walgreen drug store at 7th and J streets in downtown Sacramento, 1949.

Hilda in front of our first new apartment together, at 39th and J street, Sacramento, California. Rent was $95 per month.

Pilot School graduation day, Bainbridge, February 15, 1951. I am second from right.

Top: Me with my nephew and niece Jimmy and Jackie Marsh, posing in front of the '51 Olds Convertible, at my home in Enid, Oklahoma, summer 1952.
Bottom: Hilda and doorman standing in front of the Dorchester Hotel, London (1950).

209

Alert duty at RAF Station Lakenheath in England, 1958. Left to Right: Me (co-pilot), Ed Bailey (pilot), Ray Barrett (Rad-Nav).

Taken same day as preceding photo, my B-47 in a smoky jet-fuel-assisted takeoff (JATO), a technique used on short runways to provide more thrust on takeoff by use of small rockets.

My B-47 Crew at March AFB. I am on the left in the foreground, with my co-pilot Andy Miller standing next to me.

Brothers Tom and Lyle with me at my home in Riverside, 1961.

Me with daughter Barbara on left, and son Jimmy on right, at home in Omaha, 1963.

Our home in Omaha, Nebraska.

Transitioning to civilian life. Portrait photos both taken around the same time, 1964, in Omaha, Nebraska. I waited a long time to wear the scrambled eggs on my visor, and was sad to give them up.

Part Three: Civilian Years

Setting down Roots

We arrived in Sacramento in May of 1965, ready to begin our new civilian life. We moved temporarily into a small apartment in Rancho Cordova and had the moving company store our shipment until we found a permanent place to stay. We also left the '57 T-Bird in storage in Omaha.

Right away I started looking for work with the banks in town. I learned right away that anyone wanting to be hired into a management training program had to travel to San Francisco and apply there, since that was where most California Banks had their headquarters. I applied to United California Bank,[176] Bank of America, Wells Fargo and other smaller banks. I ruled out BofA almost immediately because of the attitude of the personnel department. They required applicants to fill out an application and leave it with them, and then wait for them to make the next move ("Don't call us, we'll call you."). On acceptance of an application, the next step was a scheduled meeting with one of their personnel department employees. That meeting was followed by a waiting period and then another meeting, and then another, and another, and so on. Every meeting involved waking early, driving all the way to San Francisco, and being gone all day. UCB, on the other hand, called one day to invite me to come to San Francisco for interviews with several of their top-ranking personnel all at once.

---

[176] UCB had regional headquarters in San Francisco, but its corporate headquarters were in Los Angeles.

On days when I interviewed out of town, Hilda would be stuck in the house all day with the kids, and when I finally arrived back home, there would be a list of errands waiting for me. Hilda was absolutely wonderful throughout this period. She was totally supportive and did everything to make my job search easier. After nearly three months of looking I still had no offers, and I began to widen my search to other major area employers such as Aerojet. But they were really only interested in people who had political influence with the military brass in Washington, D.C., and if you didn't, they basically did not have a position for you. Meanwhile, I was persistent about contacting the banks.

During this period we were having a great time as a family. We used the weekends to search for a rental house close to a school, since Barbara would be starting at kindergarten that fall. We found a nice little house on Alegre Court in Rancho Cordova, moved in and had all our stored items delivered to us. The T-Bird stayed in Omaha for the time being.

I knew that UCB was getting close to making an offer when quite unexpectedly, one of the smaller banks made me one. I had decided I really wanted to go to work for UCB, but needed to respond to the other bank. At this time, my old B-47 co-pilot George Harbaugh (who had himself earned a business degree from CSU San Diego), was working in the personnel department at Convair Astronautics and I thought he would be able to give me some good advice. He recommended that I go to the person I was dealing with at UCB, tell him that I had this other offer I needed to act on, but really wanted to work for them and needed a prompt decision. I called the man from UCB and used the exact words George had recommended; he was silent for a moment, and then asked me to come to San Francisco to meet for lunch and pick up my written job offer. I met with him, we had our two-martini lunch, and I was hired.

My training was set to begin at the branch located at the corner of 21st and K in downtown Sacramento. It was the end of July 1965 and after those three months of job hunting I wanted to take a vacation with the family, so I negotiated a start date of September 1, 1965, and took off the month of August. I used part of this time to travel back to Omaha, take the T-bird out of storage, install a new battery and drive it out to Sacramento. That solved our transportation problems, since I could now travel to interviews while leaving Hilda with the Olds VC.

I had set goals to retire from the Air Force, complete my bachelor degree and start my banking career by my forty-first birthday, and just made it with a week to spare.

United California Bank

I reported to the 21st & K Street branch of UCB ready to go to work. My starting salary was $400 a month. Even combined with my monthly Air Force retirement pay of $425, it was not quite enough to cover all our expenses at first, but after training and a couple of salary increases we lived very comfortably.

Bank branch management involved not only making loans but also management of all personnel and functions. Each bank branch was virtually a complete, fully functioning, self-contained business unto itself. A banking career was still widely respected back in those days. If he was doing his job correctly, a bank branch manager was regarded as a leading figure in his community, empowered with personal decision-making authority and personally accountable for results. It was not like it is today, with branch managers sitting next to the dog food racks in supermarkets and without any judgment or decision-making authority. This work has been stripped of all its former dignity. And in my opinion, all the modern technological "advances" with centralized "service" centers and telephone banking have done nothing to improve the industry or make it more profitable. Without personalized, direct contact--a relationship and communication between a bank officer and a customer--appropriate credit decisions are not possible. If an honest, comprehensive research or measurement of this were possible, I am convinced it would bear me out. The massive bank failures and bailouts of recent times are at least in part a consequence of the depersonalization and consolidation of the banking industry.

There was still a quaint notion back when I started that in order to be able to effectively manage something, you first had to have a clue about what it was you were managing. When a bank signed you on to become an officer, the training it invested in you was extremely thorough and spanned several months. The first part of my training involved spending a few weeks in each operational function to learn them, beginning with the teller line. Hilda had been a teller in several of her past bank assignments, so I was pretty familiar with what tellers do. But I was a good sport and let them teach me. It was fun to begin with and the bank personnel were very helpful.

I met lots of different people, became closely acquainted with my customers and made lasting friendships with many of them. One in particular is my good friend, John Houston, who has been my barber continuously for the past 46 years. Believe it or not, during that entire span of years, only twice have I had haircuts from anyone other than John (one was performed by John's brother, David, who works in the same shop with John). John was just twenty-two years old when I met him at his shop at 20th & K streets, just a block from my branch. Being recently retired from the Air Force and still sporting my flat-top, butch military hairstyle, I needed someone who knew how to do that kind of haircut and John was a rare expert at them. I would plan my vacation and any other necessary travel so that I would never have to get a haircut from anyone else. John became a bank customer, and besides that we have enjoyed a lot of golf and pheasant hunting together. I have never heard of anyone who has had the same barber for as many years as I have.

After completing the operations phase of my training (in the spring of 1966), it was time to move into the credit phase. This required a couple of months' training at the

Northern California region headquarters in San Francisco. It would have been impractical to drive to San Francisco every day to participate in the training, so I rented an apartment on a month-to-month basis, two blocks up the hill from the bank on California Street.

The credit training was more rigid than operations training, but still very enjoyable. Classes were conducted on the second floor on the south side of the building. From our vantage point, we could look out the windows and observe construction of the new Bank of America building.[177] We watched it start out as an enormous hole in the ground, and gradually rise up as floors were added. UCB's San Francisco headquarters was very small by comparison. Also nearby was the short-lived San Francisco Playboy Club,[178] just three blocks down the street. We found time to get acquainted with the club and "bunnies," and see some of the shows. I still have some souvenirs from the bar there.

One of the things that made my visits to San Francisco interesting was the fact that my mother now resided there. After a long period of widowhood, she had remarried and relocated to San Francisco with her new husband, a man named Bill Hunter. She had met Bill while living and teaching school in Southern California. They had moved together to San Francisco (after briefly residing in Oregon) and were managing the Mart-Motel located at Ninth & Mission. Before, Bill had been a San Francisco resident for many years of his life and owned a small boat that he used to take people on cruises out on the bay. He was retired, and they had very little income to live on. They owned a four-door Nash Rambler but didn't want or need it in the city, so they decided to lend it to

---

[177] Formerly Bank of America Center, it was that bank's landmark, 52-story world headquarters until 1998. It has been renamed to 555 California Street and is owned by a consortium of investors, the largest among them being Donald Trump.

[178] Founded in 1965, it existed only briefly during the mid- to late-1960s.

me and have me take care of it for them. Now I was up to three vehicles. Sometimes I would drive the Nash to the credit class in San Francisco, but usually I would drive the T-bird there and leave it parked at the motel garage right next to the office. This arrangement was quite convenient, and spared me from having to leave the car out in the open or pay for parking.

Mother and Bill lived in an apartment right behind the office. A door in their living room opened right into the motel lobby behind the counter where they would check in the guests. It was several blocks to my apartment from there and uphill all the way, but I enjoyed the exercise. I would run down the hill on Friday evenings, hop in the T-bird and head for home in Sacramento for the weekends.

I got to meet some of the high-level bank executives during my training in San Francisco. One of them, the chief of the personnel department, wanted me to stay in San Francisco and go to work for him there, but I told him that I thought it would be better if I got some branch experience before I took on any headquarters job. After the initial training at the 21st and K branch and finishing the credit class, I was transferred to 10th and K, where I went to train as a loan officer.

My new boss, Tony Westra, was a big guy who had played football for the University of Michigan. Besides managing 10th & K, he was also UCB's regional manager for the Sacramento area. He was a good trainer for me and gradually allowed me greater autonomy and responsibility as time went on. At this time, both Westra and Sacramento's mayor, Walter Christensen, were working hard at getting the K Street Mall project going. He had me canvass all the businesses along K Street between 7th and 16th Streets to see if the owners were interested in having a mall. Those visits opened the dialogue for me to win them as customers for UCB, and I was able to bring in quite a few. But as far as the mall idea went, only 29 percent of them wanted it to be built there. This was not what the project champions wanted to hear, and they were determined to get the mall built one way or another. Next, pressure was applied to owners of the commercial properties on K Street (many of whom were absentee landlords based in Chicago or other parts of the United States). At the end of all their campaigning, Tony and the mayor somehow got the official support rate for the mall up to 74 percent and it got built. I personally thought the mall was a horrible idea. Sacramento's downtown area was fine just as it was. It had angular parking, thriving businesses and a real homey atmosphere. After construction of the mall, downtown Sacramento deteriorated rapidly, and it has never recovered. Now more than forty years later, the mall and a lot of the rest of midtown still look like a ghost town.

For the brief period I was assigned to the 10th & K branch, I frequently worked out at the Elks Club[179] gym nearby during my lunch hours. I had been a member of the Elks since joining in 1956 in Riverside, and really enjoyed keeping up the fitness program I had started in my early days in the Air Force at this gym, which was very well equipped and just a five minute walk from work. I should mention that I had received a whopping $50 a month pay raise about six months into my bank career. I asked Bob Houghton, the personnel manager in San Francisco who hired me, how on earth they could possibly afford such a gigantic raise. It really irked me when he explained that they had taken my Air Force retirement pay

---

[179] Lodge No. 6 met at the Elks Club building at 11th and J streets downtown from the 1920s until declining membership forced it to sell the building in 1972 to local development magnate Buzz Oates and relocate to the Florin Road area. The building has since changed owners several times, and is now called Elks Tower.

into consideration when setting my compensation level. Around mid-1967, my management decided I was ready for additional responsibility, and they transferred me back to the 21st & K office as assistant manager. At that time, the manager was a Canadian named Stuart Matheson, the same person who gave me my initial training when I first started with UCB. He was a very good guy.

Just prior to this however, bank headquarters had been sending me strong signals that I would likely need to transfer very soon to the San Francisco Bay Area for more training. In the locations they were contemplating sending me, parking would have been a big problem for my four vehicles (by now I had added a used Chevy pickup with a chassis-mount camper to my "fleet"). I resolved that I would need to get rid of one of the vehicles. I couldn't really sell Mother and Bill's Rambler since it was still theirs, and we needed the Vista Cruiser and camper for family travel. Reluctantly, I decided that the T-bird would have to go. In retrospect, that was a terrible mistake that I deeply regret making to this very day. It was in mint condition and only had about 60,000 miles on it. I found an employee at Dalton Motors who was interested in it for his daughter to use at college. While he was over to the house to look it over, I was on the verge of sending Hilda outside to tell him I had changed my mind and it wasn't for sale. But my thoughts turned to all the parking problems and expenses in San Francisco, and I just decided to go through with it. I went outside, accepted the $1,200 cashier's check he had brought with him, and gave him the title and the keys. Not only did I lose a car that I absolutely loved to drive, but I lost a valuable

223

classic in the making. Last I checked, the price on vintage 1957 T-birds peaked at around $300,000! On top of all of this, I never did get transferred to San Francisco after all, and could have hung on to the T-bird forever.

Sometime in the spring of 1969 I got a call from Bud Powers, one of the executives who had initially interviewed me at UCB headquarters, to say they were looking for someone to fill the manager position at the branch in Pittsburgh, California. Pittsburgh is a small delta town about 70 miles from Sacramento. I thanked him, but said I preferred to stay in Sacramento, having just spent $10,000 on a house. I also liked the Sacramento area quite a lot. He was okay with my answer, and took the opportunity to let me know that everyone had a good impression about how I was doing. He was quite complimentary, adding that I could stay right where I was and easily become the manager of the 21st & K Branch someday. He also mentioned that my branch had been a consistent money-maker ever since it first opened around 1959.

In the '60s, one of the standard perks that went along with a branch manager job was a 100 percent-sponsored country club membership. That was a great benefit, because the bank not only paid the membership and dues, entitling the member to unlimited use of the club, but the monthly meal and entertainment tab as well. So for example, the 10th & K branch manager position went with a membership at Del Paso Country Club (considered to be the most exclusive and elite club of its kind for our area). At the 21st & K branch, Stu Matheson had a sponsored membership at North Ridge Country Club in Fair Oaks. Stu invited me out to North Ridge to play golf from time to time. I was not very good, but could negotiate my way around a course passably. I got more and more involved in golf and improved my game as time passed. At 21st & K, we also had a lot of customers who belonged to North Ridge. Stu was transferred to a branch in another city and got replaced by an Englishman named Glen Bythel. Glen was an avid golfer and immediately took over the branch membership at the North Ridge Country Club. He brought me out with him also, and the two of us got along very well.

A lot of deal making naturally took place on golf courses all across the country, but with the women's movement, sponsored country club memberships came to be associated with gender discrimination. Later, when I became a branch manager myself, UCB headquarters directed me to investigate and report on whether or not North Ridge discriminated against women. I don't remember the exact year, but at the time of my investigation the club had a female general manager, and 39 proprietary female members. The same standards and investigations were applied to women as men (e.g., credit background checks, etc.). Memberships were granted to any women who were qualified. The bank was not going to continue to sponsor entertainment perks for their branch managers if the country clubs were found to discriminate against women. I was able to prove that at least at North Ridge, there was no discrimination so the bank continued to sponsor my membership. A fellow member who managed a branch for Bank of America was not as lucky. BofA conducted a similar investigation of North Ridge, and decided to cut his sponsorship to just 50 percent of entertainment expenditures. Ultimately, this great tradition has fallen by the wayside as banks have moved to eliminate all employment benefits for the sake of cost savings as well as political correctness as the industry gradually moved to "robotic" banking.

The bank transferred Glen Bythel to Marysville in April 1973. I was made a Vice President and became manager at 21st & K. branch. This is what I had wanted all along, and I enjoyed the new responsibilities. Glen's secretary and I did not get along that well, and after discussing the issue with personnel she was immediately transferred to another branch.

Another employee serving as our new accounts representative, Suzanne Aguilera, became my secretary. She and I got along really well (her dad was retired Air Force), and she eventually went on to become a VP and branch manager.

My promotion meant that the bank's membership at North Ridge Country Club passed to me. I have been a member for 38 years now and I really enjoy playing golf there regularly. I have golfed all over the world, and can say that North Ridge is one of the finest clubs anywhere. When the kids were growing up they all took golf lessons there, and now my grandson Ian is active in the junior golf program. My granddaughter Carolyn worked for a year in the restaurant at the Club. It has an annual invitational golf tournament called the Ridge Runner. Members invite a guest to play three rounds on three consecutive days, and there is a gala dinner party on the last day of the tournament (always a Saturday night). I have played in that tournament for 36 of the past 38 years. I have had three holes-in-one on the eighth hole, the last of which actually occurred during the 1992 Ridge Runner tournament. My guest and I won the Ridge Runner in 1991. I have had some good luck on the five-pars at North Ridge also, and have eagled three of them. I had another eagle on a four-par hole at the Ancil Hoffman Golf Course during a tournament there.

1273 Gary Way

By the summer of 1967, Barbara had finished first grade at a nice little school[180] near our house and Hilda and I thought it was time for us to start looking for a house to buy. I didn't want to buy into the local housing market if I was going to be transferred out of the area, so I checked with personnel in San Francisco to see if I could count on remaining in Sacramento for a while. The answer was yes, so Hilda and I started shopping for a house. We worked at this for about a month. We had two basic parameters: first, that the house not require a lot of work, and second, that it be located fairly close to a good school. Barbara was going into second grade and it was time for Jimmy to start kindergarten. After some searching we found exactly what we wanted. It happened to have been featured as "Home of the Month" in the Sacramento Valley Homebuilder Magazine, August 1962 issue (the year of its construction). It had about 2,400 square feet, four bedrooms, two and a half baths and a terrific layout, with a good-sized swimming pool. A separate structure to the main house included an oversized garage, a large recreation room, office and workshop, and had its own separate heating and air conditioning units. This structure was separated from the main house by a covered breezeway, and joined together by a common roof. Hilda could look out through the dining room window and watch the kids walk to and from the Del Dayo School, just one short block away. The backyard had a pool

---

[180] Williamson Elementary School.

and concrete deck, and no grass to mow. Hilda taught kids to swim in that pool for the next 30-plus years. We paid $35,000 for the home. We used $10,000 of savings to apply as a down payment and financed the balance. When we bought it, we enclosed the breezeway and made a few other changes, so our total investment in the house came to about $38,000 altogether. At the peak of real estate prices some 40 years later, the house was valued at $750,000.

During the 1960s, Tom piloted many different types of planes for the Air Force. During the Bay of Pigs invasion and the Cuban Missile Crisis, he refueled fighter aircraft from his KB-50. Some of his greatest flying experiences were in the C-124. The United States had built an ice station[181] and airstrip on a floating ice mass in the Arctic Circle, and Tom used to fly missions there. Because the ice mass was not stationary, it could be difficult to find the ice runway, and the extreme weather conditions near the North Pole made finding it that much harder. Other trips in the C-124 included hauling a ground-controlled approach unit ("GCA") to Argentina. The U.S. Air Force had sent some planes and personnel to participate in joint exercises with the Argentine Air Force, and the GCA unit was needed to provide the arriving American planes with an instrument approach. Note that the C-124 was

[181] Known as "T-3," it was built for joint military-civilian scientific research.

an enormous cargo plane capable of hauling huge loads, but was propeller-driven and had nothing even close to the hauling capacity of a jet-powered C-5[182] or a C-17.[183]

Tom stayed in the Air Force for about 13 years altogether. Sometime in 1967 or '68, he called to tell me about an opportunity he had to work for United Airlines, and he wanted my advice about whether to leave the Air Force to take advantage of it then, or stay put until he could qualify for retirement. I advised him to go with United. I think he had already made up his mind to take the offer anyway, but just wanted to bounce it off me. When he first began his career with United Airlines, they allowed Tom to take furloughs to continue to fly the C-124 on missions for the Air Force. On these flights he was typically hauling cargo to Europe, Vietnam and other places. The museum at Travis AFB has a C-124 on display, and because of his vast experience flying that aircraft, Tom would sometimes get asked to give visitors tours and answer questions. He wrote an article for the museum newsletter describing one interesting experience he had in the C-124. Tom and his crew were assigned to transport Charles Lindbergh's red-winged "Sirius" aircraft to Osaka, Japan, for Expo '70. The Sirius is a single engine floatplane that Lindbergh and his wife Anne Morrow flew in 1931 from New York to Nanking, China. The aircraft had to be dismantled and made to fit inside the C-124. Tom hauled it from Andrews AFB in Maryland to Osaka via Hawaii and Wake Island. They delivered the Sirius in February 1970 and returned to Osaka to bring it back to the States in September of the same year. When the Air Force quit flying the C-124, Tom transferred into the Air Force reserves and concentrated entirely on his commercial flying.

---

[182] The Lockheed C-5 Galaxy has been used by the USAF since 1969 and is one of the largest cargo planes in the world.
[183] Boeing C-17 Globemaster III, a large military transport aircraft.

Sometime in 1968 I got a call from Bill Hunter. He said to me, "You've got to get me and your mother out of here!" That evening around 9 p.m. the bell had rung in the office of their motel and Mother had gone to attend at the front counter as usual. A thief pointed a handgun in her face and demanded she give him all the money in the register. Mother opened the cash drawer, and the thief reached over the counter to stick has hand in the drawer to take out all the cash. Just as this happened, Bill appeared in the doorway with his .22 revolver, and Mother slammed the drawer on the criminal's hand, shouting, "Get out of here, you son of a bitch." The thief looked up and saw Bill pointing his gun at him, turned around and fled out the door. The experience was frightening for both of them, and they both agreed it was time for them to get out of San Francisco.

Hilda and I went out searching for a place for them, and bought a duplex located on the southwest corner of Morse and Whitney in Sacramento. It was a nice, small duplex with a one bedroom on one side and a two on the other. Mother and Bill moved into the one-bedroom side. By this point, Tom and Jane had divorced. Tom was living in Long Island and flying routes out of the airports in New York City. Jane took their kids to Sacramento in 1968 and moved into the other side of the duplex. I thought it was a good arrangement for them because Jane worked, and my mother could watch the kids during the day.

Not long after that, Tom bought a house on El Nido Street in Arden Park for Jane and the kids. It had a small guest house in the back into which Tom moved Mother and Bill, leaving my duplex empty. So, I was forced to look for new tenants for the duplex. Bill and Mother both chain-smoked and the walls of their side of the duplex had become totally covered with stains. Even after three coats of paint, the walls still had a smoky appearance. We got the place re-rented and things went along okay for a while. But the tenant on the two-bedroom side, a divorcee with two small children, became delinquent with her rent payments. She had a good job with an insurance company, and I knew she could afford the payments. I found out when she got paid and I got into the practice of following her to her bank when she cashed her paychecks, demanding the rent right there on the spot. I grew annoyed with having to go to all this trouble, and the last time I met her at the bank to collect the rent money, I said to her, "You've got thirty days to get out of my duplex." After that, we sold it. If it was family, it was a pleasure, but outside of that, I really never enjoyed the experience of being a landlord.

Tom got remarried while he was living on the East Coast. His base of operations was switched to San Francisco International Airport, and they moved to Sonoma, California, where they bought a 13-acre ranch, I believe in 1973. There was an old guest house on the property, and Mother and Bill moved in there. Tom's wife brought her three kids from her first marriage, and Tommy Jr. and Kim moved in with them

231

also. Initially, the place was sort of dumpy-looking with a bunch of ramshackle old houses, barns and other structures strewn all over it. Besides that, there were old wrecked cars all over the place (mostly Ramblers and DeSotos), which made it look like a junk yard. Like me, Tom had grown up fixing up old cars and learned mechanical skills from our dad. But unlike me, he retained a genuine interest in those activities well into adulthood. At some point Tom refurbished a beautiful, vintage gull-wing Stinson we rode in together. He kept it at the ranch, taking off and landing in a field adjacent to his property (he later donated that plane to an aircraft museum).

It turned out the ranch was "haunted" by a ghost, and everyone in Tom's family as well as my Mother claimed to have experiences with it, but we never saw anything. They kept horses on their property, and our kids really enjoyed visits there because their cousins let them ride them. Tom did a lot of entertaining and had some really fabulous parties out at their place, including an annual pig roast they did for many years. While our kids were all still living at home, we visited them a lot for Christmas and other occasions. Over time, Tom fixed up the property and made it into quite a lovely estate.

Tom always had street smarts I lacked along with a good head for business and he has been successful at lots of different ventures. One was a really outstanding Mexican restaurant he bought ("Jorge House"), where the kids all worked during their teen years. He stayed with United for 31 years before retiring. Tom's health was always pretty good, but in 2006 he had a four-way heart bypass operation. I visited him several times at the hospital in Santa Rosa. He is now using a pace-maker. He got to do some really wonderful things with his flying career which in fact really exceeded my own experience. I was just a little envious of him for this, but truly, I have always been extremely proud of my brother for all his accomplishments, and love him very much.

232

Family Life

Sunday evening was family night out, and we almost always went to either of the officers' clubs in town at Mather or McClellan. Mather's OC hosted an outstanding Oktoberfest party every year for a long time with very good entertainment, and we had some quite memorable times at those. We traded our first camper for a green 1969 Ford 250 pickup (at the time, less than a year old) with a slide-in camper While the kids were growing up, we took a really big driving/camping vacation somewhere every year, traveling all over the western states and Canada. There were a few favorite destinations we returned to many times, like Sea Cliff State Beach in Aptos, California, or Prairie Creek Redwoods, near Eureka.

Our most ambitious road trip ever happened in 1976. Barbara was about fifteen years old, Jimmy about thirteen and Susan ten. We let Jimmy plan the entire three week itinerary, and after exploring about the fifth cave on our trek, I think the girls wish we hadn't. We headed straight north through Nevada and Idaho to Yellowstone, sight-seeing along the way to Canada. We were stopped at the Canadian border and subject to a complete inspection by the Mounties. I was growing a beard on that trip, but I didn't think we looked that dangerous. The inspector was a woman and she went through the camper very deliberately, like she was looking for something in particular. I had brought a twelve-gauge automatic shotgun and some shells with me, but I knew that it was legal to carry long guns in Canada (hand guns were prohibited). The inspector noted the shotgun with no comment, finished the inspection and let us resume our journey. The International Peace Park (Glacier on the U.S. side, Banff on the Canadian side) is really one of the most beautiful places on Earth. We spent some time at Lake Louise, and Jimmy waited until he had paddled Susie out to the middle of the lake in a canoe before tormenting her with sound effects from the movie "Jaws."[184]

From there we continued eastward on Canada's Highway 1. When we got to Regina, Jimmy had contracted such a bad intestinal flu that we had to take him to the hospital. As the doctor examined him, Jimmy suddenly vomited all over everything. The doctor (what a guy) never flinched or changed expressions, but only said to Jimmy reassuringly, "Well, if you can't be sick in a hospital, then where can you?" He gave us some medicine that quickly cured Jimmy, and when I asked him what we owed, he simply replied, "Nothing; medicine is free here in Canada."

We continued on eastward in Canada, turning south around Lake of the Woods back into the United States at Minnesota and on to Wisconsin. This was the first time I got to show the Forty to the whole family. It was summer, very hot and muggy. The Forty is a pretty densely-forested property with a lot of hills, and we set up our camp on the top of one of them. We had our dachshund Mitzi with us, and the kids and the dog immediately ran out into the woods and started having fun. Before long I heard them screaming that Mitzi had fallen into the creek. I raced down to the creek and saw Mitzi being carried downstream by the current. I ran downstream along the bank and found a place where there was an opening in the brush. I had to lie down and hook my

---

[184] "Jaws" had been released in theatres that year and was the rage with kids.

234

feet on some brush to keep from falling into the creek. When Mitzi floated by, the only thing I could reach was her snout. I gripped her muzzle and swung her back over my head and up the hill. Then I scrambled up to make sure she didn't roll back down into the creek. What a fiasco! In spite of the heat and the king-sized mosquitoes, we had a good time at the Forty.

There were a couple of families with whom we did a lot of that kind of traveling and who had kids near in ages to our own. We went on a lot of camping and beach vacations near Lake Tahoe with the Meyers, Chokan or Lee families for snow and skiing vacations in the winter. We had several opportunities to treat ourselves to live dinner shows at Reno or South Lake Tahoe, experiencing such artists as Elvis Presley, Liberace, Sammy Davis, Jr., and others.

The kids' favorite vacations were our visits to Lyle and Phyllis' place in Garden Grove, mainly because from there it was only about a five-minute drive to Disneyland. In 1996, Lyle and Phyllis sold their place in Garden Grove and moved to Nampa, Idaho (near Boise) where their daughter Vicki was living. She later left the area, and in 2003, Lyle and Phyllis relocated again to Custer, South Dakota, where Phyllis has a lot of family. Lyle stayed in good health physically, but he is nearly blind now and he suffers from acute short-term memory loss. I still talk to him by phone frequently, and he can still remember the good old days (in fact, when I was getting close to finishing this book, he was able to provide some details I was missing). Lyle has been a great brother and friend, and we have shared many great times together.

We eventually sold the camper and bought an RV, but kept the pickup. I taught the kids to drive as soon as they were old enough, and used our Ford 250 pickup because they had a bit more steel around them if there was an accident. Barbara became an excellent driver. She was at the wheel of the camper on a return trip from a vacation we took back east, when a car just ahead of us lost its muffler and tailpipe. It happened too quickly for Barbara to avoid running over it. But she kept a cool head and did a great job of controlling the truck. A few miles later, the left rear tire went flat and she had to pull over on the freeway. As they grew older, the kids began losing interest in family vacations. We kept the motor home for quite some time, which actually became Jimmy's residence for his first year at the University of California, Davis (1979-80).

As my income grew (both through bank raises and cost of living adjustments to my Air Force retirement pay), I calculated that we could afford to own a small boat for fishing and water skiing. We bought a small fiberglass outboard boat and began making excursions on the Sacramento River and Folsom Lake. The kids were still small and light, and that boat was enough for us at first. But as the kids grew, this changed. Fully loaded, it had a freeboard of only about four to five inches. I realized that if a really big wave came, or if the kids started to move around too much, water could pour over the sides into the boat and sink us. Besides safety concerns, the kids became more interested in water skiing and the small outboard engine just did not have enough horsepower to pull adult skiers. We traded it in for a new and much larger (17-foot) boat with a 150 hp Mercruiser inboard/outboard engine. In the mid-1970s we began renting a slip at the Brown's Ravine Marina at Folsom Lake, where we left the boat for most of each year (hauling it back to store in our garage during the winters). There had been a long wait list to obtain a slip, and we thought it would take years before we would have our own. But when a severe drought hit California (1976 to '77) and Brown's Ravine became a mud flat, a lot of tenants pulled their boats out and canceled their slip rentals.

A fun family we went boating with the most was the Cantrells. Ron Cantrell was an architect, and I first met him because he was a bank customer. His wife Jackie and his kids were in the same age range as ours, and they got along well together. The Cantrells had discovered a very nice secluded spot on the north side of the lake where we would always go and set up a sort of base camp with a pop-up awning. We all called it Cantrell's Beach. Small groups of us would go out and ski while the others stayed at the beach. The kids all became very good skiers. I never learned to slalom (single) ski, but Jimmy and Susie did; Jimmy learned some stunt skiing also. When we were done skiing, we usually took the boat to the south fork of the American River to troll for rainbow trout, German brown trout and kokanee. It was very relaxing and about the best way to spend a whole day in the hot Sacramento summers.

Besides "Ahno," there was one other nickname Hilda had for a long time for which we have Ron to thank. One day on Folsom Lake, while we were setting up at Cantrell's Beach, Ron was observing Hilda barking out orders of the day to all the kids. When she was finished issuing orders, Ron said "Okay, kids, the Warden has spoken, so go do your work." After that, whenever she was being especially bossy with the kids or myself, she'd get a "Yes, Warden." The Cantrells got in the habit of referring to, or addressing her as "Warden." We let the nickname slip in the company of social friends who found it so playful and charming that they started calling her or referring to her in conversation as "Warden," instead of "Hilda." Whenever one of our close friends, Jack Lee, phoned the house wanting to speak to her, he always asked for the "Warden." The nickname sometimes got shortened to just, "Ward." At first the name really annoyed her, and she angrily protested that it was undeserved. But the nickname stuck, and a point was reached when there was nothing she or anyone could do about it. I believe she got used to it and eventually even came to find it amusing herself. I know we all did.

At the end of a wonderful day spent at Folsom Lake on our way home, we frequently stopped on Sutter Street in old Folsom, where an entertainment group put on a melodrama play and variety show at the old Gaslighter Theatre there.

The family had a lot of great times together while the kids were small and growing. But once they were grown and busy traveling or raising their families, the RV and boat went into disuse. California had another severe drought that began in the late 1980s which prompted me to cancel the slip and sell the boat.

Fraternity and Community

Freemasonry

I had been raised to believe that Masons were somehow superior. Everyone in my family loved the Masons and of all the folks we knew and respected, most were members of the Masonic Order. Several of my uncles were Masons and I was aware that a large number of our founding fathers were also Masons. I had wanted to join for years but never lived in one place (or in the case of March AFB, was never on the ground) long enough to support a Masonic schedule. But once we settled in Sacramento and I had my bank job secured, I decided to look for a lodge to join.

I made some inquiries and found out about a lodge named Provident[185] that met in downtown Sacramento near my office.[186] The Master was a retired Air Force master sergeant who had many connections at Mather AFB. His name was Everett J. G. Chapman and he was one of the most dedicated Masons I have ever known. Chappie has been deceased for several years. I believed I met all the requirements to be a candidate for Masonic degrees, so I asked to join[187] and passed all the investigations. At the

---

[185] Provident Lodge merged with Three Pillars and now meets at a temple in Elk Grove.
[186] At the Masonic Temple, 1123 J Street.
[187] Masonic regulations prohibit lodges from soliciting new members.

beginning of 1966, Wilbur Holtzclaw became master of the lodge and he was there to preside over all my degrees. I was made an entered apprentice on February 16, passed to fellow craft on June 27, and raised to Master Mason on September 26, shortly after my forty-second birthday. I was told there were 114 Masons present at my third degree. The Ben Ali Shrine Chanters provided the music and the Scottish Rite degree team conducted my third degree ceremony. I really felt honored by this. I attended lots of meetings and began to "go through the chairs." I found out soon enough that for some, Freemasonry is a total way of life, and can be quite demanding on a brother's time. I felt that I could not balance such a strong commitment with the demands of my new career, and I withdrew from the line (at the time I held the office of Senior Deacon). I still attended meetings and spent as much time as I could at functions.

There are two ways to progress to higher degrees in accordant bodies. One is via the York Rite, and the other the Scottish Rite, although there is no restriction against being a member of both. In Sacramento in the 1960s, a prevalent but inaccurate view was that the York Rite existed mainly for Jewish brothers to advance their Masonic careers,[188] and they did indeed seem

---

[188] This was ironic, considering that only after completing all the York Rite degrees, Masons may proceed into the Order of Knights Templar, which requires strict Christian belief and observance (and is the only masonic organization I know of that emphasizes any one religion over any other). Today no one even remembers this perceived distinction between Scottish and York Rite Freemasonry, much less practice it.

to exhibit a preference for the York Rite. The Scottish Rite was generally thought to be for everyone else, although Jewish brothers also did join Scottish Rite as well. I entered the Scottish Rite route, which delivers an additional twenty-nine degrees beyond the three earned in blue lodge (4th through 32nd). These additional degrees are considered to be merely honorary. The 14th, 18th, 30th and 32nd degrees are acted out in quite an elaborate ceremony. Respectively, I received these special degrees on consecutive days ranging May 22-25, 1968. The rituals were very well done and I was impressed. The 18th degree (Rose Croix) was the most interesting of all. My neighbor, Paul Granquist was an actor in that ritual; we became better-acquainted as a result of this. Later on, Paul would persuade me to join the Ben Ali Shrine[189] and the Shrine Marching Patrol. I joined the Shrine on December 14, 1968.

I was never extremely active in the Scottish Rite, but did become quite involved with the Shrine. The marching patrol was quite a group. We wore those distinctive costumes with our scimitars and we marched in parades all over central California. Usually we performed at fairgrounds, but lots of times on the streets of Sacramento. We marched in the July 4th parades along with the Shrine Horse Patrols (that was sometimes very interesting as we would try to miss the horse droppings and still keep in step) and the Keystone Cops

---

[189] Back then, a prerequisite for joining the Shriners was to pass all the Scottish Rite degrees, however this requirement has been dropped.

(another Shrine unit). The kids enjoyed watching us perform at those parades. The patrol would have parties several times throughout the year, the best and most elaborate one being the annual Christmas party. Hilda would always get a new gown to wear at that party each year, and I have a series of photos of her standing next to me in my tux and fez at those events. We really enjoyed those times. Patrol membership has declined, but a few active members still march in parades. Many of the men I knew have passed away and many of those still above ground can no longer march. Brother Lyle joined the Masonic order, went through all the Scottish Rite degrees like myself, and remained a lifelong member. Brother Tom joined, but it wasn't for him and he dropped out without completing all the blue lodge degrees.

As they got older the kids all became involved in Masonic youth groups, the girls in Bethel 159 of Job's Daughters, and Jimmy in DeMolay. Barbara was elected Honored Queen of her Bethel in 1977. Susan was her musician and played the piano at all the meetings and ceremonies. I think they had a good time and learned from that experience. I am proud to say that Jimmy and I belong to the same blue lodge, Natoma No. 64 (I demitted from Provident Lodge and we both joined Natoma Lodge together in 2003). One of the great things about this lodge is it has plenty of (ex-) Air Force guys. Jimmy served as lodge treasurer for four years and we attend stated meetings and dinners together.

Daedalians

The Order of Daedalians is a non-profit fraternity of military pilots. It honors as its founding members all who were commissioned officers and rated as military pilots prior to Armistice Day, November 11, 1918. There were originally 14,000 WWI pilots. In the early years active membership was open only to the founding members and their descendants. The Daedalians program is dedicated to fostering the spirit of patriotism, integrity and good character in the nation's youth and supporting them in military careers as pilots. In the early 1950s, as founding members began dying off, membership was authorized for active and retired commissioned officer military pilots. A qualified applicant must be nominated by an active Daedalian for membership. Sam Byerley was a member, and he invited me to join. The order depends on donations to fund a comprehensive and varied scholarship program. I have enjoyed being a member over the past twenty years or so. Our group meets once a month for lunch at the Dante Club in Carmichael, where we always have an excellent speaker. I was able to get Eddie LeBaron (of NFL football fame) to speak to us at one of our meetings. We award our scholarships to worthy ROTC students from Sacramento State University. Our numbers continue to decline because our membership is aging and because of the general lack of time or interest younger people have in involvement in fraternal and service organizations.

Service

Shortly after going to work for the bank I found that belonging to a service organization was a good way to meet new prospective customers and that the bank would at least partially cover the expense. As I started to look around for a club to join I found that the Fort Sutter Lions Club was always looking for new members and that many of our customers were already members. I paid the fee, the bank reimbursed me, and I became a member. This was in 1966 and I kept my membership until about 2003. We had a lot of fun over the years. I was president from 1975 to 1976 and represented the club at the national convention in Hawaii in 1977. Every year we had our Past Presidents' Barbeque at William Land Park, the only time we could enjoy rib eyes that Yubi Separovich had marinated in a coveted secret recipe which he jealously guarded. For several years, we held our local district convention at Konocti Harbor/Clear Lake. We would sometimes have as many as six hundred people there and it was a great time for the whole family. Sometimes I towed the boat along, and we stole some time to water ski and fish while there.

Sometime in the mid-1970s, the club sponsored a summer exchange student program with Japan. Some of our members agreed to host student guests (who were dependents of Lions Club members in Japan) for two to four weeks at a time and then the kids would go to someone else's home in another city for a few more weeks before returning to

Japan. We hosted a boy, Masahiro Ogasawara, and a girl, Kumiko Tanabe, both about thirteen years old. We were able to take them water skiing and on trips around California. They enjoyed their stay very much and did a lot of crying when they had to leave to go home.

Fort Sutter Lions Club was great fun. We had around sixty members and we had our weekly lunch meetings at the Rosemount Grill. We always tried to have an interesting speaker for each of our meetings. I was able to persuade a retired Judge, a TV station announcer, the Sacramento County district attorney and others to speak at our luncheons during my term as president. But the most interesting speaker of all was an SR-71[190] pilot, Capt. Harold B. "Buck" Adams, who had just established the speed record from London to Los Angeles. I was acquainted with some folks at Beale AFB and arranged for him to speak at our club. He gave a presentation that showed how they readied the aircraft in England as well as highlights of that trip. To my knowledge, that speed record still stands.[191]

A lot of the members of that club became close personal friends. President Reagan appointed one of our members, Lee Galloway, to a judicial post in Washington, D.C.; many of our other members were pillars of the Sacramento community from all walks of life. One was the editor of the *Modesto Bee* newspaper, another owned a thrift company.

As with all service and fraternal organizations, membership declined as young people coming up were too busy to bother with this sort of thing, to the point that we had a real hard time getting even ten people out to the meetings. I left the Fort Sutter Lions in 2006.

---

[190] Lockheed SR-71 Blackbird, an advanced, "black ops," long-range, Mach 3+ reconnaissance aircraft used by the USAF from 1964 to 1998.

[191] 5,447 miles, from London to Los Angeles in a world-record 3 hours, 47 minutes, 39 seconds at an average speed of 1,435.59 mph.

Because of their broad connection to their local communities, bankers from my generation attracted numerous invitations to serve on the boards of directors of various non-profit organizations, and I certainly received my share of solicitations. Such work may not always seem very glamorous, but I and people like me believe it is part of our duty to our community to devote some measure of time to such service, and it can actually prove a fun and interesting opportunity. One very good friend and bank customer asked me to serve on the board of Sacramento Goodwill Industries. Most people are familiar with their thrift stores; these are their outlets for selling donated clothing and other household items. Perhaps not as well-known is the fact that the net proceeds from the stores are used to provide training to disabled folks so they can become employable and find work to sustain themselves. Such individuals are also employed by Goodwill itself to clean and repair donated items before they are resold in their stores. This does help disabled people overcome at least some of the disadvantages they face and gain some measure of independence and self-respect. Sacramento Goodwill had several stores and was pretty well-organized. I agreed to serve on this board and did so for several years. I was made board chairman in 1995, which was the year our national president retired and had to be replaced. The folks at the national headquarters in Washington, D.C., decided to hold a convention in Indianapolis to elect a new president, and Hilda and I traveled there with the Sacramento Goodwill president to attend. The citizens of Indianapolis really like to show off their race track[192] to visitors. I don't remember how many of us Goodwill representatives from all over the United States attended the convention, but there

---

[192] The Indianapolis Motor Speedway, home of the Indy 500 race.

were a lot and we needed several charter busses to take us to the track. I remember that even on the freeways, traffic was stopped to allow our bus caravan through. One of the demonstrations we saw at the track was a car traveling at 220 miles per hour. The new president we elected was a celebrity named Fred Grandy, whom many readers will remember best from his role as Gopher in the 1970s television sitcom "The Love Boat." He also served as a member of the U.S. House of Representatives from the state of Iowa. I got to converse with him quite a bit during that convention. He is a real nice and likable guy and everyone thought he was a good choice.

During my tenure on the board of Goodwill Sacramento, we trained a lot of people and were fairly successful. One disappointing outcome for me was the fact that we did not get the contract to place employees in the commissary at McClellan AFB. As a military retiree, I shop there regularly. They employ disabled people through "Pride Industries," another large non-profit organization with a mission similar to Goodwill Industries.

Civilian Flying

Although I was no longer doing it for a living, I continued flying as a civilian pilot and kept my license current.[193] When we first got to Sacramento, I inquired at the Sacramento Executive Airport about flying programs I could take to stay current. I discovered back in 1965 that a very close friend from my 15th Air Force Days at March AFB, Dick Oster, was chief pilot there at Patterson Aircraft Company ("Patco"[194]). I completed a program with him that allowed me to add an instructor rating to my civilian pilot license. I already had my instrument rating. Now all I had to do was to keep my annual flying physical current. I found a doctor and reserve Air Force colonel named William Dugdale who would become my primary physician and perform my annual physicals for the next forty years. He became a great friend as well. We went on several trips together with the Air Force, as we both served on the military/business committee of the Sacramento Chamber of Commerce. Bill and I golfed together at many benefit tournaments in Las Vegas supporting Big Brothers of Sacramento. I started doing a lot of flying on my weekends.

Sometime in 1968 or 1969 I met a fellow named Andy Lavra at the Sacramento Executive Airport. Andy managed the maintenance operation at the Georgetown Airport, was

---

[193] The pilot license is still current, but I stopped getting annual physicals in 1997.

[194] Aircraft sales and rental company located at the Sacramento Executive Airport.

also an engineer at McClellan AFB,[195] and owned a 250 Comanche.[196] He needed some money to finance his Georgetown operation, and was looking for partners to purchase a co-ownership stake in his Comanche. I and another fellow, a doctor named Chunn, took him up on it, and the three of us became equal one-third owners of Andy's Comanche. We kept it at hangar #45 at the Executive Airport. It was red and white and flew beautifully. The plane was also relatively very inexpensive to own because Andy could do the annual inspections for us up at Georgetown for just $30 (such inspections normally cost almost $1,000 back then).

I took that plane many times to Campbell River[197] for fishing expeditions. Another trip I remember in that plane was when the whole family flew down to Ventura, California, to visit Hilda's sister Margie and her family. Hilda was in the back seat with Susan and Jimmy, and Barbara was in the front with me. When it was time to contact the ground radio to give them our position report, I wrote it all out and gave it to Barbara, and she gave the information to the ground station over the radio.

---

[195] This base was established in 1935 as a supply and logistics depot and served as a staging base for the Doolittle Raid on Tokyo. In 1995 it was marked for closure under BRAC, and the Air Force ceased operations there in 2001. Today, the U.S. Coast Guard operates an air station and there's still a National Guard Reserve presence there, but the rest has been converted to an office park.

[196] A four-seat, low-wing, all-metal light aircraft with retractable landing gear. Together with the Twin Comanche, these planes were the core of the Piper Aircraft Company's line-up until a flood wiped out both production lines in 1972.

[197] On Vancouver Island, in British Columbia, Canada.

Through banking I got to know a lot of aircraft owners. One of the first important customers I met, a man who became a very close friend of mine and has been ever since, is a pilot named John Didier. There was a time when I took the Comanche to Denver with John, his nephew (then age twelve), and my son Jimmy (age eight). After the stop at Stapleton, I had planned to fly on to Wisconsin with Jimmy to visit relatives, and then return back through Denver again to pick up John and his nephew for the trip back to Sacramento. Shortly after takeoff for Wisconsin, Jimmy got airsick and really messed up the plane. We gave up on Wisconsin and went back to the Denver airport. We ended up having a great time staying with John and his family. His son Chris, about two years old at the time, went to the Air Force Academy, had a great career flying some of our most sophisticated fighter aircraft, and retired a lieutenant colonel.

Another customer, Ray Stevens, owned a Cessna 182.[198] One day in June 1970 he invited me to fly with him and an instructor pilot from Patco to Campbell River. On June 6 I caught a 30-pound Chinook salmon which qualified me to join the elite "Tyee" club. I was "hooked," and flying/fishing trips to British Colombia or Alaska became an unbroken annual tradition for the next thirty-five years. Over time our annual pilgrimage expanded as we added planes, pilots and fishermen to our group; one year we had five airplanes carrying nineteen fishermen.

---

[198] A high-wing, single-piston engine, four-seat aircraft in production from from 1956 to 1985. Production resumed beginning in 1996.

Floyd Tarpenning is another flying and golfing friend I have known for many years. He flew his Piper Cherokee Six[199] in our formation to Campbell River and was also in our party at several Big Brothers tournaments in Vegas. Like me, Floyd had a banking career before he retired. I still usually see Floyd and his wife Helen once a week for lunch at the Elks club, and we still golf together regularly. We have become very close personal friends over the years.

Another great friend was a local businessman, a Texan named Carlton Harrison. He owned a Mooney M20[200] that he let me fly regularly, and together we spent many happy hours flying all over the skies, taking trips from salmon fishing in British Colombia to short trips to Las Vegas. Most of my Sacramento pilot friends had far less flying experience than I did, and everyone picked my brain for information.

Sam Byerley retired and moved to Sacramento in 1971 with Jessie, his first wife (of thirty-plus years), but he did not remain married to her for very long after that. When he got to Sacramento we renewed our friendship and we began to do lots of flying, fishing, hunting and golfing together, all the way up to his passing in 2004. Besides taking his bass boat out to all the reservoirs within a two-hour drive of Sacramento, Sam was with me on many of our salmon and halibut-fishing expeditions to Campbell River. Sam and I did a lot of pheasant hunting in the sloughs and rice checks from Dixon to Beale, and he helped me teach my son to shoot. He was really such a great friend and became a real mentor for the kids, who regarded him as an uncle. I remember Sam encouraging Susan after she had been an officer in the Air Force for a while that she could become a general if she wanted to. Sam remarried a wonderful woman, Darlene, and

---

[199] Piper PA-32 Cherokee Six is a fixed-landing-gear, light aircraft with six or seven seats.

[200] A piston-powered, propeller-driven general aviation aircraft with a low-wing and tricycle gear.

we socialized with them a lot over the years. Hilda taught their grandson to swim in the pool in our backyard. And Sam was with me the day I shot my first hole-in-one on the eighth hole[201] at North Ridge, in July 1985, which was reported on the sports page of the *Sacramento Bee*.[202]

There was one challenging flight returning from Campbell River I should mention. We were leaving the Campbell River Airport en route to Boeing Seattle[203] in the Twin Cessna 310. Sam Byerley was copilot, and we had a full aircraft with six people on board. On our first takeoff attempt, a bush pilot came in buzzing the runway right at us as we were taking off. In order to avoid a collision, we had to brake suddenly, get off the runway and abort our takeoff. After assuring ourselves there weren't any more planes coming down on us, we taxied back to the runway and took off. During that flight, I noticed we weren't able to get our airspeed higher than 160 miles per hour. As we were approaching Seattle and going through the pre-landing checklist, I asked Sam to put down the landing gear, but we discovered that it was already down (and had been for the entire two-hour flight). I think the experience of almost being taken out by that reckless Canadian must have

---

[201] Which is a 185-yard, three-par.

[202] The paper made a mistake and said that I had used a 5-iron when I had actually used a 5-wood. My neighbor and golfing buddy Paul Granquist saw that article and called me right away, saying I couldn't hit a 5-iron 185 yards on the best day of my life. I had to tell him he was right, and that the *Bee* had erred.

[203] Boeing Field, officially King County International Airport.

unnerved both of us, and we had forgotten to raise the gear after takeoff.

Another pilot friend, Stan Jelinick, owned a 260 Comanche, which is basically the same as my 250 Comanche, but with a slightly larger engine. We had flown in his plane to Campbell River with our two sons, both named Jimmy and both about sixteen years old at the time. When we took off from Campbell River on the first leg of our journey back, Stan was having compass trouble, and he made a turn that would have taken us right into the side of a 5,000-foot mountain. I told Stan, "We can't do this." With an errant compass, we could not fly IFR,[204] and the clouds and fog created conditions almost as bad for flying VFR.[205] We took the airplane down to 500 feet, and kept it close to the ground all the way back to the United States. On entering U.S. airspace, we needed to find Jefferson County International Airport[206] to go through customs clearance. At this time, Jefferson County International was basically just a dirt landing strip in the middle of an evergreen forest. A rainstorm had kicked up with high winds, and the airplane was being buffeted wildly in the turbulence. Even at our low altitude, navigation was extremely difficult, and we had a tough time finding the airport. We actually had to put down at several small landing strips in the general vicinity of Jefferson County International

---

[204] A qualified pilot must submit a flight plan under "Instrument Flight Rules" when meteorological conditions make flying and navigation entirely dependent on the use of avionic instruments and electronic signals (i.e., no visual references). To fly IFR, your instruments obviously have to be working.

[205] Visual Flight Rules are in effect when weather conditions allow a pilot to fly and navigate by visual reference (i.e., to landmarks on the ground).

[206] This airport is located near Port Townsend on the Olympic Peninsula.

before we found it. At one of the places we landed, we stopped in the front yard of an elderly couple. The man came out and said to us, "I suppose you think you're at Jefferson County Airport?" This couple invited us in for pie and coffee. We waited for the weather to improve a little, getting our bearings before taking off again and finally finding Jefferson County International. After clearing customs, we proceeded on to Seattle and landed there on a "gyro out" approach.[207] From there the compass worked okay and the weather was clear for the rest of the trip back to California.

The branch performed well and was consistently profitable. I took my duties very seriously. I was bringing in a lot of valuable customers, some of whom had airplanes. My flying hobby turned out to be a pretty useful networking tool. Knowledge of my flying and aircraft ownership spread among bank management, and I almost started moonlighting as a sky chauffer. Our regional manager called me one day and asked if I could fly him to visit the branch in Eureka. How could I refuse? We took the Comanche. The personnel officer came along with another regional employee who had a pilot license. He was a good pilot but did not have a lot of flying experience. Then our bank president John Barley started flying up from Los Angeles and I would take him on branch

---

[207] Or "no gyro" approach: A radar approach/vector provided in case of a malfunctioning gyro-compass or directional gyro. Instead of providing the pilot with headings to be flown, the controller observes the radar track and issues control instructions "turn right/left" or "stop turn" as appropriate.

visitations. This way, he could hit up five to six branches in a single day and save a lot of time by not having to drive. This went on for several years. One time I had rented a brand new Cessna 206[208] for a trip for him. We were coming in to land at the Susanville Airport, and the crosswind was so strong that I knew it would be impossible to put down on the runway. As we were coming in on final approach the wind blew us quite far from the runway, and I landed the plane on an earthen runway aligned with the wind direction. Barley and the regional manager we had along with us never knew what happened. When we left Susanville for Redding, the wind had shifted and we were able to takeoff on the regular runway with no problem. Barley looked down at all the rocks and rough terrain below, and said, "On our next trip, let's get a two-engine plane." That was fine with me, because I loved to fly the Cessna 310[209] and the bank paid for it, so it worked out for everyone. After that we always rented the 310 for the bank, and we even took it on several of the annual fishing trips.

I enjoyed owning and flying the Comanche, and I sometimes wish I still had it. On December 2, 1973, Andy Lavra was

---

[208] A high-wing, single piston-engine utility aircraft in production since 1962.

[209] A six-seat, low-wing, twin-engine monoplane produced between 1954 and 1980. It was the first twin-engine aircraft that Cessna put into production after World War II.

working on a Bonanza[210] up at the Georgetown Airport for a local attorney. He completed whatever repairs he had been working on and decided to take the aircraft for a test hop. The plane caught fire on takeoff, and Andy was unable to get it back on the ground. He wrapped it around a tree at the end of the runway and it burned up completely with Andy inside it. After that, Dr. Chunn and I had a meeting, where we agreed that it would be too costly for us to keep the Comanche, so we decided to sell it.

One especially memorable vacation was a trip Hilda and I took to Spain in 1977. We had kept in touch with friends from our time at March AFB, including a couple who lived across the street from us in Riverside, Bill and Betty Henderson. They owned a time share in Spain and invited us to join them for two weeks. I had, of course, visited many parts of Spain with the Air Force, but Hilda had never been, and I looked forward to showing her some of the wonderful places I'd seen.

We flew from Sacramento to New York City and from there to Madrid on Iberian Airways, continuing from there on another flight to the Mediterranean. We had been in a spacious 747 from New York but we were packed in like sardines on this smaller two-engine jet. When we finally got to our destination, Bill met us. We were very tired, and one of

[210] Hawker-Beechcraft Bonanza, a general aviation light aircraft that has been in continuous production since 1947, longer than any other aircraft model in history.

our bags was missing. We thought we'd never see it again, but the airline delivered it to us at Bill and Betty's condo (an hour's drive from the airport), which was quite a surprise. Their place was located approximately halfway between Barcelona and Malaga and about three miles in from the coast. It had two bedrooms, two bathrooms and a wet bar, and was very well-furnished. The condos were built half underground and some of the rooms had no windows because the walls were built directly against the hillside. They were situated amid two eighteen-hole golf courses that were designed by the late Spanish golf pro Seve Ballesteros and were absolutely beautiful with palm trees and other ornamental gardens everywhere. We managed to get in a few rounds of golf, and did a lot of sight-seeing.

We also visited Barcelona and Toledo. Toledo is a very ancient city with a Roman aqueduct still in operation. The streets of old Toledo are so narrow that we were able to look directly into the second-story bedroom windows of houses we passed from the top of our double-decker tour bus. We hoped to be able to visit the island of Majorca while there, but didn't get the chance.

We paid several visits to a casino close to Bill and Betty's time share, which was located right on the water. I was impressed with the relaxed way they gamble there. Being used to the way they try to rush you into spending all your money quickly in Las Vegas this was very different. The blackjack dealers, for instance, wore nice uniforms and they would say, "Carta, Señor?" and they didn't mind if you took minutes to decide whether you wanted a card or not. We spent about a week with Bill and Betty and then flew back to Madrid to spend some time there.

The hotel where we stayed was very close to the old part of Madrid, near the Plaza Mayor. I still own a couple of oil paintings of this landmark that I purchased on a previous trip, and now Hilda was walking in some of those scenes.

There we had dinner at Restaurante Botín a three-story (all underground) restaurant that has been in continuous operation since the year 1725 AD. The rooms are all decorated with pictures or paintings honoring famous matadors who have conquered bulls, as well as famous bulls that have killed matadors. It specializes in suckling pig and lamb, along with many other unusual dishes. In the 1990s, Jimmy was able to visit that restaurant with his wife Vera while in Spain on business. We visited too many wonderful places together in Madrid to recount here.

Now for the trip home. I have had some frightening experiences onboard airplanes before, but the takeoff from the Madrid-Barajas Airport tops the list. It was a fully-loaded Boeing 747 (Iberian Airways), it was July and very hot. The aircraft had to be at the top of its weight limit, because it was completely full of passengers and had to be carrying enough fuel to buck the headwinds all the way to New York. I always time the takeoff roll on my watch whenever I fly. If the aircraft doesn't begin to rotate in 30 seconds after full power is applied, and doesn't leave the ground in 35 seconds, it can be an indication of engine malfunction. If the weather is very hot, or if the airport is at a high elevation (like Denver or Mexico City), you have to add a few seconds. The altitude at Madrid is not very much above sea level, but it was quite hot so I figured the aircraft should rotate in 40 seconds and leave the ground in 45 seconds. I was seated by the window on the left side of the plane. We taxied out and got into takeoff position.

Everything seemed normal. The pilot advanced the power for takeoff, and I started timing him on my watch. After 40 seconds we were still solidly on the ground. After 50 seconds, still solid on the ground. After one minute and five seconds, the pilot finally yanked the plane off the ground just as we came upon the end of the runway, which I watched pass underneath us through the window. That was the most frightening takeoff I have ever seen. The rest of the trip was uneventful, and we got to New York City and back to Sacramento without a problem.

Prime of Life

I would have three different careers in my productive lifetime, namely the Air Force, banking, and real estate (the latter of which will be introduced later), and each of my three kids entered one of those fields. Barbara became a real estate agent and has made a good career for herself in property management as well as in the sales/brokerage end of it. Jimmy went from college to banking; he didn't stay in banking, but has followed a career in corporate finance. Susan joined the U.S. Air Force, and retired last year at the rank of lieutenant colonel, same as mine when I retired.

Barbara

Barbara seemed to enjoy school when she first started, and she did very well. When she got older, we had her IQ tested (which was customary in the 1960s), and she scored 147 (her brother and sister had similar scores later on). She was good in math and got up to 90 words per minute on a manual typewriter without error.

We had two Ford station wagons in the 1970s, which we sometimes allowed Barbara to take to high school when she got her license. She was in a big hurry to be done with high school and accelerated her studies so that she could graduate from Rio Americano High School in three years instead of four. After that she took some junior college classes here and there, eventually earning an associate in arts degree in business management from American River Community College (ARCC), graduating together with her mother in 1984 (Hilda earned her associate in arts degree at the same time).

When she was about eighteen, Barbara was in a big hurry to move out of the house and be independent, which is typical for a girl in her late teens. For a time, we worked out a compromise by setting her up in the rec room and making it into a small apartment. A little later, she moved to an apartment near Arden Way and Fair Oaks Blvd. During this period, she accepted a marriage proposal from a boy she was dating, but as the date drew near, she started having misgivings. I advised her to call it off. I'm not sure if that is what convinced her, but she did decide to call it off about four days before the wedding date.

In 1982 she married a man named Mike Miller. Mike had served in the Air Force and attained the rank of staff sergeant before being discharged. He was older and had been previously married to a Taiwanese woman with whom he already had two children. A short time after marrying Barbara, they both gained custody of the two kids, a girl named Beverly and a boy named Mike, Jr. Barbara and Mike's marriage lasted for seven years and ended in divorce. But a bond had formed between the kids and ourselves, especially between Hilda and Beverly. Hilda treated Beverly like a daughter and loved her very much. Beverly wound up moving in with Hilda and me and living in the same rec room Barbara had on three separate occasions. (Beverly married a CHP named Tim Brown, and they have three sons.) When Barbara divorced, Hilda and I took her to Campbell River on a short vacation. I tried to talk her into going back to college and getting a degree, but she chose not to pursue a bachelor's degree.

I thought Barbara would have made a good CPA and might have been very successful with her own accounting firm. She would eventually own a couple of different successful businesses of her own, but did not choose accounting. Barbara began working in real estate, work that has proven to be quite well matched to her skills and interests.

Barbara married Craig McKnight on October 20, 1990. Like Mike, Craig had been married and had a son and daughter, the latter of whom he had custody of. Paige was just three years old when Barbara became her stepmother, is now twenty-five years old, has given us a great-granddaughter, Ellagrace Cecilia. I just learned that she is expecting again. In 1997, Barbara founded her own property management company, Residential Property Management. In early 2000, she and Craig rented a ranch house near the intersection of Auburn Blvd. and Winding Way that had lots of horse stables, paddocks and a barn, and they opened a boarding operation which they named Green Acres. All this kept them busy until 2002, when they sold everything and left the Sacramento area.

My other two kids would take jobs that involved a lot of world travel and permanent overseas assignments, but for the first forty years, Barbara never moved away from our particular zip code, much less the Sacramento Area. In July 2002, however, she and Craig decided to relocate to his hometown of Scranton, Pennsylvania, after spending an enjoyable vacation there. She became a licensed real estate agent and has built a very successful career there. I have visited them several times, and I am glad to say they all seem to be leading very happy lives together.

Jimmy

From the start, Jimmy did well in school. He passed first grade, skipped second grade and moved right into third. Skipping second grade was Hilda's idea. She seemed to think about the kids' education as a competition, or a race against their peers, and she wanted them to be ahead of the group. I suppose it was similar thinking that drove my mother to enroll me early in the first grade. I did not agree with moving Jimmy up a grade, but I lost that argument. I do think that it was socially disadvantageous, being a newcomer and the youngest in his new class, and leaving behind a group of kids he had been fitting in well with. Jimmy adjusted alright, and continued to score well in school.

We knew about an accelerated learning program (mentally gifted minor, or MGM") available in the San Juan Unified School District at a school near Del Paso Country Club called Pope Avenue School. Jimmy transferred there when he entered the sixth grade (his sister Susan transferred with him at the same time, into the second grade). It was another social adjustment for Jimmy, but he did well there also. He went on to the same middle and high schools as Barbara (Arden and Rio Americano). I think he might have been better off if he had been a year older than he was when he started college in the fall of 1979.

I remember several interesting stories from Jimmy's growing up years. One was when he was about twelve years old and had an argument with Hilda. He had locked himself in his bedroom and pushed a heavy dresser against it (Hilda was on her way with a skeleton key). He opened his bedroom window, popped out the screen, and escaped out the window, after which he fled on foot to a neighbor friend's house. He contacted me at the bank, told me what had happened and asked if I could pick him up and bring him home. I said, "Sure," and when I picked him up, I told him to hunch down in the back seat of the car so I could get him into the garage without anyone seeing him. I had already phoned Hilda from the bank, and once we had both stopped laughing, we had decided that would be our plan. Hilda had cooled down by then, and struggled not to smile and show a stern face to Jimmy when he came inside. I don't remember just what the argument was about anymore.

Sam Byerley and I took Jimmy along on many of our pheasant hunting trips. The first was when he was about ten years old. When we shot our first pheasant that day, and he saw the blood and the unconscious pheasant convulsing, he became really upset and started crying. When he was a little older (about fourteen), I taught him how to handle a shotgun and shoot pheasants. At that point, he no longer got upset and was really ready to enjoy the sport.

A good friend of mine, Mike Drake, had a Brittany spaniel named Sally which he used to let us borrow for some of our hunting trips. Jimmy and I used to go over to Mike's house very early on a Sunday morning and, without waking or disturbing Mike's family, take Sally out of her pen and load her into the car. Sally was always excited to see us coming because she knew she was in for a day of hunting. I remember she was always exhausted when the day was over. Mike also came pheasant hunting with us sometimes, and came on several fishing trips to Campbell River. We took Mike and his seven-year-old son, Sean, with us in the Cessna 310 on one trip to Canada. We dropped Sean at Walla Walla, Washington, and picked up Mike's uncle to continue on with us on our fishing trip. We stopped again in Walla Walla on the return flight to drop off his uncle and pick up Sean. That boy grew to a height of six feet nine inches and became a great college basketball player. Mike and his wife were with us on our last fishing trip to Campbell River. Another in our group, Don Clark owned several airplanes, one of which was a King Air 90.[211] Don had just received his instrument rating and he wanted me to be along when he took his first instrument flight. We went to Campbell River and fished for three days without one of us ever getting a bite. That was our last trip to Campbell River.

Jimmy was accepted into UC Davis and began studying there in 1979. He double-majored in economics and international relations, graduating on schedule with his bachelor's in the spring of 1983. The day of his commencement ceremony coincided with the last day of the Ridge Runner golf tournament. In one of the biggest mistakes I have ever made which I regret to this day, I chose to finish the tournament rather than attend his commencement ceremony (in part also because I knew I wouldn't be able to smoke there). The president of North Ridge that year, Carl Di Capo's own son Bill would graduate in the same ceremony (Jimmy and Bill were friends). Notwithstanding his office at the club, Carl made it clear that there was nothing important enough to keep him from watching his son graduate, and he would therefore not be participating in the Ridge Runner. He made the correct choice. I knew it at the time, and even though Jimmy said then that it would be okay for me to go to the Ridge Runner instead and has never complained since, I

---

[211] Beechcraft King Air 90, a twin-turboprop aircraft.

believe it was important that I should have been at his graduation.

Jimmy was at that age in a young man's life when he craved adventure. He wanted to take a year or so off during his college years or after graduating and go hitch hiking across Europe or trek across South America. To "hippie" around the third world was something I told him I would not support, and I tried to convince him to wait until he could be sent to places like that with style and status. If he had had the money to do that sort of traveling, he probably would have gone, but he didn't so he instead went straight to work after college.

Jimmy had worked twenty to thirty hours a week at the Bank of America branch in Davis during his undergraduate program. BofA hired him on to the credit training program and sent him to live in Sonoma County. He worked in Petaluma, Santa Rosa and Sonoma, and did both consumer and commercial credit. What he wanted was to get into international banking, but without more education and experience, that was a hard field to break into. He determined that to accomplish what he wanted to in his career, he would need an MBA, and he was accepted to and enrolled in UC Berkeley's program in 1985. An old friend of mine from First Interstate, Clint Luhmann (whose son had earned an MBA from an Ivy League school), mentored Jimmy and helped him with his application process. Jimmy's classes met in the evenings in San Francisco; he was able to get a transfer with BofA to the city, and worked full-time for three years while earning his MBA. In the spring of 1988 I watched him graduate with his class at California Memorial Stadium.

Some months before graduating he had been hired by Hewlett-Packard as a financial analyst in Palo Alto and he moved to the South Bay Area. He began traveling a lot, including to international destinations, and his second assignment with H.P. (in 1989) was as the country finance

266

director in Brazil, where he worked for over two years. When he got there, the Brazilian employees jokingly told him that single American men who spend any amount of time in Brazil never leave single, and predicted he would marry a Brazilian girl. He didn't believe them and we didn't either, but how wrong we all were. He married a Brazilian girl named Vera Abreu (whom he met at H.P.) on February 16, 1991.[212]

Hilda and I flew down and spent the entire month of February in South America. Rio de Janeiro is tied with Hong Kong for the most beautiful city I have ever flown into. It turned out to be one of the greatest vacations we ever had. First we landed in São Paulo and Jimmy flew with us from there to Rio. Vera was already in Rio, and we were to meet her at the U.S. Embassy. I remember our cab circled the block a couple of times, but Vera wasn't yet finished with her appointment. So we stopped and waited at the curb outside the embassy. Just then, a big city bus jam-packed with people came screaming around the corner at too high a speed to make the turn. It skidded right into the magazine kiosk I was standing next to, pushed it off its blocks and slammed it into the exterior wall of the embassy. I thought that was the craziest thing I ever saw, but Jimmy just laughed, explaining that was how things worked down there.

There was another time we were all walking down a street in a driving rainstorm looking for the shop where we would be fitted for our morning suits, with strong winds and torrents of rain pouring down the streets like they were rivers. The wind blew some tree branches into some power lines above our heads. A transformer mounted on the power pole exploded with a deafening noise, and we could feel the concussion from the explosion. An electrical fire ensued lighting the tree, wires and power pole on fire. Living in

---

[212] In fact they had eloped on August 3, 1990, while vacationing in California; February 16 is the anniversary of their marriage ceremony.

Brazil, Jimmy had gotten used to chaos, and did not seem to find that unusual either.

Jimmy and Vera got us checked in to the Intercontinental Hotel in São Conrado (south of Copacabana and Ipanema), and then left for the Santos Dumont Airport[213] (they were headed for Natal, in the northeast of the country). We stayed in Rio for their Carnaval celebration, and had a reserved table on the parade ground, the Sambodromo. We also got to visit the statue of Christ the Redeemer that stands watch over the city, and took a sky ride to the top of the iconic Sugarloaf Mountain at the mouth of Guanabara Bay.

Back in São Paulo, the wedding went off beautifully, with only one exception. One of the bridesmaids was late and after waiting for her for two hours, they went ahead with the wedding. Vera's father joked that her late arrival was necessary, as everything had to proceed exactly as had the rehearsal on the previous day (this same bridesmaid had shown up late for that also). Jimmy must not have paid attention when I told him what a bad idea it was for me to have brought my mother with me on my honeymoon; not only did Vera have to put up with her mother-in-law but her father-in-law as well as we all traveled together to Iguaçu Falls (the most voluminous waterfall in the world, quite spectacular) in the south of Brazil, as well as Paraguay and Argentina. Jimmy's best man Dave Fairfield and his wife Beth were with us for the whole trip also.

Vera's family members were all extremely welcoming and gracious, and they all seemed to be pretty well heeled. Her cousins and siblings seem to all be doctors, engineers, or other highly technical professionals. One of Vera's aunts, Rose, is an English professor, and although she had never

---

[213] Brazilian schoolchildren are taught that Alberto Santos Dumont, for whom the airport is named, invented manned, controlled, powered flight a year before the Wright Brothers' triumph at Kitty Hawk (i.e., Brazil invented aviation).

visited an English-speaking country when I met her, she was perfectly fluent with just a twinge of a British accent, and she acted as our interpreter.

Since the vacation in South America, I have seen several of Vera's relatives on visits they have made to the States over the years. I have also maintained regular correspondence with Vera's father, Wilson de Araújo Abreu, for the last twenty years. A few years younger than I, he had joined the Brazilian Army at age seventeen in 1944 and transferred to Brazil's Air Force officer (cadet) training program in 1945. Wilson was on a training track similar to my own. Besides Canada and the United States, Brazil was the only other country from the Western Hemisphere to contribute troops to the allied war effort. Previously, on an occasion when Adolf Hitler had been asked whether he believed Brazil would enter the war on the side of the allies, he had jokingly remarked, "Brazil will declare war on Germany when the snakes in Brazil start smoking pipes."[214] But in 1942, Brazil did declare war and sent its Brazilian Expeditionary Force to fight in the ground war in Italy. The Brazilian soldiers' battle cry was "A cobra vai fumar" ("The snake will smoke now"), and the emblem they wore on their uniforms was the image of a pipe-smoking snake. As with my brother Lyle, the war ended before Wilson got to see any combat action.

---

[214] Every Latin American government eventually declared war against the Axis powers in WWII, but most South American governments of the time (including Brazil's) were fascist dictatorships that initially sympathized with the Axis countries, and declared war only in the spring of 1945 when it became clear that the Nazis' defeat was inevitable. After the war, these countries famously became havens for fugitive Nazi war criminals escaping prosecution.

BRASIL

We had an interesting experience on the flight home on Pan Am.[215] Our stewardess was a retired Air Force officer's daughter. We got acquainted and she gave us a hint that after the plane leveled off at altitude and the captain announced that passengers could unbuckle their seat belts, there would be a rush of all the Japanese passengers from the seats in the front rows to the rear of the airplane, where they knew they would be able to find five empty seats in a row to make into a bed for the long flight to the United States. The stewardess fixed up seats for Hilda and me so we would have our own "beds" before anyone else got there to claim them.

Jimmy was transferred to H.P.'s Latin America region headquarters in Miami in late 1991, and Vera was already pregnant. Their first child was born, a beautiful girl they named Carolyn, on February 3, 1992. Hilda and I went to visit them several times while they lived in South Florida, and when Carolyn was about three months old, we took her, Jimmy and Vera on a cruise to the Bahamas. Carolyn was the only baby on the boat, and Vera was still breastfeeding her. H.P. transferred Jimmy back to California later that year, and they moved to a nice little house they bought in San Jose. Their son, whom they named Ian, was born on December 4, 1995.

In the mid-1990s, Jimmy had a position in H.P. for a couple of years that occasioned him to spend two weeks a

---

[215] Pan-American World Airways, which was at one time one of the largest airlines in the world, went out of business later that same year, in December 1991.

270

month in either Mexico City or Guadalajara. He invited Hilda and me to come with him on one of his trips there in 1995. He had to work during the day while we went sight-seeing, and we had another great vacation. A Tapatio[216] friend named Adolfo Tavizon who had worked with Jimmy in Brazil and who was also a groomsman at Jimmy's wedding had left H.P. to become the Latin America region controller for ITT Sheraton. His office was at the same Sheraton Maria Isabel property where Jimmy always stayed on his trips to Mexico City. When we got there for check-in, we were ushered into a special room for VIPs, where a pretty Mexican girl told us we were being upgraded to a suite. Adolfo gave us the normal H.P. company rate for any ordinary room, but we learned that the daily rate for this suite was $2,400. The suite was two stories with the bedrooms on the second floor of the suite. On the first floor we had computers and a conference table that would seat twenty people plus other elegant accommodations. We were on the fourth or fifth floor and our balcony was at about the same elevation as the golden statue of the guardian angel of the city atop her high pedestal. Hotel staff people came around each evening to ask if we would be needing butler services. We found out that our suite was the very same one where Arnold Schwarzeneggar had stayed during his filming of "Total Recall," and that Bill Gates had stayed there recently also.

Jimmy hired us a secure taxi driver who met us each day to take us someplace. We visited the Toltec pyramids to the north of the city, the Zocalo, or main downtown plaza that has Aztec ruins, the capitol and the National Cathedral, the Anthropological Museum (Mexico's Smithsonian), and the military academy in Chapultepec Castle (which was the scene of the last battle of the Mexican-American war, and Mexico's surrender). We also rode down to Guernavaca, a charming

---

[216] Nickname for a Mexican born in the city of Guadalajara.

271

village in the mountains south of the city. The food there was absolutely delicious, much better than any Mexican food we had ever tasted in the United States. We visited a Catholic church in Mexico City that had so many pure gold pictures and decorations in the walls that the building was slowly sinking into the ground. Each year they would have to shore up certain parts of the floor. Our trip to Mexico City was a rich and memorable time.

Jimmy left H.P. and moved to the Sacramento area, where he used his knowledge of the languages, economies and business environment to become Oracle Corporation's Latin America regional controller for several years. He has also been involved in several technology startups, management consulting, and work in several non-profit organizations. He and Vera divorced last year after twenty years of marriage.

Susan

Susan was two and a half years old when we moved into the only home she has any childhood memories of. Hilda made sure to give her a very early instruction in swimming. Back in those days, most people just had the common sense to realize that a swimming pool in the backyard could be a hazard for small children. But instead of erecting an unsightly, eight-foot-high iron fence around the pool, we just told them not to go near the pool alone and taught them to swim. We didn't leave loaded guns around in the house where kids could get them either. Because people from my generation had plain common sense, few of us ever had any real problems with accidental injuries or death from pools or guns, and if it ever happened it was truly an unavoidable freak occurrence. Susan was an enthusiastic swimmer and spent so much time in the pool each summer that her blond hair turned lime green from the chlorine, before green hair became the fashion with young people.

Susan figured out at a very early age that I always had chewing gum on me (this was to cover my smoking). When I came home from work and went to empty my pockets on my dresser, Susan always followed me back there wanting to mooch some gum. So my nickname for her became "Gum Chum." Susan was the only one of our kids who had any cavities when they were young. Hilda and I believed this may have been related to the fact that in Riverside, where Barbara and Jimmy spent their first couple of years, the drinking water was fluoridated, whereas in Omaha and Sacramento, where

Susan spent her first years, it wasn't. As mentioned, Susan did most of her primary schooling in the MGM program at Pope Avenue School. When she got to Arden Junior High School, I usually drove her to school in the mornings on my way to work, and every Friday she and I had a special breakfast "date" together at IHOP on the way, where she always ordered their silver dollar pancakes.

Susan went to Rio Americano like the other two kids and, like her sister Barbara, finished in three years, graduating in 1983. She took some classes at ARCC. One day in 1984, she had driven our Ford 250 pickup to school and it was stolen from the school parking lot. The thieves had it for a couple days, but fortunately we recovered it. They had flipped the toggle switch on the dashboard to change from the main gas tank (when it ran dry) to the auxiliary tank, not realizing that in those old models, the toggle switch only changed the readout on the gas gauge. To actually switch between tanks, there was a brass butterfly valve on the floor beside the driver's seat, which was hard to see and hard to turn. They ran out of gas near the corner of Hazel and Madison. They pushed the truck into a Shell station, and certain they must have plenty of gas in the tank, told the attendant that the fuel pump needed to be replaced. When the attendant checked the fuel pump and saw that it was brand-new, and further noted that all the lug nuts except one had been removed from each tire, he deduced that the truck must be stolen, and alerted the sheriff's department immediately. I had obviously already notified the sheriff myself that the truck had been stolen, so they called me to go out and recover the truck. The thieves were probably going to take it somewhere, strip it and set it on fire, but their plan was thwarted thanks to their ignorance. They never showed up to retrieve the truck and were never caught or punished.

Because Hilda would have most preferred Susan to remain close to us for college, she was quite perturbed that

Jimmy (who had a successful experience at UC Davis) managed to persuade her that she had to leave town or would probably never finish college. She decided to transfer with the units she had completed at ARCC to UC San Diego, graduating in 1987. She also decided she wanted to become an officer in the Air Force, and got involved in ROTC through San Diego State (because it was not offered through UCSD). Because I was a retired officer, the ROTC director allowed me to administer her oath of office and pin her at the ceremony where she was commissioned a second lieutenant. I got to pin her at subsequent ceremonies also as she moved up through the ranks.

Susan was sent to Sheppard AFB near Wichita Falls, Texas, for three months of basic training, after which her first permanent assignment was at Travis AFB. We were lucky that for the first several years of her Air Force career most of her assignments were at California bases near enough to Sacramento that we could get there to visit her within a day's drive or less. In January 1988, Susan married an officer she met at Travis named Jerry Thompson. Not long after that, she was sent to Osan Air Base in Korea, where she served for about a year from 1989 to 1990. Hilda and I were able to spend a week visiting her (as mentioned previously). We rode a C-5 from Travis, stopping at McChord AFB[217] in Tacoma for fuel, then on to Anchorage AFB in Alaska, where we stayed overnight. It was bitter cold, and the plane had to be de-iced before we could board it the next morning and take off for Iwakuni,

[217] This base was merged with the Ft. Lewis Army Base in 2010, and is now administered by the U.S. Army as Joint Base Lewis-McChord.

Japan. We had a sumptuous dinner at the officers' club and spent the night in the BOQ. The next day, we proceeded to Osan.

Susan was a transportation officer and was able to track all our movements as we proceeded along on our journey. When we landed at Osan, she was the first one up the ladder to greet us, which was a very special welcome. Susan came home from Osan to an assignment at Castle AFB in Merced, where she and Jerry bought their first house together. While stationed at Castle, she was sent on a three-month TDY assignment at the USAF Base at Riyadh, Saudi Arabia (April through June 1992). Susan entered the Air Force OSI[218] program, and after training in Washington D.C., in early 1993 she was transferred to Vandenberg AFB where she solved her first murder investigation.

Barbara and Susan both had been around horses a little as children (for riding lessons and whatnot) and I think they were both always interested in horses. It is interesting that both of them became horse owners at different points in their lives. Vandenberg had a horse boarding facility with stables and riding arenas and Susan acquired two horses while she lived there. She has been a horse owner ever since, and this has been a very satisfying hobby for her.

Susan was transferred to McConnell AFB in July 1996. Hilda and I went to visit and helped her shop for a home to buy. She

[218] Air Force Office of Special Investigations: A Field Operating Agency of the USAF that uses special agents to identify, investigate and neutralize criminal, terrorist and espionage threats to the USAF and Department of Defense (working collaboratively with other military and non-military intelligence and investigations agencies).

bought a five-acre ranch in Mulvane, Kansas, a town near Wichita which has been her permanent residence ever since. Jerry was serving as an Electronic Warfare Officer in a B-52 crew in 1992 when he decided to resign his commission and enroll at Fresno State to train to become a physical therapist. The marriage didn't work out, and ended in divorce.

In Wichita, Susan met and became engaged to a fellow Air Force OSI officer at McConnell named Peter Hall. They were married in his hometown on Long Island, New York, on Christmas Eve 1998. Hilda, Jimmy and I were able to make separate flights to be there for her wedding. Susan's childhood best friend Jennifer Renick also came out for the wedding. Everyone in the family had heard my war stories about listening to "Opus One" on BBC radio on our flights back from combat missions, and at the wedding, Susan and Pete did a special jitterbug dance to that tune for me, which they had especially choreographed and practiced in the days leading up to the wedding. I felt much honored by this.

Pete is a terrific guy, and I am very proud to have him as a son-in-law. Hilda felt very much the same way. Susan and he have had a very compatible and happy marriage these past thirteen years. During one of Pete's active duty tours (which was in Afghanistan), he arranged for an American Flag to be flown over the U.S. Embassy in Kabul on my birthday and on Armistice Day 2007, which he later presented to me along with a commemorative plaque.

Susan came to my 381st Bomb Group reunion in Arlington, Virginia, in 2007, and was the keynote speaker at our

Saturday night dinner. I administered her oath of office to become a lieutenant colonel there at a hotel near the new Air Force museum just before she delivered that speech (she had been promoted the day prior). Susan retired on her 45th birthday, February 26, 2010, at Andrews AFB. Several of Hilda's East Coast relatives, as well as Jimmy and his son Ian, were able to make the trip out for the ceremony and visit.

First Interstate Bank

Soon after I was made manager at 21st & K, I decided I could use some more education. I enrolled in evening classes at ARCC, and proceeded to take all the management courses in the catalog. Then I found out that ARCC's course offering included everything necessary for a real estate degree, and that became my goal. A friend and UCB colleague, Walt Laun, attended night classes with me. Like me, Walt was a retired Air Force officer who had piloted P-47s[219] in World War II.

Walt and I befriended Art Irvine, one of our instructors at ARCC, and often we would go to his home after class for a drink. Besides teaching night classes, Art owned a big camera & photography store located on Alta Arden Expressway. Two or three of us went trout fishing many times at local reservoirs, like Comanche, or deer hunting around Mt. Shasta, usually in my camper. Walt was an excellent chef and did all the cooking on those excursions. Walt became my Assistant Branch Manager, after which time he got promoted and became manager of UCB's Freeport Branch. He and I flew my 250 Comanche together several times, typically to the airport in Sonoma,[220] where we would stop in and pay a visit to my brother Tom at his ranch. In that timeframe, Tom was based out of San Francisco International Airport and flying DC-10s for United Airlines, mainly routes to Hawaii, New Zealand and Australia.

---

[219] Republic P-47 "Thunderbolt," nicknamed the "Jug," one of the main fighters used by the USAAF and its allies in WWII. It was very effective not only in aerial combat, but ground attacks also. A modern-day counterpart in that role, the A10 Thunderbolt II, takes its name from the P-47.

[220] Charles M. Schulz – Sonoma County Airport, named after the "Peanuts" comic strip cartoonist.

When credit cards were first introduced into the banking system, UCB initially got the MasterCard.[221] Part of our job was to sell this product to customers. Consumers picked up on the cards right away but some merchants were skeptical and took a little more persuasion. Business owners thought that the 3 percent discount would cut too deeply into their profits. After a while business owners relented, assuming that not everyone would use cards for purchases, and the discount would be offset by savings in collections and bad debt. In one example, I had a customer who owned a chain of retail clothing stores all over Northern California and Oregon called Pauline's Dress Shops. He also had an airplane that we had been flying regularly. He asked me if I could fly with him to Ashland, Oregon, where he proposed to gather all his store managers to hear a presentation I would give on the new MasterCard program. I did this, and was able to convince all of them to promote MasterCard.

I started using the credit cards regularly myself, and I did find it convenient not to have to carry as much money around with me all the time. But to me these cards only made sense if the entire balance was paid off each month. Otherwise, the cardholder would basically be living beyond his means, something to which I was always philosophically opposed. I believed these cards could be dangerous for undisciplined people because of the exorbitant interest rates charged. I am proud to say that in all the decades credit cards have been around, I have never once allowed a balance to roll for a single monthly cycle, nor paid so much as a dime of interest. It is distressing to see how America has changed during my lifetime from a patient, frugal, saving culture to the "I want it all, and I want it now" culture that expects

---

[221] Originally "Master Charge," it was first promulgated by UCB along with a few other California banks (Wells Fargo, Crocker and Bank of California) and some East Coast banks, as a competitor product to Visa International, which was owned by BofA.

everything to happen on borrowed money people can't afford and can't pay back. This applies not only to individuals, but all levels of government as well. With a national debt now over $14 trillion, this situation is a greater threat to our society than any other today.

UCB's holding company, Western Bancorporation, owned banks in several western states, despite old laws restricting interstate banking.[222] When the federal government began deregulating banking in the early 1980s,[223] many in the industry believed it to be only a matter of time before all barriers to interstate banking were totally eliminated. My bank leadership shared in this belief, and they wanted to be perceived to be at the forefront of this trend. In 1981, Western Bancorporation changed its name to First Interstate Bancorporation, and the names of its subsidiaries in each state (including UCB) were changed to First Interstate Bank ("FIB"). I am not sure whether our leaders thought that the idea of a larger, more geographically spread-out bank would appeal more to customers for some reason, that it would convey to competitors the notion that we were a force to be reckoned with, a combination thereof, or some other reason(s). Within California alone, there were several banks already larger than or as large as UCB, namely BofA, Wells Fargo and Security Pacific, and several larger banks on the East Coast (Citibank, Chase Manhattan, etc.). Perhaps there was something useful about First Interstate Bancorp having a single, unified marketing theme across its holdings. We in the trenches just sort of went along with it, trusting that there must be a good reason for the change. The 1982 Douglas Amendment did create loopholes to some provisions to the Bank Holding Company Act, but total deregulation of

---

[222] The 1927 McFadden Act, and the 1956 Bank Holding Company Act.
[223] E.g., the 1980 Depository Institutions Deregulation and Monetary Control Act, and the 1982 Garn-St. Germain Depository Institutions Act.

interstate banking would not come until passage of the Riegle-Neal Interstate Banking and Branching Efficiency Act of 1994. FIB was bought out in 1996, and its name is hardly remembered by anyone anymore (much less UCB's).

Jack Lee and I formed a partnership back in the mid- to late 1970s to build a spec house at 222 Cimarron Circle in Folsom in what was then a brand-new housing development. Our timing was not good, and unfortunately the project was unsuccessful. The United States was at the lowest point of Jimmy Carter's stagflation economy, and under his inept Federal Reserve Chair Paul Volcker, interest rates were higher than they have ever been in my lifetime. These conditions killed the housing market. We had five families ready to buy the house, but none could qualify for credit because the calculated payments, with the prevailing 22 percent mortgage rates, were too high for anyone to afford.

I wound up selling my interest in the spec house to Jack, who held onto it until he was finally able to unload it at a loss. The general contractor we had hired to build it was Jim Hoppe, someone Hilda and I had met through Jack. Hoppe was born and raised in Minnesota, joined the Air Force and served as an aircraft mechanic in the Vietnam War. When he left the service, he settled in the Sacramento area and became a true master of all trades. He is one of those rare individuals who not only knows something about, but is expert at nearly every construction trade, whether electrical, plumbing, mechanical or carpentry. He has built entire housing projects from the ground up, but has always worked independently and also done remodels and repairs (that's how Jack ҡṋ⸺ him). I admit that his skills have come in very handy whenever I have had problems with the house, and Hoppe has been a great help to me in that regard. But besides that, he has become one of my very best friends over many years. He is a friend to the whole family, actually. He and I get together regularly on Fridays for clam chowder at North Ridge, and Char and I get together with him and his wife Lisa for dinner as well.

In 1976, my secretary Suzanne was promoted and transferred to the Sacramento Main branch at 10th and K. I began recruiting her replacement and ended up hiring a new secretary named Charlene Kaufman. Charlene was naturally very good at customer relations and knew exactly how to handle our most valued customers. I remember one of our wealthiest customers would come in about once a week wanting to cash a $3,000 check so he would have some "walking around" money for his weekend. While he sat conversing with me at my desk, she would go around the branch to do his banking for him. UCB owned Giants season tickets at Candlestick Park right behind the home plate, which we frequently dispensed as gifts to our best customers. Charlene always knew exactly who should get them. She was a serious, dedicated and well-qualified professional who brought special licensing to the position (notary, insurance, etc.). She was involved in the Professional Secretaries International Association and served as president for two years, which gave her the opportunity to travel to and host international conventions. She was an absolutely great secretary, and worked with me until I left FIB.

Over the course of a long banking career, I was privileged to be able to get to know many people who were or became very successful and influential businessmen in Sacramento. When they were first getting their start in business, I was their banker, and perhaps the first person to believe in them, the first person with any inclination to give them a chance and help them get started. You could say I was just doing my job, but it left a lasting impression on many of these great people, and I have enjoyed some wonderful relationships that lasted well after my retirement, even up to today.

One customer I met right when I became branch manager was a recent law school graduate named Randy Paragary. He had decided that he didn't want to practice law, but wanted instead to go into the restaurant business. He told me his plans, I believed him and I gave him the loan he needed to start things up. We had to renew it a couple of times, but he repaid everything and went on to become one of the biggest restaurant owners and most influential business leaders in the area. On many occasions I would stop by one of his restaurants and Randy would exclaim to his personnel that without me, he would have never been able to get his businesses going. I thought such flattery to be exaggerated, but the appreciation was always nice to hear.

I made the loan to open the first Marie Callendar restaurant in the Sacramento area, which is still in operation on Arden Way. Initially it was unsuccessful but it soon became profitable, and the owner opened a second restaurant on Freeport Boulevard near the Executive Airport. Now there are several locations of that franchise all over the area. It used to take only around $35,000 to start up a restaurant like that; today you'd need about a half a million.

My approach to lending was simple: I based my loan decisions on what I perceived to be the quality and honesty of the person requesting to borrow money, rather than the chance the business would likely succeed or fail. This approach may not have been typical, but I certainly wasn't the only lending officer leading by his gut. In banking, we used to speak of the "eyeball test," and there were plenty of seasoned bankers who would swear that was the most important consideration of all when making a loan decision. You had to look the customer in the eye, in person, read their expression, and decide for yourself whether this was someone to be trusted or not. For me, this approach worked beautifully. In a thirty-year, highly productive banking career and many millions of dollars of loans, my total career write-offs were less than $50,000.

I had all kinds of customers, from grocery stores to law firms to heavy construction companies. One customer in particular, Bruce Brooks, became one of my best friends and was involved in many different kinds of businesses. Bruce was a USC geology graduate who had worked for the large oil companies before starting his own oil and gas exploration company, Capitol Oil. Besides this, Bruce owned Mercantile Bank, some real estate assets, and a Polynesian-themed restaurant and club near the Executive Airport on Freeport Boulevard called the Zombie Hut. Bruce was not just an empresário, but also an amateur entertainer whom we would often see there playing piano and singing.[224] He became one of UCB's best customers. When I met him around 1975, he owned a Super 340[225] that we took to different golf courses in Monterey, Palm Springs and elsewhere. We played a lot of golf at his club, El Macero Country Club, and mine, North Ridge. Bruce came to the Big Brothers tournaments in Las Vegas with us.

---

[224] Bruce's closer was always Frank Sinatra's "My Way."
[225] Riley Super 340, a 1972–1975 Cessna 340 aircraft converted by fitting two 310hp Continental TSIO-520-J/-N engines. Also known as R340 Super.

Bruce used to say that he had "made a lot of millionaires." That is because he invited friends to join partnerships his firm assembled to finance new oil and gas explorations. I was invited in on some of these ventures but I always refused while he remained my customer because I believed it could be a perceived conflict of interest for me to make investments with a company to which I was also issuing credit. Instead, I watched others make small fortunes participating in those gas and oil well partnerships. Of course, it was a risky investment, because the exploration could result in a find of nothing (in which event the partners lost everything but the tax write-off). On the other hand, a relatively small commitment of a few thousand dollars for 1 percent of a new drilling could result in an income of $15,000 a month, which could last for many years before the well was fully depleted. If you invested in several, you were bound eventually to strike it rich. Bruce's consortia were a clever and sensible way for his company to avoid putting all its own eggs in one basket, and spread the risk around. At one point our banker-customer relationship changed such that there was no longer any ethical conflict, so I started taking Bruce up on his offers to join in on some explorations. Hilda and I hit some dry holes, and some others that were successful, but we never got any super-productive ones. I still have 1 percent ownership in one well that has been producing income every month for the last thirty years.

Crime Fighter

During my nineteen years at 21st & K, we had about six attempted robberies. Thankfully, no one ever got hurt at our branch. In one of the robberies, after coming in and holding up a teller, the bandit bolted out the back door of the bank with me chasing right after him. He dropped the gun he was carrying as he left the building. A customer had left through the same door before the thief, and I saw that the thief was going to run right past him. I shouted out, "Hey Les! Grab that guy!" Les grabbed him and pinned him up against a fence. Using a pen, I picked up the gun he had dropped (so as not to damage any fingerprints). The gun turned out to be only a toy. Now the police were on the scene and they took charge (the tellers had all pressed their alarm buttons right after the bandit left the teller line). On another occasion, a bandit came up to one of my tellers and demanded money. She just said, "No" and walked away. Surprisingly, the bandit just gave up and left the bank.

During my time again at 21st & K, no less than ten crimes were committed against families of bank managers in our northern California region. The bandits would typically kidnap the managers' wives and hold them for ransom. Of the ten kidnapping incidents, six were committed against families of managers who worked for UCB. It never happened to my family, but I decided anyway in 1976 to go with a friend, Stan Waggoner, to the Sacramento County sheriff, to obtain a concealed weapon permit. I have had that permit continuously for over thirty-five years.

We had a customer named Rahawi, a Middle Eastern immigrant who had some sort of acute mental illness and believed the bank was stealing money from his account. While in jail for some crime he committed, he put out a $10,000 contract on me and another employee at my branch, hiring a fellow prison inmate who was about to be released. But when this criminal was released, instead of carrying out the hit on me, he instead went directly to the authorities and told them about Rahawi's plot. We never found out what ultimately happened to Rahawi, but were nervous about his potentially being released one day on probation. I kept a real close relationship with the sheriff department after that. I supported every sheriff, no matter who got elected, and knew and got along very well with all of them. I even served frequently as a volunteer to work at one of the sheriff offices from time to time, right up to March 13, 2000.

In August of 1980, Sacramento's Chief of Police Jack Kearns summoned a group of us to hear an idea he had about getting the people of Sacramento involved in crime control and prevention. He asked my good friend, Ray Thielen, Coroner George Nielsen and some others of us to form a committee and produce a plan. Ray had been a major in the Army Intelligence Corps, had retired, gone through law school and was an attorney. He was a member of Valley High Country Club, where we had golfed together many times. The result of our meeting was the creation of the Sacramento Citizens' Crime Alert Committee. I was the committee's first treasurer and served on the board of directors for several years. I remember getting a $200 donation from the Sacramento Footprinters for a checking account opening deposit. We struggled our first year to attract donations, but in that time helped solve one murder case and recover almost $500,000 worth of stolen property. People were encouraged to call in and report on the crimes. They could remain anonymous and receive rewards (now as much as $1,000). Our program is given air time on all the local TV networks during their news broadcasts. As a free public service, they show photos and sketches of criminals, report on the crimes they committed, and provide the phone numbers for people to call. During my tenure with the committee, our biggest challenge was always securing enough money from donors to pay the rewards. I floated the idea once to organize an annual golf tournament fundraiser, like the ones that worked so well for the Big Brothers organization (those usually netted about $15,000 from one tournament). Unfortunately, I got little support for my idea. One small-minded committee member sarcastically suggested that we take a coffee can out to the Haggin Oaks golf course with a sign on it asking for donations, so people could put some quarters in the can. At any rate, the program has been very effective and is still an important tool for fighting crime here in Sacramento, and I am happy to have been able to be a part of it.

River City Bank

In the 1970s the country was changing fast, and some in the generations after mine were embracing the hippie counter culture and taking on an attitude of distrust and hatred toward our military. This was in part a reaction to the very unpopular Vietnam War (because of the way the government completely botched its execution) and its aftermath. A liberal element emerged that developed the very false notion that the United States was somehow to blame for all the suffering in the world. No longer were our military people regarded as heroes and liberators. Now they were baby killers, tools for an evil, imperialistic regime. Not everyone thought this way, but this malignant mindset spread, and we all had to deal with it. It was really a most unfortunate development in our society and probably the worst thing that has ever happened to American culture. With some, my military background and personality automatically engendered disdain and resentment. There was a day in 2001 when I walked into the American River bank branch in Fair Oaks and ran into a teller who used to work for me at 21st & K. She related that back in the 1970s, many of the branch employees had given me the nickname "the Colonel," which they derisively called me behind my back. I know I brought a military bearing and command style into my management approach. That was all I had known over the previous two and a half decades of my working life. People my age expected and respected that, but for some younger people it was a turn-off.

The several civil rights movement strains gave rise to a similar, parallel victim ideology, which blamed all the misfortune of underprivileged groups on a conspiracy of white, Anglo-Saxon, Protestant (WASP) males intent on repressing and exploiting them. I was impartial and fair to people. I was an effective staff manager and offer no apologies for how I managed, except that I was perhaps too trusting of people, and not alert to just how far they would go to try and damage me personally.

I retired from First Interstate Bank in October 1984, but it was not by my choice. Certain members of my staff conspired to get me fired, a fact that I became aware of too late to protect myself. We had a few employees who had been with the bank for a long time, and for this reason alone felt entitled to be promoted. This attitude of entitlement is common in the business culture of Sacramento; it seeps in from the unionized, state civil service mentality so prevalent in Sacramento (the state government has long been the largest employer in this area). In my view, these employees were really not capable of handling any additional responsibility at all, and I believed their promotion would not have served the interests of the bank. My whole focus was on maintaining good customer relationships and achieving a profitable bottom line. (In my last year at FIB, my branch earned a net profit of $770,000.) The few employees who thought I had wronged them brought false and secret complaints against me, and the bank foolishly sided with them. America had fully entered the era of anti-establishment political correctness we now live in. It has been very like the era of the Salem witch trials – all anyone had to do was level an accusation at someone, and they were guilty until proven innocent.

FIB's local leadership, terrified of being perceived as politically incorrect, caved to the pressure, made me a scapegoat, and terminated me. They did so without an investigation, and without a single shred of evidence that I had unfairly held anyone back. I immediately sued FIB for wrongful termination, and immediately I won. In the end I received a cash settlement and got to keep the North Ridge Country Club membership. And although I had only nineteen years and two months with the bank, I was given credit for the minimum twenty years for full retirement benefits. Several old friends in the bank who strongly disagreed with the way the bank handled the whole situation came out from San Francisco and assisted me with my retirement arrangements. I was ultimately vindicated and landed on my feet, but I very much regretted that a handful of disgruntled incompetents could ruin a great career of so many years, after all my dedication, hard work and great results. I had just turned 60 years old in September of 1984. First Interstate was bought out in 1996 by Wells Fargo Bank, so my retirement checks now come from them. I was acquainted with the president of Wells at the time of that acquisition, and he personally saw to it there was no interruption in my retirement benefits. The 21st & K branch struggled after that. FIB tried placing a series of different branch managers into my old role, none of whom was ever able to manage it profitably. I have it from other ex-employees that it lost money and had to be closed. The last tenant to occupy the building where my old branch was has gone out of business, and the building is empty and up for lease.

A couple months before I retired, Hilda was diagnosed with breast cancer, so we were dealing with that problem already when my forced retirement occurred. After retiring from the bank I started receiving calls constantly from former customers who needed a banker. I was still on the board of directors for the Sacramento Citizens' Crime Alert Reward Committee and happened to mention this to fellow board member Jim Birmingham. At the time, Jim was an employee of River City Bank, a local independent bank. He phoned me the next week to ask me if I would be interested in working for them. I agreed, and went back to work in December 1984, after being idle for only two months. I explained very carefully to the RCB president that I had sued my previous employer and won. His only comment was "Hmm, retired, and money too." I was assigned to an office on K Street, right across the street from First Interstate Bank's Sacramento main branch at 10th & K. My customers were pleased to have me back out of retirement, and I was able to immediately build up a portfolio of over two million dollars. I had a really good time working for RCB for the next ten years.

When I moved to RCB, a lot of valuable customers moved with me, and Bruce Brooks was one of them. His businesses were prospering, and in 1986 he decided that he should upgrade to a better aircraft. He decided to buy a Lear 35,[226] and asked me for $2 million to finance the purchase. I got the financing through committee with little difficulty (although one parochial member remarked that we had "no business loaning money on airplanes") and RCB financed Bruce's Lear.

Around that time, I had arranged for the chairman of RCB's board to meet Bruce. Before, I remember asking Bruce if he had ever met him, to which he replied, "No, he has never had the pleasure of making my acquaintance." That was the sort of comment you would expect to hear from Bruce. Both he and the chairman had gigantic egos, and I looked forward apprehensively to a very interesting meeting. On our way to lunch, I informed the chairman about the huge balances Bruce had on deposit with us, which together with the Learjet financing made him one of RCB's very largest customers. The lunch meeting went without a hitch. On the way back to the bank the chairman asked me if he did okay and I told him that he did fine. The presidents of UCB and FIB used to ask me the same sorts of follow-up questions after making joint customer

---

[226] Learjet Model 35, a jet built for business and military transport, powered by two Garrett TFE731-2 turbofan engines with a cabin capacity of six to eight passengers. When used by the United States Air Force, these planes carry the designation C-21A.

calls. The most important and beneficial outcome of all this was that I was now going to get to fly Bruce's Lear! From Sacramento it only took us 55 minutes to get to Las Vegas and the golf course; that was a trip Bruce and I took many times together.

I am pretty sure Bruce wanted me to go to work for him and manage his bank, although he never mentioned it in direct terms. I remember a conversation I had with him about his bank and my success at First Interstate. I believed I needed the backing and assets of a bank much larger than his to achieve the kind of results I did there. I also preferred keeping Bruce as a personal friend, rather than to have him as a boss, and always demurred to these oblique solicitations.

Around 1986, a man named Hugh Smith became a customer of mine at the River City Sunrise branch. Hugh had an Air Force career and was a full-bird colonel when I met him. Although not a doctor himself, his job was to manage the military hospitals at the Mather and McClellan AFBs. This was actually his last Air Force assignment before retirement. Besides being a successful businessman, Hugh is a terrific golfer and has been my guest at the Ridge Runner for the last eighteen straight years. He and other friends of his have traveled with me several times to Sitka for salmon and halibut fishing in recent years, and we have also taken some ocean liner cruises together. I really admire Hugh's astuteness, and I like being able to bounce ideas off him because I know I can always rely on him for good advice. I have really enjoyed knowing him and consider him to be one of my very best friends.

I used to own more shares of RCB (it's not traded on the open market), but sold most of it. I have hung onto 100 shares just for fun so that I can attend the annual shareholders' meetings, which I always do. This gives me a chance to reconnect with some of the great people I worked with there, and I always feel happy and flattered to hear that

294

many old customers remember me and talk with appreciation about the support I gave them while I was working.

Transitions

I had been flying regularly with rental airplanes from Patco and with John Didier. I had also been flying often with Carlton and must have logged more than 300 hours in his Mooney before he met his tragic end in it. It was March 1985. He and I had been in Las Vegas on one of our annual trips for the Big Brothers golf tournament. Carlton did not play golf but had business in Vegas. I was going to fly back to Sacramento with him instead of returning with the rest of the golfers in our group. We got the Mooney started up, and were going through the before-takeoff check, when I found that the altimeter was malfunctioning (it would not accept the setting). The altimeter is a critical instrument that has to be working properly before takeoff in order to fly safely and legally. Since we couldn't set the altimeter, I told Carlton I would not fly the aircraft. The Big Brothers had already departed Las Vegas, so we caught a bus back to Sacramento.

Carlton returned to Las Vegas to have the altimeter repaired, after which his idea was to fly himself back to his home in Denton, Texas (he had sold his Sacramento business in 1978 and moved there). He left Las Vegas for Denton on March 15, 1985. The next day, I got a call from his wife to tell me that Carlton had crashed the Mooney and was dead, and asked if I would be a pall bearer at his funeral. I spoke to the FAA investigators; he had run into weather just west of El Paso and received instructions from the ground controllers to descend to a lower altitude. The altimeter must have still been malfunctioning because he was already at a lower altitude and wound up flying his plane right into the ground. His wingtip had dug a long, straight trench in the desert floor leading up to the half-mile area over which the wreckage was strewn. Perhaps he had seen mountains rising very close outside his side window and swerved abruptly to get away from them, not realizing he was cruising only a few feet above the ground. It was such a violent crash that his wedding band had been pinched flat into a gold stick. We buried that along with his remains in Denton.

I told RCB that Carlton was such a close friend that I would have to take a few days to go to his funeral in Denton. Before leaving, I was discussing Carlton's accident with a mutual friend from Patco who just shook his head and said that Carlton was the nineteenth personal friend he had lost to an accident in a light aircraft. This comment proved significant, because while at the funeral, I happened to glance down at the license plate on the hearse that carried Carlton's coffin and it read "JFG20." I'm not superstitious, but I confess that seeing my initials and the number 20 on a hearse following that conversation at the Executive Airport made me wonder if it could be an ill omen. That was how a long and wonderful friendship ended. We had flown many places together and I really missed him. I kept flying.

Sometime in 1982, Mother left from Tom's place in Sonoma and moved in with us in Carmichael (Bill Hunter had died in February 1981). At this time, Mother was ill. She lived with us for only about six months, during which time Hilda cared for her like a hospice nurse. Eventually, Mother's condition worsened to the point that we could no longer provide for Mother's care ourselves, and in 1983 we moved her to

Mountain Manor, a convalescent home in Carmichael. The kids and I visited her there frequently. She stayed at Mountain Manor for about ten months, and then had to be moved again. Her health continued to deteriorate rapidly, and she died on May 5, 1985. I made arrangements with a local mortuary to have her prepared to be transported back to Wisconsin, and I rode on the same flight with her to Madison. We had both taken our first airplane ride together, and now we had made her final one together again. From Madison we traveled by cab to the mortuary in Portage. On May 9, we buried her at Pacific Cemetery in her plot next to Dad. With her death and Carlton's happening so close together, not so long after I lost my job at FIB, late 1984 to early 1985 was an extremely tough transitional period in my life.

The Burglary

To me, the grief and heartbreak caused by a burglary are exceeded only by a death in the family. No one died, but it is devastating to think about criminals breaking into your home when you are away, taking everything you have of value and walking away scot-free. Our loss was total. Items taken included all my guns, televisions, cash and jewelry. The thieves took my old service uniforms and war memorabilia, including the A-2 jacket with hand-painted Hell's Angels insignia on the back, the one I had worn in all those combat missions. Some of the stolen items could have been fenced at a flea market for a few dollars, but to me they were priceless treasures that held immeasurable personal value. To add insult to injury, the thieves loaded all the loot into my Lincoln Mark VII and made off with it along with everything else.

Here is how it happened: I left work at the bank in the Natomas area around 5 p.m. on Friday, January 22, 1993. I didn't notice anything unusual until after I got on the freeway at the intersection of Highway 50 and Highway 99. I can't say exactly where another vehicle started following me – it could have been near the bank or shortly after I left the bank. But as I entered the freeway I noticed this older-looking gray pickup truck behind me. It followed me all the way to my house in Carmichael. When I pressed the remote control to open the garage door just a half block from home, the dull grey pickup was still right on my tail. I turned into the driveway and the truck slowed almost to a stop as the driver took a careful, slow

299

look at the house before taking off to the west on Shelato. Leading him right to my home was probably one of the dumbest things I have ever done. In retrospect I should have led him to a grocery store parking lot and called 911.

The next day was Saturday and Hilda and I had planned to go to San Francisco for an overnight stay at the Marines Memorial,[227] where we had been members for years. It had a great restaurant, the rooms were nice and it was located near the center of town, walking distance from Union Square and other attractions. Saturday morning, we took the Town Car and left the Mark VII in the garage. I had purchased the Mark VII for Hilda for our 41st Anniversary. The trip was fun; we had a fine dinner at the Memorial and just a great night in the city. We got up Sunday morning, ate a late breakfast, packed up and headed back to Sacramento. The cell phone rang as we were heading down the hill towards Vallejo. It was Susan calling from Bolling AFB in Washington, D.C. She said that Barbara had been trying to call to tell us that our house had been burglarized and lots of stuff was missing. We finished our conversation with Susan and contacted Barbara; she couldn't say right then what all had been taken.

When we arrived at home, we could tell that the criminals tried initially to break into the house through a high small window in Barbara's old room because of the cracked pane we found. The side fence comes in right under this window. A neighbor's tom cat had been jumping up there and spraying his scent all over the window, and to discourage him, I had hammered a flat board on top of it with a bunch of nails sticking up. I remember the last time he tried to jump up there, because I heard him let out a loud scream. The tom cat

---

[227] The Marines Memorial Club in San Francisco, California at 609 Sutter Street (at Mason), is a private social club for United States Marines and other veterans of the United States Armed Forces.

never came back. My improvised cat trap seems to have also been inconvenient for the burglars. A small consolation for what ensued is the thought that it surprised them as much and in the same way as it did the cat, and I hope they got tetanus from the rusty nails.

After that, they just went around to the back door leading into the kitchen and pried it open. We found the back door latch broken. Hilda had left her set of car and house keys on the kitchen table, making it very easy for the criminals to steal it. Although the Mark VII was Hilda's car, she had been driving the Town Car more, so a lot of my stuff was in the Mark VII. My briefcase was there, which had my honorary sheriff's badge, my concealed weapons permit, some photos, a checkbook and other banking materials. They had hours of uninterrupted privacy to carry out the burglary, knowing that no one could witness their movements. After loading up the Mark VII, they just backed the car out of the garage, closing the door behind them, and drove away. It was probably the smoothest burglary they ever committed.

The criminals who hit our house were professionals who knew exactly where to look to find the most valuable items. In my top dresser drawer they found all our gold and diamond rings and other jewelry. They found the eight or ten $100 bills that I kept handy for an emergency. Also taken were two sets of fifty commemorative Jefferson two dollar bills.[228] Each bill had a stamp with the flag of each of the fifty United States and seal from the post office where we stood in line to have them authenticated on the first day of reissuance of those bills in 1976. They had a face value of just $200 but were worth much more as collector's items. So, the thieves' cash haul was over a thousand dollars. Hilda did not wear her wedding ring all the time and she had left it on the dresser. Our rings had

---

[228] The two dollar bill had been discontinued in 1966, but they were reintroduced in 1976 for the U.S. bicentennial.

been specially made; hers was quite wide and mine the standard width. Each ring contained about ten small rubies, spaced evenly around the ring. I would later spend $500 for a jeweler to make a replica of Hilda's stolen wedding ring for her. My Masonic ring with diamonds was taken, along with a lot of other jewelry.

They casually browsed very selectively through my closet, taking my WWII bomber jacket, my formal Air Force uniform, and a special hand painted Hawaiian shirt. Those items would probably bring the most money at the flea market where they usually try to sell this kind of property. They did not take any other items of clothing. The next important items were the guns. They pried open the gun cabinet and from there took a Remington 1100 automatic 12 gauge shotgun, Jimmy's Browning 12 gauge (one of the last ones manufactured in Belgium), two .22 rifles, a first-generation Colt .45 revolver and several other guns. One gun that was very special to me was my Remington 30-06 with a Leopold scope. With that gun, I could shoot the ace of spades out of a playing card at 250 yards. This was the gun I used for deer hunting. They left the 30-30 rifles and a couple other guns. Maybe there was no good secondary market for these guns, but they probably just ran out of room in my car.

They sat at my bar and drank some sodas, they must have realized that we were gone for the night and they could take their good old time. Sometime during their time here they defecated outside on the concrete decking next to the swimming pool, and left behind some of those blue paper towels they used to clean themselves, the kind gas stations provide patrons for washing their windshields. They seemed to want not only to rob me, but to taunt me.

We were in shock after we got home and began to find out the extent of our losses. After the sheriff completed their report, we stayed in close contact with them over the course of the entire investigation. Since I had been working closely with the sheriff department over the years I think I got somewhat better treatment than most would. I was told that one the deputies had said, "Doesn't he understand that we don't even investigate burglaries?" to which a deputy who knew me replied, "Yes, but this man is a friend and we are going to follow up on it." I suppose most law enforcement people figure that insurance companies reinstate burglary victims the value of their losses, so why even bother with it?

Inside the briefcase I had left in the Mark VII, the thieves must surely have noticed my concealed weapons permit and honorary deputy sheriff badge. Perhaps for that reason they became wary and decided not to touch the checkbook that was there. About ten days after the burglary, I got a phone call from an individual who said he was a contractor from Auburn. He said he had been working in the south area and, as contractors often do, had been searching inside a big trash dumpster on the south side of the Florin mall for a piece of scrap lumber when he found my briefcase inside it. He had opened it, found my name inside and was calling to return it to me. I met him, got the briefcase back, and verified that nothing had been taken from it. That was another mistake that I made; I should have taken a deputy sheriff with me to verify who this individual really was. These criminals were very professional and seemed to know every move in advance.

After about a month I began to wonder if they were ever going to find the car. I had been talking to USAA, which as usual had been very cooperative all along. Another two weeks or so went by and on a Friday the insurance company said Monday they would pay us $20,000 for the stolen car. Then at about 2 a.m. the following Sunday morning we got a call from the Highway Patrol. They had found our Mark VII, which the thieves had abandoned in the Meadowview area in south Sacramento, and they instructed me to go there to pick it up. I had made arrangements with the sheriff's department to inspect the car if it was found, to check for fingerprints and what not, before I took it to a dealer to have it fixed. I also did not want to go to the Meadowview area alone if I could possibly avoid it because of its high crime rate. So the CHP towed the Mark VII to a location given by the sheriff's department. The next day the sheriff personnel examined the car, but did not find any evidence that could help identify the burglars. I think the burglars were too smart for us. They had stripped the car. The JBL stereo speakers were gone as was all of the other sound equipment. There were some minor dents and scrapes on the outside of the car, but no major cosmetic damage. After the sheriff's people were finished examining the car, I had it towed to the Lincoln dealer and arranged for the repairs. It cost just over $8,000 for the repairs and about a month to have it all done. The dealer tried to cut corners by installing cheaper stereo and speaker gear that did not match the original equipment and would not work, and they had to remove all the inferior parts they had installed and replace them with the correct ones.

I only discovered that my lambskin A-2 bomber jacket had been taken some six months later. I was looking for it to take with me to a bomb group reunion in Seattle in July 1993. I made some inquiries and saw that WWII memorabilia collectors were trading them in the $2,000 range. I contacted USAA and they agreed to give me $1,700 for the loss. Those of you reading this who visit flea markets or shows where WWII artifacts are sold should know that a substantial proportion of those items were originally stolen from their rightful owners and their heirs before entering the collector secondary market and they are actually priceless to someone.

Of all the guns that were stolen, the only one we ever recovered was the Remington shotgun. About twelve years after the burglary, I received an unexpected phone call from the sheriff's department. They told me they had recovered my shotgun and to come to their warehouse to claim it. When I got there I just took one look and said, "That's not my gun." They insisted it was, and directed me to check the serial number. Sure enough, it was my Remington. I couldn't recognize it because the barrel had been sawn off, painted with a dull black color, and was covered with military jungle camouflage. I learned it had been found at a location in Nevada where a lot of people had been busted for growing marijuana, and they had been carrying my gun while patrolling the boundaries of their plantation. The Remington 1100 had been my favorite gun for hunting pheasants. Now all it's good for is blowing away home invaders if they ever come bursting through my front door.

It is probably a good thing that we were not home when the burglary happened. If I had heard them breaking in I would have naturally retrieved one of my weapons and would certainly have used it to protect my family and myself. If I did not hear them in time and they had guns, it could have been a greater disaster. This all took place eighteen years ago, but not a day passes that I don't have angry and bitter thoughts about how those criminals violated my rights, my property and my privacy. I can still see that dull grey pickup truck following me home from work, and I wonder what the driver of that truck is doing right now.

Jimmy, Susan and Barbara at our home in Carmichael, 1967.

Hilda and the girls posing by the family ski boat at Brown's Ravine, Folsom Lake, California.

Tahoe ski vacation, January 1974, with the Chokan and Cantrell families. One of many such trips.

Top: Hilda standing in the doorway of our first camper. Tahoe, late-1960s.
Bottom: Barbara, Jimmy, and the camper we used on so many wonderful family camping trips. Alta, California, 1972.

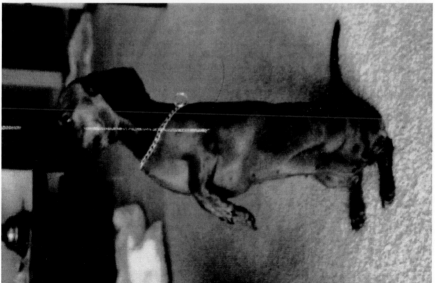

Top: Our German Shepherd, Molly, at our home in Carmichael.
Bottom: Our dachshund, Mitzi, .at our home in Omaha.

Me (sporting Ben Ali Shriner Patrol Fez) with the family at a Masonic event, 1975.

Reunion of Hilda's family at our home in Carmichael. Seated on sofa, (left to right): Eddie, Aunt Mitzi, Claire, Margie and Ann (probably Jimmy Marsh taking the photo).

Me piloting my Piper 250 Comanche on a trip back from Campbell River, B.C., Canada. The photo was taken by my friend Harry O'Laughlin in Judge Art Eisinger's Cessna.

My B-47 co-pilot George Harbaugh with his Bonanza. San Diego, 1980.

Me and Sam Byerley flying the Cessna 310 to Campbell River, B.C., Canada, 1970s.

Floyd Tarpenning's Piper Cherokee Six returning from Campbell River, B.C., Canada, 1970s.

Me piloting Bruce Brook's Lear Jet 35, 1983.

Me with John Didier aboard the governor of Colorado's private plane for a "Civic Leader" invitational tour, with General Hammond, stopping at Roswell, Albuquerque and Alamogordo, New Mexico and Phoenix, Arizona, March, 1990. (John and I were on the Sacramento Chamber of Commerce Military Committee).

Barbara posing in her regalia with Hilda and me at her installation as Honored Queen of Bethel 159 Job's Daughters. At the Sacramento Masonic Center, December 1974.

Above and below: Barbara and Hilda graduating with their "twin" AA degrees from American River College. June 1984.

This was taken of Hilda, Barbara and me on the day of Barbara's (first) wedding in 1982. She just looked so beautiful that day!

Barbara and her husband Craig holding their infant granddaughter, Ellagrace, 2008.

Me and son Jimmy, Carmichael, 1970.

Jimmy driving our boat at Folsom Lake, summer 1975.

Left to right: Floyd Tarpenning, Jimmy, Sam Byerley and me on one of many pheasant hunting excursions, 1970s.

Me and Jimmy posing in July 1994 with our catch at the Queen Charlotte Islands, B.C., Canada. Our small fishing boat was nearly dragged underwater that day by a monster halibut.

Jimmy on his 21st birthday at Folsom Lake, 1983.

Me and Hilda with Jimmy at his wedding, February 16, 1991.

Author and Jimmy in Honolulu, 1986.

Me and Hilda on Jimmy and Vera's "honeymoon" at Iguaçu Falls, Brazil, February, 1991. Seated (left to right): Beth Fairfield, Dave Fairfield (Jimmy's best man), me, Hilda, and Jimmy (daughter-in-law Vera is in the foreground).

Me with Susan at Ketchikan, Alaska. This was a day-long excursion we took while on an Alaskan cruise with the Lees. The ship's galley cook served them the same day, September 6, 1980.

Pinning Susan and administering the oath of office when she made second lieutenant in the USAF. 1987, San Diego.

Me presiding over the ceremony again, this time when Susan made captain, 1991 at Castle AFB. Susan's first husband Capt. Jerry Thompson is standing on the right.

Hilda and me visiting Susan in Osan, Korea, November 1989.

Susan's horses Breeze and Judah at the Vandenberg AFB stables, 1995.

Susan with Breeze at her ranch in Mulvane, Kansas, 1997.

Susan and Barbara with me and fellow 381st veteran Herb Kwart at the 2007 Bomb Group Reunion in Alexandria, Virginia. Susan was the keynote speaker at our dinner, and I had just administered her oath of office for her promotion to lieutenant colonel the day before.

Pete and Susan in their captain uniforms 1999.

Pete and Susan visiting Times Square in New York City on New Year's Eve, 2006.

Founding board of directors of the Sacramento Citizens' Crime Alert Committee. I am posed between Police Chief Jack Kearns and Martha McBride (wife of Judge Tom McBride). Also pictured are friends from Ft. Sutter Lions, Andy Andresen, Herb Wilson, Yubi Separovich, Ray Thielen, Cal Florence, and other founders.

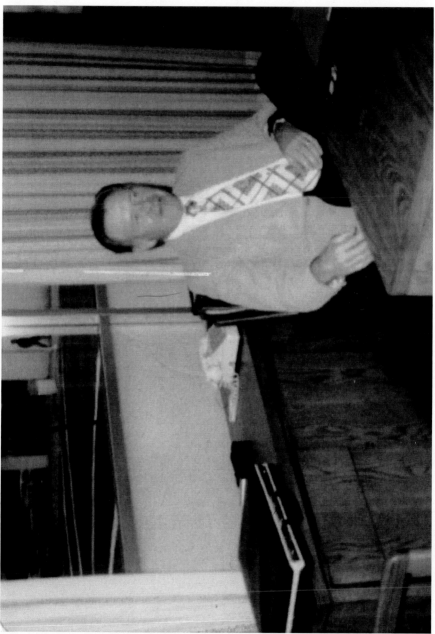

Me seated at my desk on the officer platform of UCB/FIB's 21st and K branch, where I served as branch manager for eleven years.

Me speaking to the UCB president at a branch Christmas party in the1970s.

Interviewing a customer at River City Bank.

Bruce Brooks and me with his Learjet 35 at Sacramento Metropolitan Airport, 1983.

The 1991 Ridge Runner Invitational at North Ridge Country Club, the only year I won the tournament. My partner Eric Pilagaard is on the far left, I'm on the right. In the 1992 tournament, I scored a hole in one on the eighth hole.

Hilda, Vera and granddaughter Carolyn in her grandfather's arms, just hours before we learned our home had been burglarized the night before. The photo was taken by Jimmy on January 24, 1993.

Hilda and me at a Retired Officers' Association dinner.

Part Four: "Retirement"

North Ridge

When I left River City Bank in April of 1994, I was nearly 70 years old, had visions of full retirement on three pensions plus some more money from investments, and I thought to myself that maybe it was time I quit working. That feeling went away in less than a week. My good friend Bob Bernard, a flying, fishing and golfing buddy of many years, owned Western Mortgage Company. We talked one day about all the real estate loans I had made during my banking days, and what was I going to do with myself now that I had left RCB. I replied, "Maybe nothing." But I got to thinking about my degree in real estate from ARCC, and that perhaps I should get a broker's license. I made some inquiries and confirmed that my degree and banking experience qualified me to take the broker's exam. I took the exams, got my broker's license and went to work with Bob at Western Mortgage after spending about two weeks in retirement.

Meanwhile, I had been elected to the board of directors at North Ridge Country Club in January of 1994. I had been a member of the club since April 1, 1973, and every few years the subject of making some changes or improvements kept coming up. We talked about them in 1994, got serious about them in 1995 and finally started the changes in 1996. The board had many discussions on how to get the project started, and we were divided into two schools of thought. I had financed some large construction projects during my banking career, the latest being the Creekside Dental building in

Folsom. I thought the best way to get the club improvements done was the way I always did it at the bank. We would get a scale model built, approve the design, put it up for bid, select the best bidder and get it done. The proposed improvements would cost about $4 million.

The majority of my colleagues on the board wanted to do it another way. Their approach was to throw $4 million at a contractor and see what we could get, with no plans and no scale model. Of the board's nine members, three (including myself) favored my recommended approach, and the other six favored the alternate approach. The $4 million necessitated a $9,000 assessment for each proprietary member of the club. Since we had no idea how many members would be able to pay the $9,000 up front and we could not start the project without having all the funds ready to pay for the construction, we had to get a commitment from a bank for the $4 million.

I called Andy Ware (the RCB officer who had been assigned my accounts when I retired) and told him, "We need $4 million for construction at North Ridge Country Club." The standard origination fee for a loan of this type would normally be 2 percent, and the interest rate would be prime plus 2 percent. I told Andy we wanted the money for fifteen years at prime, with no points and no fees. I said we would draw down the loan for the first two years and then begin paying it back. Many of our members wound up paying the $9,000 assessment up front, so our loan balance never exceeded $2.7 million. By securing this loan with these terms, the club saved about $600,000 in financing costs. Besides this, the club earned a huge spread between its cost of money and the 9 percent interest rate charged to members who financed their assessments. The prime rate was in the 8 percent range at the beginning of the loan, but rates plummeted and remained very low for the entire twelve-year payback period (the prime averaging about 4 percent). This provided the club with interest income of between $800,000 and $1,000,000. The improvements were completed and the loan was repaid in 2008, two years early.

Sometime around 1995 Bruce got prostate cancer. It spread fast, and he died in 1996. Watching him go down was one of the saddest experiences of my life. After accepting the fact that he had but a short time to live, he sold the Learjet and the Mercantile Bank (he had already disposed of the Zombie Hut several years earlier). By this time, his son and daughter were educated and ready to take over Capitol Oil. The last time Bruce and I got to play golf together was at North Ridge. We made it to the fifteenth hole when he said that he would have to quit. The next time I saw him was at Mt. Vernon.[229] It was a big funeral, and many of his closest friends were asked if they wanted to say anything. I was too overcome with sadness to speak and so declined. The final eulogy was delivered by Supreme Court Justice Anthony Kennedy, who had flown out from Washington, D.C., just for Bruce's funeral. It had been an absolutely wonderful friendship.

---

[229] Mt. Vernon Memorial Park and Mortuary in Fair Oaks, California.

Hilda's passing

Hilda and I both enjoyed pretty good health over the years with no real serious problems until about the fall of 1983. I think that was about the time that she developed breast cancer. She did not tell me about it until the fall of 1984. She had a small dimple or indentation on her left breast which turned out to be cancerous. Hilda's mother had died of cervical cancer at age 43, and Hilda and her siblings have been at high risk of developing cancer themselves. Hilda's brother Eddie got cancer and died a couple years before Hilda. Her older sister Anne got cancer and died about a year after her. Her sister Margie got breast cancer, which has remained in remission to this date. So far Claire and Jimmy Marsh have not reported any cancer.

Hilda had a lumpectomy operation followed by radiation therapy, and the cancer never returned. The scar was hardly visible. Her doctors checked her lymph glands and found six of the twelve on her left side to be cancerous, so they operated on those also. It was an unpleasant experience to go through because she had to keep a tube under her arm for several days to drain fluid.

Her cancer stayed in remission, but we both always believed that the radiation must have caused collateral damage to her heart. I have had radiation for prostate cancer and was informed by my doctors exactly what other tissues can sustain damage from the process. About 1993 or '94 Hilda began complaining of a throat problem, and we went to have it checked at the Travis AFB hospital. She had a thyroid operation, which was successful. Then the heart doctors told her that she should enter the heart reversal program at the UC

Davis Medical Center. This was a two-year program which included a rigid diet and exercise program. She continued the exercise even after the two years. But the throat (reflux) problems continued, and nothing seemed to help. Through all of these medical situations, we received excellent care from the local civilian and military people at Travis.

On March 13, 2000, I took Hilda to a clinic at 28th & K in Sacramento for a medical appointment she had at 10 a.m. for a barium swallow. This was a routine exam to try and determine what might be causing the throat problems she was having. When I brought her home, it was lunch time, but she did not feel like eating anything. It was a Monday, which meant it was my day to go to the sheriff station at Watt Avenue and Auburn Boulevard to do my volunteer duty. I did not want to leave her alone because she obviously was not feeling well, but when I offered to stay home she insisted, "No, I will be fine," and said she would just lie there and rest. She went to the guest bedroom (Susan's old room), and I left a phone handset and my card from the sheriff's with the phone number where I could be reached. I offered again to stay with her, but she said I should just go. So I kissed her and left. It was almost 1 p.m. and after a stop at the post office, I got to the sheriff's at about 1:15. I took an empty desk and began my duty, which was to take phone calls and reports. The calls usually were about someone losing their purse or some other petty crime. About 2:20, I answered a call with my usual, "Sheriff's office, Jim Grey, may I help you?" I heard a very faint voice say, "Hello," and nothing else. It was not an ordinary hello, but rather a concerned, troubled hello. Since I could get no other response from the caller, I hung up and called Barbara to ask her to call and check up on her mother. Meanwhile, I immediately called home, but only got a busy signal. Barbara wasn't able to get through either, it turned out, so she drove to the house right away.

Hilda had apparently phoned 911 herself before calling me, because the paramedics were at the back door but they refused to break in. Our next door neighbor, Bob Prouty, had come over to help. He knew of the place where we kept a key (in the freezer on the breezeway), but for some reason it was not there that day. Barbara let the rescue people in, and they tried to revive Hilda, but all to no avail. Barbara then called me and told me that Hilda was dead. I left the sheriff's and met Barbara at the American River Hospital on Engle Avenue, where Hilda had been taken. The hospital staff was extremely uncooperative and didn't even want to let me in to see her. Vera's doctor relatives in Brazil would later explain that Hilda died of diaphragmatic heart failure, and could not have suffered longer than five minutes. But I was not pleased about the clumsy, tenuous response by the paramedics, and wonder if her life could have been saved if I had been there.

We had plans to travel the following week to meet Susan at the Hale Koa[230] in Hawaii (Susan was coming back from an inspection trip to Japan and Korea). Now I realized with certainty it was Hilda's voice on the other line when I picked up the phone at the sheriff's office. By then, she must certainly have already placed her 911 call, and must have known what was happening to her. I believe that with the last bit of strength she had left, she called me to speak with me one last time. Not a day has passed since, that my thoughts have not gone back the sound of her final, frail "hello."

Hilda and I had already made all our final arrangements. Hilda had chosen cremation, and I had chosen earth burial. My plot at East Lawn[231] is close to the

---

[230] Hale Koa ("home of the warrior," in native Hawaiian) on Waikiki Beach on Oahu, was established 1975. It was always our favorite luxury hotel in Hawaii and I have stayed there dozens of times. It is owned by the Department of Defense, and is only for military guests.
[231] Sierra Hills Memorial Park and East Lawn Mortuary on Greenback Lane in Sacramento.

mausoleum where her ashes are stored. In the window of her little shelf, we placed pictures of her from her time in Japan, and at Susan and Pete's wedding. We had a reception for her at the house, and many friends and family came. Jimmy wrote the obituary we ran in the *Sacramento Bee*. A writer from the *Bee* took an interest in her story and published a short article about her with a picture of her on our vacation in Rio de Janeiro.

Retirement

The grief and anxiety of losing Hilda after 51 wonderful years of marriage was overwhelming, and it took years before I learned to cope with it. In November 2000, I flew to Orlando, Florida, to meet Lyle for some golf.

We met and checked into the Shades of Green military hotel located close to Disneyworld and got ready for golf the next day. Tiger Woods had played there and won the tournament the week before and his name was still on the leader board. We had a fine round of golf our first day, and then dinner. We went to bed early to get plenty of sleep to play the next day, and everything seemed normal. But I woke up around midnight, and as I tried to get up I was real dizzy. The room seemed to be spinning and I had great difficulty getting to the bathroom. I thought I might be having a heart attack so we called 911 and the emergency folks came and took me to the Disneyworld Hospital. After a cursory examination they decided I was dehydrated and that was all. The emergency crew said that they were about to get off duty and they seemed to be in a hurry to be rid of me. Remember I had been stationed in Florida for extended periods before and had never experienced any dehydration. Lyle and I left the hospital and went back to the hotel.

The next day we went to Patrick Air Force Base and checked into one on the beach houses there. Patrick AFB has several beach houses that retired or active military on vacation or TDY can rent inexpensively. The rental units are located right on the beach and are quite nice. The unit assigned to Lyle and me was one of the very same ones that Hilda and I had stayed at during some of our previous trips to Florida. After a fine round of golf at the base golf course that day we had dinner at the officers' club and again went to bed early. I woke up again about midnight, this time with pains and dizziness. We called the emergency number and the base emergency crew came and took me to the Cape Canaveral Hospital. I spent the next three days in intensive care. The room was on the second floor and I could see the shuttle launch pads across the bay. I received the best care imaginable there for the three days, after which the doctor explained to me, "Your heart is perfect. Your problem is you are experiencing anxiety attacks because of the loss of your wife." He prescribed some Metoprolol for me to take and released me from the hospital. Lyle and I went back to the beach house and decided to cut our vacation short.

Lyle and I were taking different flights home from Florida. I was released from the hospital at Cape Canaveral and Barbara flew there to meet me so that she could accompany me on the flight back to California. After returning home, a Dr. Flamm became my cardiologist. He had been the cardiology department manager at Travis AFB and is an excellent physician. He has delivered perfect care and has prescribed the correct medicines for me since I met him, and I will always appreciate his concerned attitude about my health and well-being.

One friend had said to me, "You never get over a loss of a loved one. The best you can do is to just get through it." I have found this to be a true statement.

From 1994 to '97 I was making loans with Bob at Western Mortgage. Many of my old bank customers came to me for loans, and they referred other new customers to me as well. After a couple of years the buying habits of people changed. People started using the internet in place of personal relationships, and we were able to make fewer and fewer loans. One day Bob said that he was considering closing the company because business was so slow. It cost about $800 to renew the annual corporate license; I agreed to split it with him so we could stay open for one more year. After that we closed.

During the period that I had been with Western Mortgage, Barbara had been working in property management and sales for a real estate company in Sacramento. When she found out I was leaving Western Mortgage, she asked if I would go into a property management business with her. She was an agent, but did not yet have her own broker's license, and she needed a broker in order to go into business. So, she used my license initially to get her business, Residential Property Management ("RPM"), started. Barbara had some good experience in property management and the company grew and provided a good living for her, although it never made a lot of money. After a couple more years as an agent, Barbara qualified on her own to get a broker's license, and this allowed her to branch off on her own.

At that point, I signed on with an old River City Bank friend, Charlie Miller, at his C&M Mortgage Company (he had taken over my job as the Sunrise branch manager when I left there to work at River City Bank headquarters). This business operated very much like Western Mortgage and faced the same challenges. As the major mortgage companies became almost completely computerized, our customers got more and more scarce. I made a few loans, but I was doing more traveling and was not very focused on work. My broker's license expired on December 28, 2009, and I decided not to renew it. Charlie closed C&M in January of 2009 and worked out of his home after that. I had been working out of my home all along and had only been stopping by the office to get mail or deliver documents.

So at last, at age 85, I was fully retired. But now I'm 87, and have become an author.

Charlene

I had not seen Charlene Kaufman for quite a while and on the day Hilda died I saw her at the post office, where I had stopped to mail some letters on the way to my volunteer job at the sheriff's office. I explained to her about Hilda's health and how worried I was. She would say later that I looked the saddest that she had ever seen when I walked back to the car that day. Charlene had been my secretary at the bank from 1976 to '84 when I retired from First Interstate Bank. We ran into each other from time to time in the banking world. Sometime during those years her marriage failed and she and her husband divorced.

After a while I ran into Charlene again and we started spending time together. She had a house in South Sacramento and we spent time working on it. The more time we spent together the closer we became. After a while we decided that she should sell her house.

We decided to take a trip to Hawaii together in September 2001, arriving in Honolulu and checking in to the Hale Koa on September 10th. We didn't watch any television, and when we went the next morning to choose and schedule some outings, we learned about 9-11. Our immediate plans had to be changed. We had a starting time at the Hickam AFB golf course for the next day, which had to be cancelled. Everything was shut down for a couple of days. Then everything reopened again, but with heavy security everywhere.

Despite the 9-11 tragedy, we managed to have a good vacation in Hawaii. We did get to play golf at Hickam and at the Kaneohe Marine Base.[232] We saw and got to speak with Don Ho and had our picture taken with him. He was a friendly, personable guy and a real patriot. I had seen him perform several times when he was a lot younger. He sang his signature "Tiny Bubbles" song, as usual. We visited the Arizona Memorial and the Battleship Missouri. During our visit to the Missouri, as we were looking at the place where the Japanese surrendered to General MacArthur, ending WWII, a gentleman approached us saying he was from the *Honolulu Star Bulletin* and he wanted an interview for the paper. He had already taken a picture of us. He asked us questions about 9-11 and the security measures. I told him that I didn't think emptying out old American ladies' purses would do anything to help nab terrorists. Our Hawaii trip was over the next day and as we were at the airport getting ready to leave we purchased a newspaper to see if our comments had been published. They had indeed, a full half-page worth, and we purchased several copies to bring home with us. We got home on September 25. Originally, the plan was to stop in California only briefly before leaving again, this time to England to meet up with Tom and his wife for a continuation trip to Scotland. The 9-11 incident made such travel quite complicated however, and we abandoned those plans for the time being.

As time went on we began to think about spending the rest of our life together, and decided that we should be married. We did not know when or whether to mention our plans to the kids. As Valentine's Day approached, we decided to do it on that day. So on Valentine's Day 2002, we asked

---

[232] Marine Corps Base Hawaii, Formerly Marine Corps Air Station, Kaneohe Bay.

Sam and Darlene Byerley to go with us to the justice of the peace, and we "eloped."

Sam and Darlene picked us up and did all the driving. When we got to the justice of the peace, we discovered that a lot of people choose Valentine's Day to get married. Besides being very crowded, local TV news crews were there to interview couples and film them for broadcast on that evening's 10 o'clock news. A reporter came to ask Char and me some questions, one of which was, "What do your kids think about your getting married?" to which we replied that we hadn't told them about it, but they could find out when they watched the news. Sam, Darlene, Char and I went to have dinner at the new Sheraton Grand Hotel, and Char phoned her daughter Deborah to tell her to watch the news about our wedding. We asked her husband Gene Pineau to tape it for us, which he did, and now we have the news broadcast on DVD. The following week at the club, a lot of guys came up to me to say, "Hi Jim, I saw you get married last week." It was quite a deal. After our dinner, Sam drove us to the Sterling Hotel, where we spent our wedding night.

Two weeks later, we hosted a modest reception at North Ridge Country Club. The guest list included all of our family members who could attend and several of our good friends. Bob Adams offered us a very complimentary champagne toast before we cut our wedding cake. Our son-in-law Gene videotaped the whole reception, including all the guests in attendance.

Our honeymoon was a cruise to the Eastern Caribbean. Charlene had never been on a cruise before. We enjoyed it so much that we went on a lot more after that. The following year, we visited the Mexican Riviera, and later on another that went through the Panama Canal. On that cruise, one of our ports of call was Acapulco. There, I and some others noticed a dead body floating in the harbor. When discussing this with the locals, I learned that this sort of thing had become commonplace in Mexico because of the drug trafficking. On our last cruise, we sailed to Alaska. Cruises are a very comfortable way to travel and for us they were all very enjoyable vacations.

We've done a lot of other travel besides cruises. Char has accompanied me to my bomb group reunions, and together we have visited Houston, Seattle, Washington, D.C., New Orleans, San Diego, Charleston, Nashville and other places. In 2002, besides the Dayton, Ohio, reunion, there was an additional trip many of us took to England. Charlene had never been to Europe. On this particular trip we spent most of our time in Cambridge and London. In London we toured Westminster Abbey, Buckingham Palace, the Tower of London, Piccadilly Circus and other well-known sights. I was especially pleased to be able to pay a visit to the Duxford Air Museum,[233] of which I am a founding member.

We have traveled annually to Kansas City to inspect a rental property we own there, and to visit Char's son Farron Kaufman. He was a real estate broker there and managed our property, until relocating recently to Sacramento. Our usual routine when we go is to rent a car, drive it to Joplin, Missouri, then Hot Springs, Arkansas, and back through Wichita, Kansas. Char's brother Gene and his family live in Joplin. Fortunately, their home (as well as our favorite Cracker Barrel restaurant there), was spared in the tornado that devastated Joplin last May. From Joplin we normally continue on to Char's hometown, Hot Springs, Arkansas, to visit her other brother Charles Arthur and his family and participate in her family reunions. Char attended the same high school in Hot Springs as President Bill Clinton. We enjoy Hot Springs

---

[233] This is an extension, or branch, of Britain's Imperial War Museum, located near the village of Duxford, in Cambridgeshire, England, and Britain's largest aviation museum. The American Air Museum there (completed in the 1980s) includes a section honoring its founding members.

Village (where Char's cousin Carolyn lives with her husband Rex) because of the number of country clubs and golf courses there. One of these is the Belvedere Country Club, which has been a venue for several PGA tournaments over the years. A high school classmate of mine, John Siewert, owns a time share there, and we have enjoyed visiting and playing golf with John and his wife on our visits. On our return trip to Kansas City, we stop at Susan's ranch in Mulvane to spend time with her and Pete. We always try to squeeze in a dinner at Jack's Steak House in Kansas City before taking our flight back to Sacramento. When we are not traveling we are enjoying golf at North Ridge Country Club and all of our friends in Sacramento. We reserve the Oak Room at North Ridge once a month for dinner, where a big group of friends celebrates the birthdays falling in that month.

Farron's son, Davis lives here in town; his two other kids, Jessica and Taylor, are grown and live in Oregon and Missouri, respectively. Charlene's daughter Deborah is a resource special education teacher and lives in Elk Grove, California. We lost her husband Gene recently to cancer. He was a wonderful guy and a real friend. Both of Char's kids address me as "Jim-Dad," and her three grandchildren affectionately address me as "Grandpa." Char's relatives are all wonderful people, and I have really enjoyed and appreciate these new relationships.

Getting Religion

In February 2011, Charlene and I joined Fair Oaks Presbyterian Church (FOPC). If you've read this far, you already know that I had never been a member of a church, and frankly, I never thought I would ever become one. Charlene had been raised in the Nazarene Church and after we were married she wanted us to attend church together, which we occasionally did. We began attending FOPC because it was close to home and we had several friends who also attended there. I jokingly referred to our Sunday program as "Bible Thumping." At the church services, I would hand some money to Charlene to put in the collection plate when it got passed around, and I would say to her, "Here's the ticket money."

I have several personal connections to FOPC going back years. Years before, I had attended a memorial service there for Jack Lee's wife, Sharon. Hoppe was at that service, and I learned from him that he had done a lot of the carpentry work at that church when the organ was installed. Sam and Darlene Byerley attended FOPC, and we always sat together with them. When Sam became ill and passed away, there was a beautiful ceremony for him there, and I was one of the several friends who delivered a eulogy for him. At the services we attended, we often ran into friends who were or are members of the Retired Officers Association or North Ridge Country Club.

The pastor, Rev. Dr. G. Henry Wells, gave the most inspiring sermons and was very friendly toward us. Being there felt like being with family. During the first few years I attended services at FOPC, I was able to hear the minister's words, but I couldn't understand them because my hearing was so bad. After the VA provided me with hearing aids, I could not only hear the words but I could understand them, and the services became more interesting to me.

One of the couples we know from TROA are Jim and Myra Duke. Charlene's and my attendance became more regular, and our acquaintanceship with the Dukes grew into a very close friendship. Jim Duke had a twenty-year career in the Army, served in WWII, and is about my age. Sometime around mid-2009, Jim took me aside one Sunday and suggested that I join and become a member. Over the ensuing couple of years he would remind me in a very gentle, friendly manner that he was still waiting for me to join. In February 2011, Charlene and I made the decision to join FOPC. When Jim found out about this, he was elated. The Dukes conduct Bible study classes at their home regularly, which they have been doing for the past twenty-five years, and we have attended some of those classes. The Dukes have become some of our best friends.

Pastor Wells retired fairly recently and was replaced by our new senior pastor, Kirk Bottomly, an outstanding minister and another very personable individual. Overall, FOPC is very well-managed, and Charlene and I are happy to be members. Deborah attended the service with us the Sunday we joined, and I remember her saying to me, "Jim-Dad, you are now an official Bible Thumper."

Tom, Lyle and me the very last time all three brothers were together in the same place. Taken at Hilda's funeral reception, March 2000.

My three lovely granddaughters, Carolyn, Beverly and Paige. Barbara is in the background. Taken in 2000 at Barbara and Craigs' ranch in Sacramento.

Me with grandkids Carolyn and Ian at a McClellan AFB air show. I gave them a tour of the B-17 "Fuddy Duddy" (background), but we did not fly that day.

Me with grandson Ian in front of our charter boat "Pockets"in Sitka, Alaska, July 2008.

Granddaughter Carolyn tries to teach me to text on a cell phone.

Grandson Ian and me at the North Ridge Jr. Golf Tournament, August 2010.

Lyle and me at the Hale Koa Hotel, Waikiki, Hawaii on a golf vacation, early 1980s.

Phyllis and Lyle Grey with me at their home in Custer, South Dakota, 2007.

Sam and Darlene Byerley standing with me and Charlene at our wedding on Valentine's Day, 2001, at the Sacramento justice of the peace.

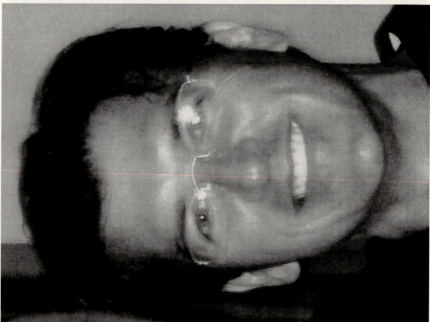

Charlene's son Farron and daughter Deborah with her husband Gene.

Jimmy and Farrons' kids visiting on Christmas Day 2010. Left to right: Carolyn, Ian, Jessica, Davis, and Taylor.

Top: Portrait photos taken April 2010 at Fair Oaks Presbyterian Church..
Bottom: Charlene and me at the 2007 Bomb Group Reunion.

Jim & Myra Duke with Charlene and me at Fair Oaks Presbyterian Church, July 2011.

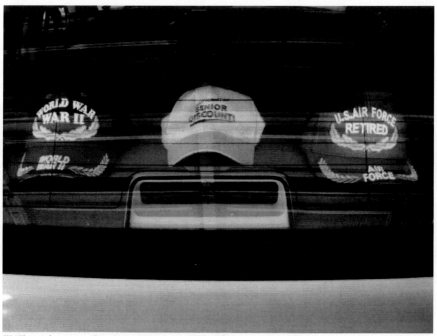

"Where's my Senior Discount?!" If you see these caps in the back window of a Lincoln Town Car, you know it's my car.

Epilogue: Vanishing Contrails

There is a proverb that says there are three things a person must do to live a good and full life: Plant a tree, raise a child and write a book. Now I can finally say I've done all three. It has been a great experience which I recommend to anyone. Everyone has their story to tell, their own living history, which is the only true and accurate telling possible. When I started this project, I never expected it to wind up as anything more than a bunch of loose pages in a file drawer. Recalling all the memories from my long life, it was amazing even to me, to contemplate what a rich and eventful life it has been. I'm pleased at the way this project turned out, and to be able to share these memories with you.

In 2004, we were fortunate to be able to get everyone's schedules coordinated so that all three of my kids and two of my grandkids could meet for a reunion in Wisconsin. The Portage branch of the Grays was organizing their biennial family reunion (several of which I had attended, but never with such an entourage). This gave us a chance to tour Wisconsin together in a minivan we rented. We traveled to Whiskey Rapids, got to see Alexander Field and the aircraft hangar where I used to loiter from age six on, the site of my home and schools, and of course, the Forty.

Flying is becoming a lost art, and before long airplane pilots may go the way of charioteers and paddleboat captains, as a short-lived, extinct oddity of human history. The last time we visited the moon was nearly forty years ago, and the space shuttle has been mothballed as of this year. Increasingly, computers are taking over the job of flying. We are already at a point where we can fly bombing missions from the comfort of a La-Z-Boy at a command center in Cape Canaveral, where Air Force drone pilots remotely maneuver their aircraft to take out enemy targets on the other side of the world. And this and last year, the Air Force tested new hypersonic, rocket-launched gliders that can travel at Mach 20. Once the technology is perfected, we will be able to strike a target anywhere in the world in just minutes.

I flew Brooks' Lear from time to time until he passed away in 1996. That's when my flying days started really tapering off. I stopped renewing my flying physicals in 1997 and was flying less and less. Whenever I did get to handle the controls of an airplane, it was always with a pilot friend. I believe the last time I flew the Citation II[234] was during a fishing trip to Sitka with John Didier in 2005. I miss it.

I have been blessed with a full and interesting life, and have gotten to know many great friends with whom I have had many wonderful, memorable experiences. I hope to continue to enjoy good health, travel and being with my family and friends in the time I have left of this life. I also still have to "shoot my age" on the golf course. I am thankful and fortunate to have such a loving, caring wife as Charlene, with whom I hope to share many more happy years.

THE END

---

[234] Cessna Citation II, a light corporate jet with seating capacity of up to ten people.

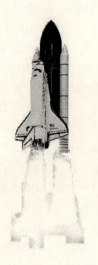

Appendices

Appendix 1: Major Events Timeline

Part One: Family & Childhood

9/8/1924:   Born in Wisconsin Rapids, Wisconsin.
11/2/1926:   Birth of Brother Lyle.
12/5/1933:   Ratification of the 21st Amendment to the U.S. Constitution, ending prohibition.
12/9/1933:   Birth of Brother Tom.
10/24/1929:   "Black Thursday" crash of the New York Stock Exchange, marking the beginning of the Great Depression.
Spring 1941: Graduated from Lincoln High School at age sixteen.
12/7/1941:   Japanese attack on Pearl Harbor.

Part Two: Air Force Years

3/15/1943:   Reported to the USAAF Aviation Cadet Center in Decatur, Illinois.
1/15/1944:   Commissioned a second lieutenant in the USAAF.
6/11/1944:   Assigned to 381st Bomb Group and stationed at RAF Ridgewell, in England.
8/26/1944:   Promoted to rank of first lieutenant, and made squadron navigator for the 535th.
11/17/1944:   Promoted to rank of captain.
5/8/1945:   VE Day (German unconditional surrender).
9/2/1945:   VJ Day (Japanese unconditional surrender).
9/10/1946:   Married B. Gloria Niemi.

9/22/1946:   Father's death.
Nov. 1946:   Transferred to post-war occupation Japan.
Sep. 1947:   Divorced Gloria.
Oct. 1948:   Typhoon Libby.
05/15/1949: Left Japan.
6/30/1949:   Married Hilda Marie Huegel.
6/25/1950:   Start of Korean War.
9/1/1951:   Began pilot training.
2/15/1951:   Graduated from pilot school.
04/01/1953: Promoted to rank of major.
7/27/1953:   Korean War Armistice.
10/01/1960: Promoted to rank of lieutenant colonel.
10/28/1960: Birth of daughter Barbara Carol Grey.
4/16/1962:   Birth of son James Hunter Grey.
11/22/1963: Assassination of President John F. Kennedy.

Part Three: Civilian Years
6/29/1964:   Retired from the USAF.
2/26/1965:   Birth of daughter Susan Grey.
3/19/1965:   Graduated with a Bachelor of General Education
             degree from University of Nebraska at Omaha.
9/1/1965:   Began career at United California Bank.
9/1/1967:   Bought home at 1273 Gary Way.
2/16/1966:   Made Entered Apprentice.
6/27/1966:   Passed to Fellowcraft.
9/26/1966:   Raised to Master Mason.
Oct. 1984:   Retired from First Interstate Bank.
Dec. 1984:   Joined River City Bank.
5/5/1985:   Mother's death.
2/3/1992:   Birth of granddaughter Carolyn.
1/23/1993:   The Burglary.

Part Four: Retirement
4/1/1994:   Semi-retired from River City Bank.
Jul. 1994:   Secured real estate agent license.

12/4/1995: Birth of grandson Ian.

3/13/2000: Hilda's death.

9/11/2001: Terrorist hijacking and attacks on the Pentagon and World Trade Center.

2/14/2002: Married Charlene Faith Kaufman.

3/31/2008: Birth of great-granddaughter Ellagrace.

Appendix 2: Combat Mission Diary

Combat Mission Diary of Captain James F. Grey
The following is an account of my thirty missions as recorded in my diary the day each mission was flown.

Mission 1: 28 June 1944
Plane: Touch the Button Nell II
Target: Reims, France (oil dumps and marshalling yards)

Very light flak about 10 minutes inside enemy coast, also light flak around Leon, France. One ship feathered #1 and aborted about 5 minutes from enemy coast. Bomb load consisted of two 2,000 lb. G.P. bombs. On the return trip we had to land at Ashfield due to weather closed in at our base. When we landed the hydraulic system in left wheel went out and we called our base for a plane to come and pick us up. Yates came and got us in "Stage Door Canteen." Flying time for Mission #1 was 5 hours.

June 29, 1944
Took off at 0500, couldn't find our formation. Flew over the wash at 28,000 for about 3 hours in a mix-up of about 800 Forts and Libs. Flying time – 4 hours.

Mission 2: 4 July 1944
Plane: The Tomahawk Warrior
Target: Tours, France (bridge)

Took off at 0430 to bomb a bridge at Tours, France. Continent covered by complete overcast. Couldn't find target so brought back our two 2,000 lb. bombs. On oxygen 6 hours. First mission that our whole crew flew together. Bond and Godfrey sick. One engine almost went out. Bobrof feathered #4 and left formation. Salvoed his bombs. Flying time 5 hours.

July 8, 1944
Bobrof reported missing in action by Squadron commander.

Mission 3: 6 July 1944
Plane: The Feathermerchant
Target: Novall, France (buzz bomb launching)

The target was a buzz bomb launching outfit. Our bomb load was eighteen 250-H.G.P.s. Ship was "The Feather Merchant." Flying time was 4 hours.

Mission 4: 8 July 1944
Plane: Me and My Gal
Target: Calais, France (buzz bomb emplacements)

Eighteen 250's! Target was buzz bomb emplacements in the Calais area. Very heavy flak. Flying time for #4, four hours.

Mission 5: 13 July 1944
Plane: Hell's Angel
Target: Munich, Germany

Ship 265. Target at Munich, Germany, city rail yards. Heaviest flak I have seen yet. One piece hit our ship in the nose – scattered glass around but didn't hurt Mac or I. Fighter hit the 24's behind us. We had P-38s, P-51s, and P-47s for escort flying way out. Flying time, 9 hours.

Mission 6: 16 July 1944
Plane: Hell's Angel
Target: Munich, Germany.
Airplane motor factory seven miles northwest of Munich. Light flak. Bombed from 28,000. Very cold. P51's escort all the way to target and out. Came back with 2 new flak holes in the wing.
Flying time, 9 hours.

Mission 7: 18 July 1944
Plane: Hell's Angel
Target: Peenamunda, Germany near Keil (experimentation center)

Took off in our own ship (Hell's Angel) and blew an exhaust stack on take-off so had to feather #2 and land and take #6115. Happened to be the ship we flew over from Maine. Target was Peenamunda, Germany near Keil. An experimentation center and hydrogen peroxide factory. Excellent results, smoke from fires up to 15,000 feet. Very intense flak. Bomb loads was 38 100 lb. incends. Flying time, 8 hours.

Mission 8: 19 July 1944
Plane: Me and My Gal
Target: Augsberg, Germany

Our own ship still being repaired. Target was Augsberg, Germany, 30 miles from Munich. An airfield and factory where they manufacture jet propelled aircraft. First day that we could see the target plainly. Leon said our bombs (10 500 lb. G.P.) hit dead center. Very accurate flak; shook us up a bit. Flying time, 9 hours.

Mission 9: 24 July 1944

Plane: Hell's Angel
Target: Help invasion at St. Lo

Target was helping the invasion at St. Lo area. Consisted of gun and tank stores. Bomb load 38 100 lb. G.P. frag bombs. Light flak. Ship was our "Hell's Angel" (265-P). Flying time, 5 hours, 20 minutes.

Mission 10: 25 July 1944
Plane: Hell's Angel
Target: Same as #9

This time we could see the ground and some of the heavy artillery fire. Bombed from 13,000 feet (lowest yet). Really got shook around. Target was destroyed. Jerry radio called to try and get us to bomb over our target. Flying time, 6 Hours.

Mission 11: 31 July 1944
Plane: Buffaloe Buf (Ship 060)
Target: Munich, Germany

They really threw up everything but their gun barrels at us. Bomb load 10 500's. Flying time, 8 hours 30 minutes.

Mission 12: 3 August 1944
Plane: In Like Errol
Target: Mulhouse, France

Bomb load was twelve 500 lb. No Flak until coast near Antwerp. Real big and accurate. Flying time, 8 hours.

Mission 13: 4 August 1944
Plane: Hell's Angel
Target: Peenamunda, Germany

Bomb load was five 1,000 lb. One ship caught fire and went down over the field area just after takeoff. We counted nine chutes and then watched the plane hit and blow up. After landing we found that there had been ten men in the ship and the tail gunner had gotten killed. Don't know who it was as yet. Pretty disheartening to start a mission with. Flak heavy at target and also Danish coast. Our own ship "Hell's Angel." Very good bombing due to CAVU weather. Flying time, 9 hours.

Mission 14: 7 August 1944
Plane: Hell's Angel
Target: Hamburg, Germany (depot)

Target was a depot halfway between Hamburg, Bremen and Hanover. Bomb load eight 1,000 lb. bombs. Heaviest load and very good results due to CAVU weather. Flying time, 7 hours.

Mission 15: 9 August 1944
Plane: In Like Errol (590 M)
Target: Paris, France (fuel dump)

Bomb load twenty 250's. Target was a fuel dump 85 miles south of Paris. We got flak holes all over the ship, several in wing and tail. One just missed Mclaren and I got one in the nose almost under my table. Worst Flak yet; came from Cain area. Good bombing results; fires with smoke up to 15,000 feet. Flying time, 7 Hours.

Mission 16: 11 August 1944
Plane: Ship#267 X
Target: Paris, France (ammo supply)

Target and ammo supply 85 miles southeast of Paris. Bomb load eight 1,000 lb. Good results. Flying time, 6 hours.

Mission 17: 13 August 1944
Plane: Egg Haid
Target: Rouson, France

Bomb load thirty-eight 100's. Target was road junction at Rouson, France. Blocked retreating Germans. very accurate flak. We had quite a few holes. Flying time, 5 hours 30 minutes.

Mission 18: 24 august 1944
Plane: Hell's Angel
Target: Leipzig, Germany (Buzz Bomb Plant)

Bomb load five 1,000. Target, Buzz bomb plant south of Leipzig. We led a squadron. High Sqdn. of the high Gp. The flak over Leipzig is the worst I've seen. Weather was good and we got a clear view of Hamburg, Bremen, Berlin, Hanover, Leipzig and Madeburg. Saw one fighter blow up over Leipzig. Our objective playing around there was to draw out the new German jet propelled fighter. We saw none. But we passed over an airfield from which 20 unidentified fighters took off to attack. They got the "wing" behind us. One waist gunner wounded by flak. We had no damage. Results – fair overshot. Flying time, 9 hours, 30 minutes.

Mission 19: 26 August 1944
Plane: Pair of Queens
Target: Essen, Germany (Oil Plant)

Load thirty-eight 100's. Target was a synthetic oil plant six miles north of Essen, Germany, and thirty miles southwest of Hanover, Germany. My first trip as wing lead navigator. Pilots were Yates and Col. Halsey. Lots of fun for a change, but somewhat more work. Good results. Made 1st Lt. Today. Flying time five hours, 30 minutes.

Mission 20: 27 August 1944
Plane: Minnie the Mermaid (Ship 614)
Target: Berlin, Germany (airstrip)

Bomb load ten 500 incendiaries. Target was an airfield six miles south of the center of Berlin. When we got halfway there we got ordered to take a target of opportunity due to weather and so bombed Emden Harbor, Germany. Just as the bombays opened the Bombay motor caught fire and we had quite a time putting it out. Then the VHF radio caught fire and the #1 engine started throwing oil. We had to drop out of formation and almost hit the lead ship's bombs. The worst luck we've had so far. A piece of flak came through the nose and made a hole the size of a baseball. Luckily it missed Mac and I. Flying time, seven hours 30 minutes.

Mission 21: 8 September 1944
Plane: Ship PFF 010
Target: Ludwigshaven

Another wing lead. Target Ludwigshaven. Bomb load five 1,000 lb. Not so good results. Altitude 30,000 feet. My 20th birthday too. Flying time, 8 hours.

Mission 22: 12 September 1944
Plane: Ship 990 PFF
Target: Brux, Czechoslovakia

Wing Lead. Target, Brux in Czechoslovakia. Our toughest mission to lead so far. Also my first encounter with enemy fighters. ME-109's; four of them flew so close that I could see the pilots plainly (a very good looking plane). No chance to shoot. Encountered them 10 miles north of Berlin. Total distance 1,300 miles. Altitude 28,000 feet. Flying time, 9 hours 30 minutes.

Mission 23: 19 September 1944
Plane: Ship #127
Target: Hamm, Germany

Flew group lead with Demegalski and Maj. Taylor. Target was Hamm, Germany in the Ruhr Valley. Bomb load two 2,000 lb. Flak very accurate. Our tail gunner got hit in the back but his flak suit stopped it. The piece went through two cans of ammunition before it hit him. Some stuff. Flying time 7 hours.

Mission 24: 22 September 1944
Plane: Ship PFF 036
Target: Kassel, Germany

My first Wing Lead and it turned out to be a division lead. Flew with Col. Leber and Capt. Yates. The Col. Chewed and chewed about a turn I made near Wiesbaden and Frankfurt. We encountered no flak at target Kassel, Germany, but plenty from the Rhine and Moselle rivers. Ship PFF 036. Flying time 6 hours, 10 minutes.

Mission 25: 28 September 1944
Plane: Ship PFF 090
Target: Magdeburg, Germany

Target was Magdeburg, Germany, 50 miles S.W. of Berlin. My second wing lead as Sqdn. Navigator. Capt. Yates (one of my best friends and the best pilot I know) finished. Wing Comdr. Was Capt. Tyson (new opp. off. [Good boy]). Very good mission. Flak was not so bad. Bomb load six 500 G.P. F-500 incendiary and smoke. Flying time 8 hours 15 minutes.

Mission 26: 8 October 1944
Plane: Ship 010 PFF
Target: Brux, Czechoslovakia

My third wing lead and that turned out to be a division lead. So about 128 B-17's were to follow where I took them. We couldn't see Brux so bombed Zwichaus, Germany. That was our secondary. About 30 miles south of Leipzig. Lt. Col. Kunkel was commander and Deme the pilot. We made a couple 360's at the target – almost got screwed up. O'cohners tail gunner bailed out over Osnabruk in the flak, and Mitchell was wounded in the arm. Now it's evening and four buzz bombs just lit in our area. One blew up only one mile away. Cripes, flak all day. Buzz bombs at night, oh well. Flying time, 8 hours 30 minutes.

Mission 27: 17 October 1944
Plane: Ship 990 PFF
Target: Cologne (Koln) Germany

Deme – pilot with Maj. Taylor as Grp. Commander. My 4th wing lead. Target was cologne, Germany. The first time I've ever seen red flak, but it was all inaccurate. Mission went very good. Flying time 6 hours.

Mission 28: 28 October 1944
Ship 196 PFF
Target: Munster, Germany

Deme pilot. Major Taylor was Group Commander. Target was Munster, Germany. Marshalling yards. Mission went quite well. Route in over Zuider Zee. Flak very accurate. Weather very bad. Contrails and clouds and haze. My 5th wing lead and 10th or 9th credit lead. Flying time 5 hours, 30 minutes.

6 November 1944

Our most disastrous day since 4 July when Bobrof went down over France. Levitoff and his crew went down over Hamburg today and we lost three other ships from the Group. A burst of flak burst over the astrodome and shattered the nose of #3 engine. Newsome said he saw the co-pilot slump down in his seat. Later he counted six chutes.

Mission 29: 21 November 1944
Plane: The Alamo
Target: Merseburg, Germany

Target was a synthetic oil plant at Merseburg, Germany, 30 miles south of Leipzig. Bomb load was 10 500's and 4 incendiaries. Mission went well until we got to the target and then rode into a front. Contrails were very heavy. We dropped the incendiaries on an airfield just north of Frankfurt. 398th got hit by fighters. Johnny Wallace was leading the 91st. It was my 6th wing lead and 10th lead altogether. Flak was very accurate. Pilot – Deme; Co-pilot – Maj. Taylor. Flying time 8 hours.

21 November 1944
My promotion to Captain came through. Youngest captain in 381st.

Mission 30: 28 December 1944
Plane: ship 196 PFF
Target: Rhine (bridge)

Bomb load: two 2,000 lb; two 1,000 lb; 2 smoke markers. Target was a bridge across the Rhine halfway between Coblenz and Cologne, Germany. The mission was almost 100 percent perfect. My assembly timing was perfect and I'm happy about it. We bombed G.H. due to 10/10 cloud. Weather was clear at 22,000 feet. The crew was Capt. Demegalski (P); Lt. Col. Briggs (CP); Capt. Angevine (VN); Capt. Grey (N); Maj. Fullick (B); 1Lt. Newsome (TG); 1Lt. Walker (NO). Very nice mission to finish up on. No flak, no fighters. Flying time, 6 hours.

One combat tour complete – now home for a while.

Appendix 3: Recommended Reading and Reference

Books

Dr. Kenneth Rowe's account of his defection and Russian and Chinese involvement in the Korean War: No Kum-Sok, with J. Roger Osterholm, **A MiG-15 to Freedom**, McFarland & Company, Inc., Publishers, Jefferson, North Carolina, 1996.

For comprehensive history of the Eighth Air Force's role in World War II (note – this book contains some factual errors, but is very complete and in-depth): Donald L. Miller, **Masters of the Air: America's Bomber Boys Who Fought the Air War Against Nazi Germany**, Simon & Schuster Paperbacks, New York, 2006.

For a fairly thorough history of the war-time 381st Bomb Group (the author was our chaplain): James Good Brown, **The Mighty Men of the 381st: Heroes All**, Publisher's Press, Salt Lake City, 1984.

Films

A renowned documentary film account of the final mission of the first B-17 crew to survive 25 missions over Europe and return to the U.S. Contains scenes with actual combat footage. **The Memphis Belle: A Story of a Flying Fortress.** Dir. Maj. William Wyler. Starring the crew of the Memphis Belle. Paramount Pictures Inc. 1944; and:

A fictionalization of the preceding documentary film. *Memphis Belle*. Dir. Michael Caton-Jones. Perf. Matthew Modine. Warner Bros. 1990.

Acclaimed film about Eighth Air Force aircrews flying daylight bombing missions against Nazi Germany and Occupied France: *Twelve O'clock High*. Dir. Henry King. Based on novel by Sy Bartlett and Beirne Lay, Jr. Perf. Gregory Peck. 20th Century Fox. 1949.

Internet

Official Site of the 381st Bombardment Group (Heavy): **http://www.381st.org**

Index

Burtonwood Airfield. *See* RAF
    Burtonwood
Buzz Bombs, 43, 54, 369

C

C-124 "Old Shakey", 88, 228, 229
C-17 Globemaster, 229
C-45 "Twin Beech", 110, 201
C-47 "Gooney Bird", 94, 98, 102, 118
C-5 Galaxy, 229, 275
C-54 Skymaster, 88, 103, 117, 128
California State University, Sacramento
    (CSUS), 167
California State University, San Diego
    (CSUSD), 275
Cameron Park Country Club, 147
Campbell River Airport, 252
Capitol Oil, 285, 337
Carnaval 1991 (Brazil), 268
Carr Field. *See* San Angelo AAF
Carswell AFB, 189
Castle AFB, 122, 178, 276
Cessna 182, 250
Cessna 206, 255
Cessna 310, 252, 255, 265
Cessna Citation II, 363
Cessna Super 340, 285
CFB Gander. *See* RCAF Station Gander
Charles M. Schultz (Sonoma County)
    Airport, 279
Chase Manhattan Bank, 281
Chicago O'Hare Airport, 156
Christensen, Walter (Mayor of
    Sacramento), 221
Churchill, Sir Winston, 43
Citibank, 281
Civil War, U.S., 4
Clinton, William Jefferson, 349
Cold War, 60, 144, 163, 171, 189, 192
Columbia Army Airbase, 36
Columbia Metropolitan Airport. *See*
    Columbia Army Airbase
Compensation Bonus Act of 1936, 8
Council on American-Islamic Relations
    (CAIR), 190
Crosby, Bing, 58

Cuban Missile Crisis, 228

D

Daedalians, Order of, 158, 163, 243
Dai Ichi Seimei Building, 124
Davis, Jr., Sammy, 235
Davis-Monthan AFB, 147
D-Day, 27, 42
Decatur County Industrial Air Park. *See*
    Baingridge Air Base
Del Dayo Elementary School, 227
Del Paso Country Club, 136, 224, 263
Depository Institutions Deregulation
    and Monetary Control Act of 1980,
    281
Disneyland, 176, 235
Disneyworld, 342
Distinguished Flying Cross (DFC), 93, 149
Dorsey, Tommy, 57
Douglas Amendment of 1982, 281

E

Eielson AFB, 171, 178
Eisenhower, Gen. Dwight D., 43, 56, 142
El Macero Country Club, 285
Elizabeth II, 145
Elks (Benevolent and Protective Order
    of), 26, 222, 251
Ellington Field, 59, 90, 91, 92

F

Fair Oaks Presbyterian Church, 351
Fairchild AFB, 119
Fairfield-Suisun AFB, 118
Fairfield-Suisun Army Air Base, 103, 105,
    117
Federal Aviation Administration, 296
First Interstate Bank, 279, 281, 291,
    292, 346, 366
Fonda, Jane, 58
Fort Sutter Lions, 244, 245
Francis E. Warren AFB, 168
Freemasonry, 193, 239
Fukuoka Airport. *See* Itazuke Air Base

G

Gable, Clark, 30
Gander International Airport. *See* RCAF
    Gander
Garn-St. Germain Depository
    Institutions Act of 1982, 281
Gaslighter Theatre (in Old Folsom), 238
Georgetown Airport, 248, 249, 256
Gimpo International Airport. *See* Kimpo
    Air Base, Korea
Glenn Miller Orchestra, 57
Gobel, George, 24
Godfrey Army Airfield, 39
Grand Review, 4
Grandy, Fred, 247
Great Depression, xi, 10

H

Hale Koa Hotel, Hawaii, 340, 346
Harlingen AFB. *See* Harlingen Army
    Airfield
Harlingen Army Airfield, 29, 30, 31
Hawker-Beechcraft Bonanza, 256
Heihachirō, Tōgō (Imperial Japanese
    Fleet Admiral), 15
Hell's Angel, 44, 45, 57, 369, 370, 371,
    372, 373
Hickam AFB, 103, 346
Hickam Army Airfield, 103, 118
Hiroshima, 97
Hitler, Adolf, 19, 22, 48, 175, 269
Ho, Don, 347
Holocaust, 124
Hondo Army Airfield, 31, 32
Hope, Bob, 58
Hungarian Revolution (1956), 175

I

Imperial War Museum, Duxford, 349
Indian Springs AFB, 164
Indianapolis Motory Speedway, 246
Italian POWs, 95
Itazuke Air Base, Fukuoka, Japan, 108,
    111

J

Japanese Empire, 9, 52
Japanese unconditional surrender, 125,
    138
Japanese war crimes, 22, 124, 126
Japanese-American internment in
    WWII, 125
Jefferson County International Airport,
    Washington, 253, 254

K

K Street Mall, 221
Kadena Air Base, Okinawa, Japan, 121
KB-50 Aerial Tanker, 180, 228
KC-135 Stratotanker, 182, 190
KC-97 Stratotanker, 169
Kearns, Jack (Sacramento Chief of
    Police), 288
Kennedy, Anthony (Supreme Court
    Justice), 337
Kennedy, John F., 192
    Assassination, 189
Kimpo Air Base, Korea, 161
King County International Airport, 252
Kinloss Air Base, Scotland. *See* RAF
    Kinloss
Kirtland AFB, 163, 164
Kitty Hawk, 5, 268
Kogenei Country Club, Tokyo, 123
Korean Armistice, 161, 192
Korean War, 122, 137, 138, 139, 161,
    162, 168, 366, 379

L

Lackland AFB. *See* San Antonio Aviation
    Cadet Center
LAX International Airport. *See* Mines
    Field
Learjet Model 35, 293, 337
LeBaron, Eddie, 243
LeMay, Gen. Curtis, 189
Liberace, 235
Lincoln High School, 6, 18, 167, 179, 365
Long Beach Airport, 158

385